Utopia and Terror in Contemporary American Fiction

This book examines the quest for/failure of Utopia across a range of contemporary American/transnational fictions in relation to terror and globalization through authors such as Susan Choi, André Dubus, Dalia Sofer, and John Updike. While recent critical thinkers have reengaged with Utopia, the possibility of terror—whether state or non-state, external or homegrown—shadows Utopian imaginings. Terror and Utopia are linked in fiction through the exploration of the commodification of affect, a phenomenon of a globalized world in which feelings are managed, homogenized across cultures, exaggerated, or expunged according to a dominant model. Narrative approaches to the terrorist offer a means to investigate the ways in which fiction can resist commodification of affect, and maintain a reasoned but imaginative vision of possibilities for human community. Newman explores topics such as the first American bestseller with a Muslim protagonist, the links between writer and terrorist, the work of Iranian-Jewish Americans, and the relation of race and religion to Utopian thought.

Judie Newman is Professor in the School of American and Canadian Studies at The University of Nottingham, UK.

Routledge Transnational Perspectives on American Literature

EDITED BY SUSAN CASTILLO, *King's College London*

Utopia and Terror in Contemporary American Fiction

Judie Newman

Routledge
Taylor & Francis Group
NEW YORK   LONDON

First published 2013
by Routledge
711 Third Avenue, New York, NY 10017

Simultaneously published in the UK
by Routledge
2 Park Square, Milton Park, Abingdon, Oxon OX14 4RN

*Routledge is an imprint of the Taylor & Francis Group,
an informa business*

Library of Congress Cataloging-in-Publication Data
Newman, Judie.
  Utopia and terror in contemporary American fiction / Judie Newman.
    p. cm. — (Routledge transnational perspectives on American
literature ; 21)
  Includes bibliographical references and index.
  1. Utopias in literature.   2. American fiction—21st century—
History and criticism.   3. Dystopias in literature.   4. Terror
in literature.   5. Fantasy in literature.   6. Transnationalism in
literature.   I. Title.
  PS374.U8.N49 2013
  813'.609372—dc23
  2012039014

ISBN13: 978-0-415-89912-3 (hbk)
ISBN13: 978-0-203-55597-2 (ebk)

Typeset in Sabon
by IBT Global.

Printed and bound in the United States of America on sustainably sourced
paper by IBT Global.

This book is dedicated to the memory of
Ellis Edward Newman, 1924–2010

Contents

Acknowledgments

In writing what follows I have incurred many debts, too many indeed to name individually here. The responsibility for any errors is of course entirely mine. I am grateful especially to my colleagues in the School of American and Canadian Studies, University of Nottingham, and to the students in my "Fictions of America" course in the last three years. Among individuals who helped with specific queries, suggestions, or criticism, I take this opportunity to thank Shashikala Assella, Celeste-Marie Bernier, Gloria Cronin, Diletta De Cristoforo, Paul Grainge, Robert Hillenbrand, Graham Huggan, Rhodri Jeffreys-Jones, Yvonne Jerrold, Matthew Jones, Richard King, Ruth Maxey, Maria Ryan, Jack Ruttle, Lyman Sargent, Liz Statham, and Graham Thompson. In the absence of almost any secondary criticism on most of the authors discussed, anonymous manuscript readers' responses and audience comments were especially useful. I am grateful for invitations to speak at the British Association for American Studies Postgraduate Conference, 2008; Staff Research Seminar, University of Leeds, 2008; American Literature Association Conference, San Francisco, 2010; Jewish American and Holocaust Literature conference, Miami 2010; American Literature Association Symposium on Crime Fiction, Savannah, 2011; and American Literature Association Conference, San Francisco 2012. I should also like to thank the editors and publishers of the scholarly journals listed below for the opportunity to try out pilot versions of material which is developed in the book. " 'Rotten with perfection': The Entelechial Fictions of Kim Edwards," *Comparative American Studies*, 8, 1 (March 2010), 22–38 (Maney Publishing); "Blowback: André Dubus III's *House of Sand and Fog*," *Critique: Studies in Modern Fiction*, 51, 4 (2010), 378–393 (Taylor and Francis); "Updike's Many Worlds: Local and Global in *Toward the End of Time*," *The John Updike Review*, 1 (2011) 53–67 (The John Updike Society and the University of Cincinnati Press); "Pictures From an Exhibition: Dalia Sofer and the Jews of Iran," *Contemporary Women's Writing* 2012; doi:10.1093/cww/vps001 (Oxford University Press); "The Black Atlantic as Dystopia. Bernadine Evaristo's *Blonde Roots*," *Comparative Literature Studies* (*Special Issue Comparative Perspectives on the Black Atlantic*, 49, 2 (2012) 281–295 (Pennsylvania State University Press).

Reprinted with permission. I gratefully acknowledge financial support from the University of Nottingham Research Committee and the Dean's Fund, and the School of American Studies, for funding attendance at conferences and research time. A special debt is due to the staff of the Hallward Library, University of Nottingham, particularly the Inter Library loans staff, for invaluable assistance in tracking down materials. I have been very fortunate to work with Liz Levine as my editor. Thanks go once again with feeling to Alice Newman, Chris Revie, and James Revie for their encouragement and support.

1 Introduction

Amy Waldman's 2009 short story, "Freedom", engages directly with the central topic of the current study: the possibility of utopia in a post-terror world. The story opens as a group of political detainees, recognisably akin to the inhabitants of Guantánamo Bay, disembark on a remote Pacific island. Formerly characterised as "so evil they had to be imprisoned on an island beyond the reach of American law",[1] they have now been reclassified as no longer "the worst of the worst" (39) and cleared for release. The snag is that no country is willing to accept them, with the exception of a select few which promise to torture them. Even Albania baulks. It is a Public Relations disaster for the incumbent American president, one of whose officials jokes that

> We need to start a new country—it's the only way. (40)

And so they do, and its name is Freedom. The Solomon Islands, hit by a tsunami and desperate for US aid, hand over Fatutaka, an extinct volcano, one of the most remote and rocky islands in the archipelago, and it is transformed at enormous expense into the world's only Muslim democracy. In go the same contractors who created Baghdad's Green Zone and Kabul's American Embassy, with tons of imported topsoil, sand and concrete, to provide it with trees, roads, a mosque, gym, post office, medical centre, and eighty-two nicely appointed bungalows for the new citizens. The resulting suburban subdivision of cul-de-sacs is reminiscent of California's Inland Empire (40) but with additional sea view. Although the new national slogan is "As Good As America™" (40) Freedom is in some respects inimical to its parent state. There is a gated community for the security guards and government personnel. "Freedom was a friendly country, but at the outset it was thought prudent to treat it like an enemy one" (40).

Deliberately constructed to a blueprint, the new community dramatizes the peculiar tension between freedom and coercion in any utopia. Like Thomas More's, the society is planned as a "product" utopia (hence the trademark on the slogan), based upon a principle (here freedom, though in other examples it might be Good or the Ideal Society) and as a result it is heavily regulated, and subject to strict social control.[2]

Waldman's story takes its inspiration from recent events which put the nature of American freedoms in the spotlight. In the story the detainees, eighty-two veterans of any number of "combatant status review tribunals" (39) including Yemenis, Uzbeks, North Africans and Uighurs, with some 500 years of captivity between them, arrive at the island no longer wearing Guantánamo-style orange jump suits ("those were so 2002" 39) but still in shackles and blindfolded by wraparound goggles. Combatant status review tribunals were held at Guantánamo Bay (controversially defined by the US Department of Justice as outside US legal jurisdiction) to confirm the status of detainees as enemy combatants. The process was the product of the US doctrine of pre-emption, the idea that threats must be defused before they are actualised, and enemies defeated who have not yet emerged. The tribunals were not trials concerned with past acts, but related to future acts, and to whether the detainee was still a threat. Effectively therefore the war against terror itself relied upon projection into the future. In the case particularly of the Uighurs, a Chinese Muslim minority, many of those cleared for release remained none the less in detention. The United States feared that if they returned them to China they would be persecuted or tortured. Although American officials made overtures to more than twenty countries for asylum for the Uighurs, none would accept them. Ironically, the Uighurs, who have traditionally suffered religious persecution at the hands of Chinese Communists, had previously viewed America as a champion of liberty. As their lawyer argued in court, "there might not be a more pro-US Muslim group in the world."[4] Freedom for the Uighurs, however, amounted to continued detention in Guantánamo, an institution memorably described by Lord Goldsmith, a British government minister, as tarnishing America's reputation "as a beacon of freedom, liberty and justice."[5]

Satire cuts in several directions in the story, targeting the very idea of utopia after terror, the American image of itself as founded on principles of freedom from religious and political persecution, and Imperialism more broadly. In their small boats, the new settlers, a whole clan of exiled Magwitches without return tickets, recall the practice of exporting Europe's problems to its colonies: English convicts sent to Virginia or the Carolinas, or (once America became the land of the free) to Australia. There is no return from the island. Fatutaka, formerly a British colony and still recognising the English monarch as head of state, has been riven by civil conflict since it gained its independence, and is a very typical casualty of empire. Richard Benson, whom the American Foreign Service assign to run the new country, recognises that his post is lowly; as an American diplomat he has "never heard of a country called Freedom" (39). But within the confines of the island he is as all powerful as any colonial authority, "a viceroy— master of the antipodes, lord of this human Galapagos." (40). A benevolent despot, Benson sets out in paternalistic terms to make the island into a home for the detainees, though in the event its evolution holds as many surprises as Galapagos.

Like many of those who invest in the idea of freedom without address-ing the reality of how freedom can be developed and lived through, Ben-son is well-meaning but fundamentally naïve. When he rebukes one of the guards for shouting at the new arrivals the guard replies that shouting is what they expect.

> They haven't shit in six years without someone telling them to and then watching them do it. . . . Free will's a muscle, dude. And theirs is as weak as your biceps. (39)

Indeed most of the men are so institutionalised that they cannot take advan-tage of any of the opportunities offered by the island. The freed man turns out to be qualitatively different from the free man (40). The restaurant remains empty; the men are so used to being forced to eat alone that they prefer solitude. Any questions from Benson recall their interrogations and are rebuffed. At roll call they refuse to answer to their names. As Abdul-lah237 explains, they insist on keeping their internment serial numbers as their true identities. The only request made is for plywood and steel mesh for home improvements; the men reconstruct the sleeping cages, seven feet by eight, to which they are accustomed. When Abdullah237 asks Benson if there is a word in English for a place "where everything was perfect, but you still felt miserable" (41), the unspoken answer is clearly utopia.

In this post-terror world narrative and utopia appear to be completely incompatible. The story also overtly questions the value of writing as repara-tive strategy. As far as the department which runs it is concerned, nobody cares "if Freedom was a happy place, as long as it looked like one" (41), but Benson continues to promote the pursuit of happiness. Assuming that tell-ing their stories would be therapeutic, he tries every means to get the men to disgorge their experiences, from encounter groups to memoir-writing classes and a wiki-history, all to no avail. At the same time, however, behind the scenes, he intercepts the men's letters, in order to censor any suspect mate-rial. The men are only going to be allowed to tell the stories which Benson approves. Once censorship is introduced every word becomes suspect to him. "Where did literal speech end and metaphor begin?" (41). If Abdullah237 says he is bored, is it a code to signal a rescue? Does Salman765's longing for his wife's stuffed peppers conceal a nefarious—or even an erotic—meaning? And as for Waheed004's poem, it is quite impossible. Every phrase seems to contain the potential for double and triple meanings. "Language took on the complexity of wartime maneuvers" (41). There is apparently no place for writing in utopia. Language cannot be policed and confined, it eludes authority, and the upshot is that the Department rules that the letters can-not be sent at all. Instead Benson keeps both reading and writing under his control, scrapping the outgoing letters once read, but composing fictitious replies himself, in the guise of mothers, brothers, sons and wives, construct-ing an external world without suffering or problems, in which Salman765's mother makes a sudden recovery from her health problems and Jamal202's little brother gets a university place. "Benson eliminated all pain and suffering, all loss and cruelty, from the responses" (41). By benevolent subterfuge he creates a utopian world, though an external one, at some remove from Freedom; "rather than trying to regulate the human reaction to difficult events, he had rewritten the events" (41). Writing creates utopia but utopia and Freedom are no longer synonymous.

When the men do decide to flex their free-will, the results are decidedly anti-utopian. Deafened by their loud music Benson introduces a system of laws, realising that "order was more easily enforced than happiness" (41). Surveillance follows and even cruel and inhuman punishment. The Bush administration had declared the detainees to be illegal combatants, unprotected by the Geneva Convention (and thus vulnerable to torture) and maintained that the President must be free to define what counts as torture.[6] On Freedom anyone who contradicts the rules is forced to listen for six hours to Verdi at high volume. "No civilised country could ever call opera torture" (41). Faced with Benson's coercion, the detainees, formerly a motley group of different ages, professions and nationalities, unite and begin to be radicalised. Bingo is condemned as un-Islamic and beards begin to sprout. Freedom is recognised overtly as a fiction. Significantly the first suicide is "suicide by book" (41). The victim weights himself down with heavy volumes and drowns. Instead of writing, the men use silence and non-verbal techniques of resistance. When Benson teaches them how to play charades they respond enthusiastically, wordlessly re-enacting the conditions of their captivity, miming forced feeding and anal probings, limping as if in shackles, hurling imaginary faecal cocktails and staging re-enacted tribunals, each with one panic-stricken desperate pleader and four stony-faced judges. Finally they reject the language of their rulers, beginning with the term Freedom itself. When they suggest a name change for the island, they offer critical variations on Utopia's original Greek meaning (no place): *La makan* (no place), *La bilad* (no land), *Bidoun* (without), *Al Wayl* (misery) and most significantly *Al A'raf*. As Edgar Allan Poe described the latter to his publisher, it is

> a medium between heaven and hell where men suffer no punishment, but yet do not attain that tranquil and even happiness which they suppose to be the characteristics of heavenly enjoyment.[7]

Although Benson extends his censorship to the Quran, locking away all copies, the hard-line Islamists come out with a majority on the ruling council and he is forced to exercise his veto. For Benson heaven has become something closely approaching hell.

On the island only the Uighurs have kept busy, carving intricately fashioned wooden furniture. Knowing how keen the government is to promote free markets, Benson proposes to export it, assuming that it will appeal to conscience consumerism, much as Western consumers will buy coffee harvested by pygmies or necklaces made by Romanian street kids. He is overruled in the name of security (40). <u>Freedom is incompatible with the free market.</u> Undeterred the Uighurs continue to make furniture which crops up all over the island, here an abandoned table for ten, there a row of bare bedframes, in groupings which silently evoke the absence of their families and satirise the claims of the island as "home". Faced with the defeat of all his projects for the pursuit of happiness, Benson decides the men must have their wives and children with them—and is promptly refused. Abdullah237 roundly declares that "He didn't want his son breathing Freedom's air" (42). America, however, manipulates desire to its own ends and works out how to use the oppression of women to its advantage, advertising worldwide for mail order brides. In a sad reflection of the conditions of women in many parts of the world, there is no shortage of volunteers to marry total strangers and remain forever at a safe distance from their families and homelands. In a horrible parody of an Islamic paradise, new brides are shipped in for the men, and they form new family groups, replete with their defiantly named children, a plethora of Osamas, Jihads, Zawahiris and Qutbs. As the years pass, with divorces, fights, suicides and murders, "Freedom became as good as America after all" (42).

Freedom begins as a joke and ends in disillusion, but the story itself does not end on quite such a pessimistic note. As a withering critique of American pretensions to freedom and democracy the story also offers a postcolonial parable, underlining the fact that <u>freedom cannot be merely given but must be won.</u> The idea of freedom does not die. At the close of the story Benson returns to witness the mass exodus of the detainees' children, six dozen teenagers in four huge boats, pushed off by their parents, and paddling furiously towards the horizon. Fairly obviously Waldman evokes Oscar Wilde's dictum that

> A map of the world that does not include Utopia is not worth even glancing at, for it leaves out the one country at which Humanity is always landing. And when Humanity lands there, it looks out and, seeing a better country, sets sail.[8]

As the ending indicates <u>utopia is not a place but the spirit of hope itself.</u> In the story when freedom becomes Freedom it dies; the concept does not survive institutionalisation. Freedom has to be kinetic, freedom from something or towards something, and is constituted in resistance. It is Benson's coercions that trigger the men's opposition; their freedom is forged in struggle. In the words of Bill Ashcroft,

> This then is the dynamic function of the utopian impulse. Not to construct a place, but to enact the utopian in the engagement with power.[9]

How does fiction enact this engagement? Waldman's story highlights, in Benson's reaction to the ambiguities of language, the slipperiness of its own method. In the story every time the word "freedom" is used, the reader has to hold two referents in place simultaneously, a concept and an antithetical realisation, generating most of the ironies as a result, and problematising the relationship between literature and utopia. In Ernst Bloch's argument all literature is inherently utopian because its whole point is to imagine a different world.[10] If, as Frederic Jameson argues in *The Political Unconscious*, narratives are socio-symbolic acts, attempts to achieve symbolic resolution of real social or political contradictions, then

> It is by narrative, by the stories that we tell, that we have a world, and it is by utopian thinking, utopian forms, utopian narrative that we may have a conception of a radically changeable world.[11]

On the other hand actual utopias have been distinctly thin on the ground in America in the later twentieth century. With the exception of a clutch of feminist works (more properly categorised as dystopias) utopian writing has largely been relegated to the science fiction side-lines in most recent accounts of the form.[12] As for the concept itself, it has had a distinctly bad press. In the second half of the twentieth century utopia was usually understood, in pejorative terms, as a contributor to totalitarianism, and its demise welcomed as a move away from abstract thinking which ignores individuality and difference. E.H. Carr criticised utopian thought as playing an adverse role between 1919 and 1939 in the policies of England and France, for example, contributing to the Second World War.[13] The miseries of Communism, the disaster of Hitler's Germany, are easily used as a stick to beat political idealists. For many thinkers (though not all) Popper's consideration of utopia in *The Open Society* marked a definitive moment in the demolition of utopia.[14] In the memorable summation of Russell Jacoby, "Someone who believes in utopias is widely considered to be out to lunch or out to kill."[15]

Of late, however, utopia has begun to get a better press. The re-evaluation of the social worth of utopia would include Rorty's 1999 case for a revival of utopian energies, describing utopia as a "most distinctive and praiseworthy human capacity".[16] Writing much earlier, Ernst Bloch, who remains a touchstone for discussions of utopia, had already expanded the concept from the narrower image of a description of an alternative society designed to evoke or facilitate a better way of life, to such phenomena as daydreams, religious visions, myths of a golden age, circuses, fairy tales, glossy magazines, travel literature, architectural utopias and social movements. For Bloch, the capacity for hope is a prime source of human creativity, dynamism and progress, and is part of our capacity for imagination. Theories of utopia have expanded exponentially beyond the literary genre to embrace critical utopias and dystopias (Tom Moylan), the desire for utopia (Ruth Levitas) and "social dreaming" (Lyman Tower Sargent).[17] Immanuel Wallerstein's appeal for a project of "utopistics", Russell Jacoby's call for a return to the role of public intellectuals, John Rawls' discussion of the possibility of realistic utopia, in a world society of liberal and decent people, and Bourdieu's call for reasoned utopianism as opposed to "bankers' fatalism" all suggest that the earlier identification of utopia with totalitarian projects has been largely superseded.[18] Although utopia remains a fundamentally contested term, even the noisy debates over the relation between ideology and utopia, usually focussed on the work of Karl Mannheim and Paul Ricoeur, have quieted, as witness, Lyman Tower Sargent's argument that despite the ways in which scholarship has played down the role of utopia and emphasised that of ideology, utopia is at least as—or even more—important in the work of both thinkers.[19]

Globalisation has also brought utopia back into the spotlight. For Patrick Hayden and Chamsy el-Ojeili, the question of how human communities can be created anew animates the engagement with contemporary globalization.[20] Utopia and globalisation are in themselves close companions. The emergence of utopia as a literary form in the sixteenth century coincided uncannily with the modern Western project of global exploration. More's *Utopia* is presented through a tale of world exploration, via its traveller-narrator, Ralph Hythloday.

> Utopia thus connotes the desire to transgress borders and to encounter other lands and peoples, to connect together otherwise disparate places and identities across the globe. In this way Utopia and globalization are born together.[21]

Globalisation has habitually been cast in utopian (or dystopian) terms. Commentators on the utopian side will tend to see globalisation as producing a world without borders, enjoying truly free trade, a progressive equalisation of peoples beyond the nation state, the free flow of information and the possibility of negotiated peace and global governance. As dystopia, globalisation is seen as polarising wealth, handing over political control to multinational corporations, eroding indigenous cultures and fostering a new imperialism based on Americanisation.[22] As Hayden and el-Ojeili argue, "happy globalization", as symbolised by the fall of the Berlin Wall, and the optimism of Friedman and Fukuyama, appeared to meet its end in Seattle in 1999; dystopian visions, haunted by terror, became more common.[23]

In its modern form therefore the utopian impulse resonates with contemporary debates about local-global penetration, the meanings of boundaries and the role of cosmopolitanism as a unifying social force.[24] But—and it is a big but—the quest for utopia has its darker underside, in the figure of the global terrorist, equally convinced of a social or religious mission. John Gray, for one, has argued that utopian politics have moved from the extremes to mainstream politics, indeed that utopianism now occupies the political centre in the examples of George W. Bush and Tony Blair.[25] Faith-based violence may be based on very different apocalyptic faiths, also shaded with utopian projections, in Gray's examples of American fundamentalism and radical Islam. With images of America as new world, paradise or utopia replaced by a terror dream, it appears that the terrorist may have gained a monopoly on the idea of paradise. The relationship between utopianism and fundamentalism is complex, including both content (visions of the good life) and structural paradigm (both stem from discontent with the now, and mount a challenge to the contemporary world). Many Islamic groups dream of establishing an Islamic state ruled by Sharia law; Osama Bin Laden's videotapes and speeches offer both a critical take on Western values and a vision of an Islamic state to come. Lucy Sargisson has argued that the particular kind of utopianism which drives religious fundamentalism is perfectionist, an authoritarian utopianism based on the notion of one truth, "the truth".[26] Perhaps in response, commentators have located a turn away from the quest for perfection towards a more modest utopianism, and an evolution from product to process.[27] The utopian wish has become more prominent than the utopian genre.

To return to "Freedom" briefly, it is important to note that America finally succeeds in pacifying the islanders (if not their children) by the manipulation of desire. The mail order brides come wafting down from the sky, soft weapons in America's cause. The questionnaire which the men have to complete to obtain a wife asks them to list the qualities they seek, as well as "Any absolute No's? (Facial Hair, Body Mass Index over 25, Previous Marriages)" (42). When the women's dossiers arrive they do not match up to specifications (facial hair abounds though nobody has requested it) but the men are wholly enthusiastic, drawing lots for first choice of wife, and then bargaining and exchanging with each other. As the wife-swapping wages, the community centre hums with the happy activity which Benson had hoped to create with bingo (42). Women are a commodity used (here, essentially, trafficked) to promote an American vision of utopia and to exploit the men's emotions. But although "Freedom" is a sharp little satire, the men's feelings remain almost as opaque to the reader as they are to Benson, whose terse classified emails back to his bosses reflect his lack of insight. The detainees don't want to inflict Freedom on anyone they love. But for Benson their opposition is strategically political rather than heartfelt: "The men have rejected family reunification. Appears to be a case of manipulative self-deprivation" (42). Narrated in omniscient third-person the story offers the reader an overview of events not unakin to Benson's own surveillance, with the men observed only from the outside, their feelings a closed book. It is a point which raises an additional concern in the present study, centring upon the commodification of emotion, a phenomenon of a globalised world in which feelings are managed, homogenised across cultures, exaggerated, or expunged according to a dominant model. Can fiction avoid playing to pre-programmed emotions? Is it utopian to assume that feelings can be evoked in the reader as a method of enacting the engagement with power? What is the role of emotion in utopian art? Among other topics, the current study investigates ways in which fictional techniques can resist the commodification of affect, and maintain a reasoned but imaginative vision of possibilities for human community. That term "affect" cries out for qualification.[28] Literary critics (wary of appearing undertheorised or old-fashionedly sentimental) have enthusiastically adopted the term "affect" to enable them to reimport a concern with emotion into their practice. But it is arguable that the term itself represents a means of managing emotion in the service of an institutional discourse. Nigel Thrift has argued that in some ways the discovery of new ways of practicing affect is also the discovery of a whole new means of manipulation by the powerful.[29]

Richard Gray's analysis of 9/11 fiction, for example, categorises all the novels which fall back upon the domestic, the sentimental, or the melodramatic as inadequate responses to the attacks, without considering why such emotional responses are illegitimate. In Gray's analysis the world of women and children does not seem to be envisaged as a positive place for literary responses.[30] It is not, however, utopian to consider that readers are entitled to their own emotions, and that one of the most important functions of literary fiction is to exercise our feelings in ways that prevent their homogenisation by a dominant culture. Scandalously, however, as we shall see in the example of the Unabomber, it is also possible for the terrorist to act in defence of spontaneous, unsocialised emotion, albeit with devastating emotional consequences in his turn.

Emotions are easily commodified. Whereas Frederic Jameson complained of a waning of affect in the postmodern world of simulacra,[31] other commentators have perceived an emotionalisation of contemporary life, the growth of a therapeutic culture and the increasing dominance of emotional labour in the economy. Liz Bondi has drawn attention to a wide range of social and cultural trends in which emotions have moved towards the centre of public life, commercial activity and consumption.[32] Arlie Russell Hochschild's *The Managed Heart*, with its analysis of the service sector in which workers are increasingly expected to produce the correct emotional experiences for customers (from comfortable flights, to pleasant dining and cheerful offices), highlighted the risks to workers' authentic identities, in the dominance of the personality adopted during the working shift in the off-duty life.[33] In some ways, of course, this management of emotion is not a new phenomenon. Nigel Thrift offers the example of the military management of affect by drilling, and in the development of small bands of brothers-in-arms, prepared to die for each other, bound together by close social bonds and learned behaviour which conquers fear and channels aggression. In this way an intense sociality acts as a structured way of producing death.[34] As we shall see (Chapter 5, below) André Dubus III's *The Garden of Last Days* pits a 9/11 hijacker (one of a band of brothers, his affect closely tailored to his mission) against a Florida lap dancer (creating an experience of emotional closeness for the client). Affect is manipulated here for divergent ends, political and economic, but both characters offer examples of a social tendency towards greater engineering of emotion (and in both cases with a utopian element).

It is important to emphasise that the emotion being produced and controlled may be located at either end of the happiness-misery continuum. Two models of feeling-management in American society are particularly germane to the discussion of utopia: the relentless creed of positivity ("Have a Nice Day!") and the compulsory grief-fest. Compulsory positivity, despite the upbeat nature of the performance, is the enemy of utopian thought and action, masking social problems and returning them to the plane of ineffectual individualism. In *Smile or Die*, Barbara Ehrenreich has decried the way in which America has opted to feel good rather than to act well. Ehrenreich lambasts the dominance of positive thinking in the public sector and the corporate world, as tending to encourage an individualised, self-centred approach to wider social failings. Diagnosed with breast cancer Ehrenreich was horrified by the ways in which "positivity" was compulsory in the upbeat pink-ribbon culture of cancer "survivors" (never "victims") and the ways in which cancer was reconfigured as a "gift". Positive thinking was promoted as a means of helping to cure the disease, as if cancer were a sign of a personal failure to think or feel in the right way. As a result, the medical and social discourse denied women the right to express fear or anger, encouraging patients to deny reality, blame themselves and submit cheerfully to the presentation of breast cancer teddy bears (a fate worse than death in Ehrenreich's book). Although the example of demon positivity in the case of breast cancer is sharpened by gendered norms which tend to proscribe expressions of female anger (prostate cancer does not usually trigger teddy-bears), the management of emotion and the encouragement of a cloyingly upbeat attitude is a phenomenon which extends right across American society. Historically America has been pathologically life-affirming, from Mary Baker Eddy to Dale Carnegie and Norman Vincent Peale, but in the contemporary period positivity has become a central plank in American ideology. Ehrenreich examines the business of positive "affect", the mood we display to others, through smiles, greetings and professions of confidence and optimism; the encouragement of positive thinking in evangelical religion (the prosperity gospel movement) and the post-rational corporate world (coaches and motivational speakers); the underlying belief that good things come to those who are optimistic enough to expect them (whether divine blessings or offers of jobs); television shows (*Larry King Live* and the *Oprah Winfrey Show*) and even the academic discipline of "positive psychology". As a result she argues that America has no mechanism for imagining the worst and is too busy accentuating the positive to tackle (or even recognise) substantial problems. Ehrenreich finds weighty support in the work of sociologist Karen Cerulo who has analysed ways in which the American optimism bias undermined preparedness and invited disaster in relation to Hurricane Katrina, the subprime crisis and the 9/11 attacks. Despite a previous attack on the World Trade Centre in 1993, warnings about another attack, a clear recognition that US airport security was inadequate, and reports from flight schools of pupils who wanted to learn how to fly a plane but were not interested in being able to land one, the American tendency to underplay the negative meant that, in Cerulo's title, they *Never Saw it Coming*.[35] Neither Dr Pangloss nor Cassandra, Ehrenreich, a long term social activist, remains committed to the belief in the ability to create a better world but cautions that we cannot wish ourselves into utopia, "and the first step is to recover from the mass delusion that is positive thinking."[36]

At the other end of the spectrum, trauma is also a highly marketable commodity. Jess Walter's *The Zero* (2007) mounts a ferocious satire on the compensation culture and the politics and economics of mourning. April, whose husband and sister have died in the 9/11 attacks, applies for Federal Victims' compensation and watches a PowerPoint presentation with her lawyer. Screen 2 covers "Pain and Mental Anguish: a quantifying formula".[37] Although "Everyone starts with a base of two-fifty" which is what the guidelines have determined each life is worth "at a base level of grieving" (169), it is possible to add extra claims for special circumstances. In April's case, however, given that she had separated from her husband Derek, the lawyer advises her to settle for $250,000. He himself is looking forward to a percentage of the award as his fee, which will include compensation for his own trauma in handling cases of compensation for trauma. He will also be compensated for "Compassion Fatigue" (174), a condition which he exhibits all too clearly. Concerned that there might be a mistress with a potential claim, he is relieved to learn that the mistress also perished in the attacks. Later when April meets her brother Gus, their encounter is filmed for a reality TV show whose producer advises her to

> Just do exactly what a normal person would normally do . . . when seeing your last living sibling for the first time since your sister . . . died such a horrible, unbearable death. This is reality; what we want is real emotions. (207)

Real emotion is not so easily accessed, however. The meeting is carefully choreographed and stage-managed by the camera crew and bears no relation to April's actual feelings which are mixed, chaotic and confused. It was April's sister, March, who was Derek's mistress, and when April phoned to upbraid her she rushed to Derek's office high up in one of the towers and died as a result (249).

Society however has clear ideas about the appropriate performance of emotion. Mourning has become so compulsory and pervasive that the news media are able to create an experience of vicarious grief. Jess Walter had spent time at Ground Zero while working as a ghost-writer on the memoirs of the New York Police Commissioner, and details from his experience feature in the novel: television news trucks going "grief-fishing", a TV crew wearing windbreakers reading "From the Ashes" and a sign in a shop reading "God Bless America. New Furniture Arriving Every Day." The central

protagonist of the novel, Brian Remy has shot himself in the head before
the novel begins and as a result his memory continually misfires, creating odd gaps and contradictions in the story. As a result, as one reader
commented, the novel rings true to that feeling of unreality which follows
major traumatic events, the sense that even something as real as death can
seem unreal, unbelievable.³⁸ Society however encourages a more systematic
approach to death. Remy is taken aback when he learns that his son Edgar
has told all his classmates that his father died in the attacks. Edgar knows
perfectly well that his father is alive but defends his action in pre-grieving
for him as a form of resistance against the generalised grief of his society, a means of insisting on the individual nature of his own emotions. He
explains that he has chosen to focus on an individual because

> General grief is a lie. What are people in Wyoming really grieving? A
> loss of safety? Some shattered illusion that a lifetime of purchases and
> television programs had meaning? The emptiness of their Palm pilots
> and SUVs and baggy jeans? (34)

In the upshot, however, even Edgar cannot avoid the social script for grief.
At the close he is so pleased to have gone through all the official stages of
grief that he cannot face appearing to regress by recognising that his father
is alive.

> I've been through all the stages of grief. You can't want me to go back.
> What, to denial? . . . Or anger? (279)

Edgar is so completely in the grip of the orthodox model of grief management, Elizabeth Kübler-Ross's stages of Denial, Anger, Bargaining, Depression and Acceptance, that he breaks off all further contact with his father.³⁹

So can fiction offer emotional resistance? Bharati Mukherjee offers a
prescient example, in "The Management of Grief", a short story focussed
on what was (until 9/11) the worst terrorist attack involving an aircraft.
On 23 June 1985 Air India Flight 182, from Toronto and Montreal to
New Delhi and Mumbai, exploded over Ireland, causing the deaths of all
307 passengers and twenty-two crew. Because it was the first flight from
Canada to India at the start of the Canadian school holidays, women and
children featured heavily on the passenger manifest. The plane was an
hour and a half behind schedule; had it been on time it would have blown
up at Heathrow. A second bomb went off less than an hour beforehand,
at Narita airport in Tokyo, on another Air India plane bound in the other
direction from Vancouver to Bangkok. The bombers may not have realised
that Canada used daylight saving time, whereas Japan did not, leading to
speculation that the two bombs were timed to coincide in a "spectacular",
a demonstration of the terrorist power to encircle the globe. Both bombs
involved "inter-lined" luggage and a "Mr Singh" who did not board.

This was an event where utopianism and terrorism coincided in different ways. Subsequent investigations revealed that the bombings were almost certainly the work of Canadian-based Sikh terrorists motivated by the desire for an independent Sikh state in India, an imaginary homeland evoked as "Khalistan", meaning the land of the pure. June was the memorial month for the 1984 Hindu storming of the Sikh Golden Temple, and the Air India 182 plane was named the Emperor Kanishka, after a Hindu ruler of India. Mukherjee and her husband Clark Blaise carried out a meticulous investigation of the bombing (drawing death threats down on their heads) which they published as *The Sorrow and the Terror*. The short story is also set against a background of multiculturalism, a dream which has triggered the immigrants' movement to Canada, but which in Mukherjee's analysis represents a degenerate utopia, degenerate because it has solidified into an ideology, and because it is multiculturalism (in her argument) which has allowed the terrorists to recruit and to carry out fund-raising in Canadian Sikh temples. Ostensibly multiculturalism accepts difference but, particularly in the Canadian "salad bowl" model as opposed to the American melting pot, it also papers over or ignores contradictions.

The event was however "utopian" in a third sense; it took place nowhere. The bombing was an "unhoused event",[40] disowned by the governments of both India and Canada. Despite the fact that ninety per cent of the passengers were Canadian, the Canadian government saw it as an Indian event. (The Canadian Prime Minister offered condolences to his Indian counterpart.) India (reluctant to put Sikh-Hindu conflict in the spotlight) dismissed it as an overseas event. It took some days for the Canadians to react officially and send Embassy staff to Ireland. Only the Irish emerged with credit, perhaps because of their own experience of terrorism, welcoming the bereaved into their homes, and offering comfort and support right away. The event became symbolic of the fact that Canadian citizens of immigrant background remained in civil limbo. Terrorism exposed the falsity of the multicultural dream and turned utopia into dystopia. However, whereas *The Sorrow and the Terror* is a non-fiction work of precise historicity, in "The Management of Grief" the facts of terror remain offstage, and the focus is upon emotion, specifically in relation to rival understandings of grief as either a universalising state of sympathy, or as a resistant cultural phenomenon, dividing rather than uniting. In the story, Judith Templeton, a Canadian social worker, recruits Shaila Bhave, whose husband and children have died in the bombing, as an intermediary with the other grieving relatives, many of whom are too shocked, hysterical, or depressed to function. She is drawn to Shaila by her apparent ability to cope, her calmness and strength. Shaila objects that,

> By the standards of the people you call hysterical, I am behaving very oddly and very badly.[41]

By Indian standards Shaila should be screaming. "We must all grieve in our own way"(183), she continues. Her own grief involves ecstatic dreams of her family, hearing voices, seeing an apparition of her husband in an animist temple, and a six month odyssey around India. Judith, however, expects the community of grieving relatives to move from one emotional state to another, following the Western model of grief management, and will reward them accordingly with state money. She is baffled when a Sikh couple reject the proper reward for right emotions, and insist on the principle of hope as the duty of a parent, refusing to accept their sons' deaths, or to sign the documentation which would allow them to collect the reward of compensation from the Canadian government. The couple's two sons died only weeks after they had brought over their aged parents from the Punjab. But despite the fact that they will soon lose all their utilities and their apartment, the parents stand their ground. The father "will not pretend that I accept" (195). Judith is nonplussed. She quotes the textbooks on grief management with their sequence of stages to pass through, compiles a chart and finds that six months after the tragedy very few of the relatives can be categorised as reconstructed. "Depressed Acceptance" (192) is the norm. "Acceptance means you speak of your family in the past tense and you make active plans for moving ahead with your life" (192). The Western model makes no allowance for cultural variation or for an active role in grieving. In this scenario grief manages the individual who moves passively through a set progress of emotions, rather than the mourner being an agent in the management of his or her own feelings. Grief is in the management chair, as the ambiguity of the title suggests, as opposed to being driven by the individual. Indian customs offer a different management model. Despite her belief that remarriage is a form of reconstruction, Judith is taken aback by the speed with which widowers have new marriages arranged for them ("it is the duty of a man to look after a wife" (190)) returning from India within a month of the disaster with young widows as new brides, and even replacement families.

The story, however, remains utopian in a hopeful sense, in its refusal to settle for the rigid definition of emotion. Louis Marin's thought (*Utopics*, translated into English in 1984) is relevant here.[42] Marin argues that utopia signifies a space somewhere between true/false, affirmation/negation, a space of neutrality in which contradictions are allowed to play off each other, rather than being resolved, or hidden in the text. Where myth dissolves contradictions by mediating them (life and death, for example) utopia does the reverse, so that happiness may be found in indeterminacy. Marin therefore finds utopia not in a perfected society but in a fictional space in which normal presuppositions of discourse are suspended. Marin emphasises the importance of spatial play in texts, identifying various works as utopic because they lack a stable ground and generate meaning from the interplay of various spaces, (in such examples as the paintings of Klee, or Pascal's *Pensées*) thus extending the term "utopia" well beyond the usual range of cultural forms considered.[43]

In the story the space of fiction is also a fiction about the absence of place. The action is constructed around a sequence of spatialised scenes set in liminal locations (in the hallway or on the stairs between rooms, on the shore between land and sea, in an airport customs area, in a shrine mediating between earth and heaven) and the central character is positioned in an indeterminate ideological and emotional state between contrasted "foil" characters who adopt firm ideological positions. At thirty-six she is too old to start again but not old enough to give up. "Like my husband's spirit I flutter between worlds" (189). Her grandmother, a young widow had opted for intense piety; her parents are rationalists, leaving her "trapped between two modes of knowledge" (189). Among the bereaved, Dr Ranganathan, a scientist, opts for Western rationalism, and begins a new life in Texas, where nobody knows his past. Shaila's friend Kusum chooses traditional religion and an ashram in Hardwar where she spends her time communing with apparitions of her family. Kusum's traditional daughter, a singer of Indian *bhajans* died in the plane. Her other daughter Pam, in love with modernity and consumerism, had chosen to stay in Canada and work at Wonderland, a theme park. Shaila herself remains somewhere between India and Canada, tradition and modernity, reason and religion. On one level the liminal locations dramatize the position of the characters as belonging nowhere, positioned between worlds and cultures. The reader wonders whether they will stand their ground in their new homeland or give up and "return" to India, for example. But in another sense liminality emerges as a source of power. On the shore in Ireland, looking out towards the location of the plane, Kusum has "the bewildered look of a sea-creature whom the tides have stranded" (184), in some interstitial space between land and sea. When they spot a head-shape bobbing in the waves both women plunge into the water, only to return disappointed to land. Yet because her sons' bodies remain nowhere, unlocatable, Shaila (unlike Kusum) has hope. In the makeshift temporary picture gallery which shows photos of the bodies, she is encouraged to identify their images, warned that long immersion in water and broken bones beneath the skin will make their faces heavier. "Try to adjust your memories" (188). When Dr Ranganathan identifies them as the Kutty boys, Shaila weeps but not from disappointment. "On the contrary, I am ecstatic" (188). Being "No place" keeps hope alive. "It's a parent's duty to hope" (186). Ireland, itself right on the edge of Europe, is a location of warm emotion. "The Irish are not shy; they rush to me and give me hugs and some are crying" (187), says Shaila, who cannot imagine anything similar happening in Toronto. She had never told her husband that she loved him, and was so traditional that she felt uncomfortable using his first name. In Ireland she manages to declare her love, in a poem floated out to sea. Liminality is also coded for agency. When she accompanies Kusum's coffins to India, a furious scene erupts in the customs area of the airport, perhaps the archetypal modern liminal space, neither in one country nor quite in another. When the customs officer is obstructive Shaila screams and swears, and then reflects that she and Kusum had once been well-brought-up young women, their voices sweet and low. Now she is prepared to outrage "customs" and act for herself.

The story ends with Shaila back in Canada, still in an apparently liminal location. Returning from a small errand in Yonge Street (once the longest street in the world) she is walking home to her apartment, equidistant between the Ontario Houses of Parliament and the University of Toronto. Before the bombing Shaila had been apolitical. Like the other Indian immigrants she "stayed out of politics and came halfway around the world to avoid religious and political feuding" (195). Now she writes letters to newspapers and MPs, one of whom advises her:

> You want to make a difference? Work on a campaign. Work on mine. Politicize the Indian voter. (196)

The story ends when Shaila, standing on the path, hears the voices of her family, "Your time has come. Go, be brave" (197). She does not know "where this voyage I have begun will end" (197) or even which direction to take, but she starts walking. Ostensibly still in limbo, somewhere between political and cultural arenas, Shaila is none the less moving forward. Until this point the story is largely recounted in the present. Now Shaila recalls the moment "last week" (196) when "I heard the voices of my family one last time" (197) and moves from the stasis of a frozen present to a past and therefore a future. What emerges from the story is a validation of the free play of the imagination in an indeterminate space, as opposed to the occupation of a fixed position, or the espousal of "black and white" views, the latter exemplified by the fundamentalist authors of the terrorist act. Marin's connection of utopia and the liminal offers a suggestive transition between "literary utopias" (formal or generic) and what Ruth Levitas would qualify as "emancipatory utopias", which place less emphasis on literary form and more upon critical content.[44] Unlike "Freedom" this story is in no sense classifiable within the literary genre of utopia, yet its content clearly engages with utopia and in its ending it moves the heroine towards social action. In the story liminality is part of the heroine's conversion to membership of a political community.

The present study focusses upon the presence of utopia, and the dynamic between terror and utopia, in literary fiction by major emerging writers in the last fifteen years. (There is nothing utopian about a bad novel.) At the risk of attenuating some of the surprises, a brief chapter outline of what follows is probably useful. Appropriately the book begins with works which focus first on utopia and then on terror, considering firstly the relation of utopia to language and symbol, and then that of the writer to the terrorist. In her short stories, Kim Edwards (Chapter 2) gives the lie to the idea that utopia has disappeared from literary fiction, taking as her topic the issue of the possibility of utopia in a globalised world. Edwards' stories concern a utopian environmental community, scientific utopianism, local utopias and the ways in which language encodes utopia, drawing on the philosophical thought of Kenneth Burke and employing a technique of pairing stories to maintain a critical dialectic. In *The Secrets of a Fire King* (2007) Edwards creates powerful images of magical other worlds (in the heavens, underwater, in performance spaces), and lushly tended gardens or paradises abound. But she also asks whether the desire for perfection is itself dangerous, and underlines the ways in which utopia depends upon the exploitation of desire. In *A Person of Interest* (2008) Susan Choi (Chapter 3) explores the links between writer and terrorist in a novel based upon the historical case of Ted Kaczynski, otherwise known as the Unabomber, who carried out a series of bomb attacks between 1978 and 1995. Kaczynski's utopian manifesto, *Industrial Society and its Future*, attacked the technologisation and oversocialisation of contemporary society, arguing for a return to the expression of real feelings rather than approved social emotion. Controversially, the novel accepts the Unabomber's critique of an oversocialised society in which affect is technologised and processed, with any inappropriate response criminalised (here in the examples of the polygraph test, institutionalised grief-fests and media-managed emotion). The novel's narrative mode, *style indirect libre*, clicks with the modern process of socialisation, permeating the individual protagonist with the imperial stance of the narrator, to produce a voice colonised by socialised processes. As a result the reader oscillates between empathy and irony in relation to the protagonist, Lee. Although the Unabomber offers a suggestive example of the literary terrorist, designing his campaign of terror around literary models, symbolism, word games and invented characters, Choi makes a clear distinction between terrorist and writer. In the novel the terrorist is unmasked by a poet. In the denouement, Choi insists on the primacy of narrative in reconnecting Lee to his emotions, and putting back together a shattered whole. Far from seeing the writer as the double or rival of the destructive terrorist, Choi reasserts the primacy of writing as a creative force.

Three chapters discuss novels about the encounter between America and the Middle East, examining the clash between different utopias— that of American human rights imperialism, that of the Islamic terrorist, and non-Western forms of utopia, notably that which inspired the Islamic revolution of 1979 in Iran, identified with the thought of Navvab Safavi. Terror appears successively in different guises, as the effects of American-sponsored terror (Chapter 4), in the American reaction to 9/11 (Chapter 5) and as Islamic terror unleashed on other minorities (Chapter 6). Chalmers Johnson has argued that attacks on America are a shock to its people because such attacks are "blowback", the unintended consequences of earlier, covert or forgotten American operations. Iran brings the issue of why Americans "never see it coming" into sharp focus. André Dubus III's 1999 novel, *House of Sand and Fog* (Chapter 4), the first American bestseller centred on a Muslim protagonist (an Iranian-American), was a finalist for the National Book Award, enthusiastically adopted by Oprah, made into a major film, and has some two million copies in print. Yet until quite recently American awareness of Iran was characterised by a combination of ignorance and wholesale amnesia, particularly with respect to American support for the Shah, his secret police and the reign of terror which they exercised. In the novel, "not knowing" is the engine of a plot which counteracts the American exploitation of gender in its propaganda machine. Where popular Iranian-American memoirs "Other" Iran, potentially serving imperialist agendas, *House of Sand and Fog* pursues a narrative strategy which makes Iranians into Americans and Americans into Iranians. In its focus on human rights imperialism, in the example of the American mission to rescue women from oppression, it anticipates the gender emphasis of its successor, Dubus's 2008 novel *The Garden of Last Days* (Chapter 5) which dramatizes the reported encounter on the eve of his mission between a 9/11 terrorist and a Florida stripper. In the novel American and Islamic rescue missions collide. A drunken wife beater abducts the stripper's little girl in the belief that he is protecting her, while the hijacker, his eyes set upon an Islamic paradise, tries to save the stripper from her degenerate Western life as a commodified sex object. The novel engages with two stories: the deployment in America after 9/11 of a retrograde story drawing upon captivity narratives, the rescue of vulnerable women, and the terror dream of the early settlers; and the clash of rival utopias, that of the terrorist, acting on his belief in one authentic truth, and that of the striptopia of the Puma Club for Men, which offers the illusion of authentic emotional connection in a fake paradise, teasing with images of economic and emotional plenitude. Baulked utopianism feeds retrograde fantasies and violence as power, fantasy and desire play out in the relation between dancer and client. In *The Septembers of Shiraz* (2007) Dalia Sofer (Chapter 6) interrogates the role of art in relation to terror, in this case terror unleashed by non-Western forms of utopia. Rival conceptions of the Golden Age, and the exploitation of art in support of those conceptions are considered in relation to the Jews of Iran and their fellow community in America. Sofer complicates any easy condemnation of one side—Jewish or Muslim, American, or Iranian, religious or secular—by a technique of juxtaposed narratives and iconic images drawn from Iranian art and photography.

The argument now moves outwards from fiction which is anchored in the specifics of time and place to dystopian novels which deform recognisable temporal or geographical locations, and draw connections between utopia and empire, the one in terms of religion, the other in terms of race. In *Toward the End of Time* (1997) John Updike (Chapter 7) interrogates the relation between religion and empire, exploiting debates in modern cosmology and drawing upon the work of Elaine Pagels and Lewis Mumford to promote the local over the global, to undermine Manichean images of global conflict and to challenge the demonological roots of American political rhetoric. In constructing his dystopic society, Updike exploits the branching paths of "many worlds theory" to transport his readers from a balkanised post-imperial America in 2020 to ancient Egypt, the Roman Empire, monastic Ireland and Poland in 1944. Each excursion into a so-called parallel universe concerns the end of an empire: ancient Egypt as the pyramids are looted, Rome as the Christians expand in all directions, Christian monasticism during the Holy Roman Empire as the Vikings appear upon the horizon, the Third Reich with defeat imminent. The excursions suggest a continuing cycle of resurgent imperialism, as the death of one civilisation contains within it the seeds of the next, but also dramatise the resistance across the centuries of ordinary people and small local communities to totalitarian forces. Chapter 8 moves beyond America (and the American writer) in a novel which also moves America geographically to the margins. In her neo-slave narrative, *Blonde Roots* (2008) Bernardine Evaristo constructs a trenchant critique of the utopian qualities of Paul Gilroy's "Black Atlantic" model, which draws positives from the effects of the African Diaspora. In her family history Evaristo, who descends from an Afro-Brazilian slave heritage via Nigeria and Britain, encapsulates the diasporic reach of the "Black Atlantic." The neo-slave narrative is a transnational genre, with examples in North and South America, Europe and Africa.[45] Evaristo makes the Middle Passage a metaphor for temporal and geographical dislocation by rearranging the geography of the globe so that "Aphrika" and the "United Kingdom of Great Ambossa", though on the Equator, lie to the north of Europa, whence "whyte" slaves are kidnapped by "blaks", to be exported across the Atlantic to work on the plantations of the West Japanese Islands. By moving everything South, Evaristo effectively transfers the Black Atlantic from Northern to Southern hemispheres, correcting Gilroy's Anglo-American bias, and relegating "Amarika" to the sidelines. Evaristo none the less follows Gilroy, however in the treatment of terror. Gilroy argues that racial terror is not just compatible with Western rationality but complicit with it. Following Gilroy, the slave's story is interrupted by an extended excursus into the thoughts of the slaver, a "blak" racist intellectual. Evaristo uses a cliff-hanger plot device to position the slaver's views between the moments of the terror-stricken slave's realisation that recapture is imminent, and the brutal whipping which follows her apprehension. The reader moves from terror to a pseudo rational creed of scientific racism and back to terror, so that the reader's anxiety over the slave's fate permeates every "rational" word with emotion.

Successive chapters have moved from the evocation of utopia, through experiences of terror, whether American or Middle Eastern, to the dystopian scenarios of Updike and Evaristo. The final chapter comes full circle, returning to the utopian image, but in the context of disaster. Chitra Divakaruni's 2009 novel, *One Amazing Thing*, sets out to investigate the role of story in relation to disaster, offering a modestly utopian conclusion. In the novel nine survivors of a disaster, trapped in a basement, combat the stress of the situation by each narrating the story of one amazing thing in their own experiences. Loosely based on Boccaccio's *Decameron*, also a disaster utopia, the novel dramatizes the ways in which story can defeat time, and open out onto other worlds. The survivors bond into a community in proportion as the disaster escalates in the collapse of material structures around them, and narrative structures also merge into each other, creating a fleeting utopia out of catastrophe and collapse. The novel offers a corrective to Naomi Klein's *The Shock Doctrine*, in which she argued for a dystopian view of disaster, categorised as an opportunity for the implementation of brutal free-market programs when the public have been disorientated by wars, coups, or natural disasters. In contrast Rebecca Solnit argued that disaster may be utopian, as her book, *A Paradise Built in Hell*, indicates in its title. After 9/11 Americans discovered, if fleetingly, that disaster involves sharing loss, danger and deprivation and produces intimate group solidarity among survivors, emotional and physical support, and an embryonic civil society.

As the outline above indicates, not only do the writers considered here still have hopes of transforming society, whether by promulgating utopian images or constructing dystopian critiques, they also employ narrative techniques which draw the reader closely into the text, doubling reader and narrator, or reader and character for example, challenging the predictable emotional scripts of contemporary society, and undermining its political rhetoric and dominant narratives. Almost no secondary criticism exists in relation to Edwards, Choi, Dubus, Sofer, Evaristo and Divakaruni, in part because these works were almost all published in the last five years, but also arguably because they resist the prevalence in contemporary American fiction of works driven by a desire to repel the reader, a phenomenon which Kathryn Hume has identified as the product of political despair. In *Aggressive Fictions* Hume paints a decidedly dystopian picture of contemporary American fiction, describing novels which make readers wish to stop reading (or wish that they had never started), works which proceed at a narrative speed which undermines the ability to interpret (Burroughs, Reed), emphasise complaint (Ozick, Dworkin, Roth), indulge in unmitigated gloom about the future (McCarthy, Pahlaniuk), or involve grotesque images (Katherine Dunn) or extreme sex and violence (Bret Easton Ellis and a host of others.)

> Not only do writers scream in your ear, but they do the mental equivalent of pissing on your shoes, holding a knife to your throat, or spouting nuclear physics at you as well. A surprising amount of the fiction makes readers feel attacked or abused by a writer who seems hostile.[46]

Hume's user-unfriendly fiction fails to mobilise sympathy, evoke shared human feelings, create empathetic characters, or embody any sense of confidence in the world or in our capacity to transform it. In contrast, however dark or critical my chosen writers may be (and they are not by any means Oprahfied examples of sweetness and light) masochist readers will remain unsatisfied with what follows.

2 Rotten with Perfection
Kim Edwards, *The Secrets of a Fire King*

Although she had won the Whiting Award, the Nelson Algren Award, the Pushcart Prize and was an alternate for the PEN/Hemingway Award for her first collection of short stories, *The Secrets of a Fire King*, Kim Edwards only came to public notice with her bestseller, *The Memory Keeper's Daughter*. Published in hardback in 2005 to merely respectable reviews, the novel came out in paperback in 2006 and stormed the market, simultaneously reaching number one in the bestseller lists of *Publishers Weekly*, *USA Today* and the *New York Times* (where it remained at number one for thirty weeks.) This success was all the more surprising, given that the publisher had decided not to push the book in hardback; sales were fuelled largely by word of mouth recommendations, and by the not inconsiderable influence of American reading groups. The novel opens in a blizzard in 1964 as Dr David Henry delivers his wife of a son Paul, a boy who is "absolutely perfect" and a daughter, Phoebe, who has Down's syndrome.[1] In a disastrous decision, David gives his daughter to a nurse to be institutionalised, and tells his wife that her daughter has died. The novel unpacks the consequences in loss and grief for the family, and tells the story of Phoebe, raised as her own by the nurse. In the opening, David Henry describes the fraternal twins as "one visibly perfect" the other potentially "defective".[2] All the action stems from this one moment of perceived imperfection, and the doctor's subsequent attempt to have only a perfect child. In the novel, marked by the central metaphor of photography, the focus is in close up on a family, with its scope extending only peripherally to eugenics and social attitudes to handicap. But the narrow focus masks a broad concern in Edwards' writing with the ways in which the refusal to be satisfied with the less-than-perfect causes irremediable social harm. In the short stories of *The Secrets of a Fire King*, intimately influenced by the philosophy of Kenneth Burke, Edwards explores the quest for perfection in a globalised, transnational world, as a form of utopianism which operates across diverse domains (ecology, language, science). In the contemporary re-evaluation of utopia, Burke has been neglected; yet his key concept of entelechy may be usefully deployed both to assert the imaginative value of utopia as a tool for critical thinking, and as a means of registering reservations about its specific realisations.

In Edwards' story, "Paradise", the narrator habitually jogs along a Malaysian tourist beach, pausing by a freestanding hotel archway.

> *Your Gateway to Paradise* was written on both sides of the arch, in scrolling letters, a puzzling claim that encompassed either the hotel or the sea, depending on where you stood.[3]

One character jokes that, according to the sign, paradise is everywhere. But the narrator sees it differently.

> No matter where you stood, paradise seemed to be the place you no longer were.[4]

As the story unfolds, the narrator realises that despite her complete immersion in local culture, she will have to leave this particular paradise, in the face of attacks by radicalised Muslim students. Global politics effaces her own anti-colonial credentials. Like paradise, Utopia is also, in Thomas More's original pun, both the good place (eutopia) and no place (outopia). In *The Secrets of a Fire King,* Edwards focusses on a utopian environmentalist community ("Aristotle's Lantern"), scientific utopianism ("In the Garden", "A Gleaming in the Darkness"), local utopias or compensatory fantasies ("The Secrets of a Fire King", "Balance", "The Way It Felt to be Falling"), the idealist NGO worker and the reality of corruption ("Rat Stories"), religious evangelicalism turned into anti-abortion violence ("The Story of My Life") and the ways in which language encodes utopian impulses ("The Great Chain of Being", "Spring, Mountain, Sea"). Images of magical other worlds (in the heavens, underwater, in performance spaces), lushly tended gardens and their reversals in degraded environments abound. While the alert reader will identify characters or settings drawn from Korea, Malaysia, Indonesia and Cambodia the locations of the stories, and the ethnic origins of their protagonists, are kept carefully non-specific. Where worlds collide, it is in a global rather than a national context. Edwards' work is influenced by firsthand experience of the potential for utopian projects to backfire spectacularly. As well as teaching English in Malaysia, and Japan, she also worked in Cambodia, in 1991–2, before the Paris Peace Accords, when Cambodia was still in a state of civil war and under US embargo. Pol Pot's forced agrarian collectivisation in Cambodia, and the attendant death rates, offers a near perfect example of a utopian project which produced the most extreme dystopian results.[5]

One story, "Aristotle's Lantern", involves a consciously utopian social and environmental experiment. The protagonist, Anna, is established as idealistic from the start, when she loses her job as a physician's assistant because she takes time out to drive a seriously ill woman to a hospital which, unlike her own, will treat the uninsured. The woman is in great pain and having trouble catching her breath; Anna empathises with the fear in her eyes, thinking that it could be her standing there, her throat closing up, fear and pain making her light-headed. Minneapolis offers a dystopian vision of traffic pollution and ozone alerts, with infants and the elderly gasping for breath without any assistance from the medical world, with its swarms of business managers "calculating and adjusting and examining the potential of every human resource."[6] When her boyfriend Jonathan calls her from the other side of the globe, she accepts his invitation to join him in an idyllic ecotourist resort, an ecologist's dream, somewhere in the South China Sea. Anna feels that Jonathan is too isolated and self-contained, and sees a chance to erase distance and reconnect emotionally across the globe in an unspoiled world.

What Anna does not know is that the resort masks an experimental community known as "Aristotle's Lantern". She demonstrates her credentials as a potential member when diving with Gunnar, its unofficial leader. Gunnar, an advocate of absolute freedom, is prone to floating off underwater in his own direction. Anna has picked up "a fragile sphere", the shell of a sea urchin:

> The inner shell of a sea urchin is a hollow globe, scored in five curved sections that taper at the ends into a small hole at the top and the bottom. *Echinodermata: Echinoidea*, whose shell is known as Aristotle's lantern. (106)

The globe falls suddenly from her hands, however, as she realises that Gunnar's regulator is trailing; he has no air. Hesitating only for a moment she passes her regulator to him, risking her own life for a man she scarcely knows. Exchanging the regulator, kicking slowly together towards the surface, the pair form one creature, with one purpose, in a kind of dance "urgent and calm, full of fluid grace" (107). Unlike the Americans, gasping for breath in fear, and abandoned by their fellows, here, in the other world below the waves, people can conquer fear, share vital resources, get their breath and move to safety together. Next day Jonathan takes Anna to the group's community centre, a magical circular atrium, half set into the cliff, half cantilevered out, and framed with high curving walls of glass. The atrium is based upon the shape of the shell and appears to represent an architectural utopia, with patterns of reflected light playing across people's faces and a fountain at its centre. Ten years previously the chain of islands had been bought by developers planning to build high-rise hotels, with comprehensive deforestation envisaged, plus a restaurant built right onto the endangered coral reef. Anna has seen similar developments in Thailand, with accompanying environmental degradation: "more hell than paradise" (111). The islands are rescued by Yukiko Santiago, a wealthy philanthropist from a Japanese samurai family, who has witnessed the devastation of war, lost half her family at Hiroshima, and having seen the worst that human beings can do, is now determined to see something of the best. She buys the islands, creates one high end eco-resort to preserve the fragile reefs and jungles, and funds a global coalition of research stations, the Sea Earth Institute, to research wave currents as alternative sources of energy. The community has grown naturally around the research station, and many of its members are refugees, survivors of war or atrocity, some of them (such as Cambodian Khemma) explicitly the result of other utopian social schemes. Now Yukiko has appointed an advisory board to guide its evolution, to see where this other social experiment will lead. Gunnar supplies the ideology:

> It is Aristotle's idea of entelechy, applied not to biology but to our human community. Entelechy—it is the science of the possible, of unlocking what is otherwise merely potential. As we see it, Anna, the ideal is like a vessel with which a community may select those possibilities suitable to its own nature—those which promise to further human development. (112)

To Anna's horror, however, she realises that she has already been the subject of an experiment. The diving incident had been staged. Gunnar had not been floating free at all; he had a plan to test her. Jonathan offers her another shell to replace the one she dropped and reminds her that "test" derives from the Latin *testa*, meaning a shell. In the Middle Ages it was also a vessel in which experiments were carried out. "The ideal is a kind of vessel too. . . . Every day here is an experiment. Every day, a test" (114). Aristotle had named this shell because its shape suggested a lantern. The community adopted the name not only because of the indigenous beauty of the sea urchins, but also because Aristotle had challenged Plato's ideal state. Plato's utopia was many good things, "but it was also static" (114). Because Plato did not allow for the possibility of growth or change, the fixed nature of his society tended to dystopia. Unlike Plato, Aristotle saw the community as a living organism, growing and changing, with politics as the science of the possible. Edwards designs her alternative world in the image of fluidity and change. Anna no longer sees the world as a "steady place" (128) but as "unmoored" (115), something that "swam and glittered and changed" (129) at every instant.

So far, so utopian. But in focussing upon the notion of entelechy as a key concept, and in the proliferating meanings of the test (as shell, trial, vessel, building, community) Edwards introduces a specific critical perspective, questioning the worth of utopian thinking. In the twentieth century Aristotle's term "entelechy" was adapted and extended by Kenneth Burke. At the risk of digressing, a brief sketch of Burke's central ideas elucidates Edwards' story and casts the utopian impulse in a more ambiguous light. Aristotle coined the term entelechy (having one's end within) to argue that all sensible things carry within them the seeds of their final states. All change means the realization of potentialities inherent in the essence of a thing, rather as if a biological organism had within it a blueprint, a plan of how it will develop.[15] In the modern period Hans Driesch, a marine biologist, applied the concept to sea urchins. Driesch had removed cells from sea urchin embryos, expecting each cell to develop into the half of the animal for which it was destined. Instead he found that each cell developed into a complete sea urchin, a fact that he ascribed to the life force of entelechy. Because sea urchins share seventy per cent of their genes with human beings they remain traditional model organisms in human biology.[8] Burke, however, appropriated Aristotle's concept to show how human motivations impel people to complete their tasks regardless of the harm they might do.[9] Artists and thinkers glimpse certain ultimate possibilities in their views of things and there is no rest until they have tracked down the implications of their insight by transforming its potentialities into total realisation.[10] Entelechy is therefore a way of describing how words can inspire people to take things (in Burke's often repeated phrase) "to the end of the line", in the drive of everything human to perfect itself. Burke characterised this tendency to drive forwards relentlessly to realize a potentiality, as a quest for perfection that was pernicious, in his central definition:

> Man is goaded by the spirit of hierarchy (or moved by the sense of order) and rotten with perfection.[11]

Man's very abilities may therefore function as blindnesses. Technology in particular represents one of the more rotten forms of perfection, since the end of the line of technology appears to threaten global disaster, whether in the shape of the bomb or DDT or the internal combustion engine. But rhetorical inventions aiming at perfection are equally threatening. Humanity faces a constant drive to follow its projects through to completion whatever the consequences. "Each specialty is like the situation of an author who has an idea for a novel, and who will never rest until he has completely embodied it in a book."[12] For Burke the capacity for language is prior to that of thought. Thought is a function of language, so man is not rational but rather a symbol making animal. Anticipating Gramscian notions of hegemony, Burke's work focusses on the problems which occur when symbols use man, rather than men using symbols. Language makes technology possible and liberates us from nature but it also makes the entelechial motive available to us. Because the human imagination can freely explore possibilities in the verbal realm that are impossible in the physical realm, we can create something that has never been. The principle of perfection is central to language; the mere desire to name something by its proper name, or to speak a language in its distinctive ways, is intrinsically perfectionist. In his work, he therefore analyses how language induces action in human beings, how the language-user's concept of perfection is revealed in language, and the ways in which language erects terministic screens so that all questions are leading questions, all select a field of battle, and form the nature of the answers by the way in which the question is expressed. As a result much of Burke's work consists of tracking down the ways in which the top (the god-term, the abstract) is always already present and operative in the bottom (the empirical descriptive term).

> For Burke, words, like theological discourse, go upward and come to a head, in God or in ultimate, perfect god terms. This is what Burke means by entelechy, the motive toward perfection that is intrinsic to language.[13]

Burke is primarily concerned with investigating the logic of perfection implicit in symbols, theologies and nomenclatures. Stan A. Lindsay gives a good example, in his study of Burke, in the terminology of the abortion debate ("unborn children" as opposed to "foetuses") arguing that the killings of personnel at abortion clinics in America indicate the entelechial rounding-out of the implications of terminology.[14] Edwards' "The Story of My Life" concerns anti-abortion terrorism, in the shape of an unscrupulous activist mother who uses her own illegitimate daughter as a symbol in the service of the pro-life movement. Burke also derives God from man's capacities as a symbol-maker, rather than deriving man and the universe from God's powers of creation, an opposition dramatised in "The Secrets of a Fire King", with its warring magician and preacher. Several of Edwards' stories concern rhetoricians and language teachers ("The Great Chain of Being", "Spring, Mountain, Sea", "The Invitation") or revolve around dominant symbols which assume anti-human characteristics—gold ("Gold", "The Invitation"), rats ("Rat Stories"), radium ("A Gleaming in the Darkness", "In The Garden"), the heavens ("Balance", "The Way It Felt to Be Falling", "Sky Juice"). "The Secrets of a Fire King" is a textbook example of the damage done when symbols use man. The revivalist preacher and the circus magician deploy their master symbols, water and fire, in a verbal duel between rival tricksters. The preacher nearly drowns the girl he is attempting to baptise; the fire-eater burns her brother, and seventy-nine others perish in the ensuing conflagration. Burke is not easily summarised and the above merely sketches the essential components of his thinking in relation to Edwards' engagement with utopia.[15] In contradistinction to the idea that utopia may induce positive political change, Burke conceives of the urge to perfection as fundamentally rotten, pernicious and destructive.

To return to our tale. "Aristotle's Lantern" apparently offers a utopian image of a better future. Since the aim of the community is to find alternative sources of energy, harnessing currents and wave systems, their work is of potentially global importance. When Anna returns temporarily to America, she makes a clear distinction between the community and Minneapolis, where litter swirls, sirens scream and the papers remind her of things she had forgotten about, murders, racial tension, car accidents. Stories about food shortages in Nigeria and the effects of oil drilling in the Arctic leave her feeling that in her own world she is helpless, as opposed to her busy and useful role in the community medical centre. In contrast to the atomised and alienated world of Minneapolis, in the community "what we did connected us" (118). Pragna argues at one point (reining in Gunnar's belief in the possibility of absolute freedom) that what frees a community must necessarily restrict the individual, but the underwater scenes in the story offer an image of freedom combined with connection. Diving with the group, Anna feels "isolated and yet bound to them, the water around us a living thing, embracing and sustaining" (106). One incident evokes the attraction and the danger of immersion in the community. Phil has been diving over the reef when he realises that he has become "narked", a condition in which excess nitrogen in the blood induces hallucination. Although he knows that getting out of the deep water would restore the balance in his blood, he continues dreamily drifting, finds a shipwreck and a human femur, and imagines that people are living below the sea, alive and talking to him. For a moment he feels wholly at one with the world, "sentient and yet diffused" (117). Nitrogen narcosis is also known as rapture of the deep. The elements of the Atlantis myth and of human connection below the waves are appealing, but the magic is none the less clearly marked as a chemical illusion. The community had believed that they could turn wave dynamics into energy and light, and change the world. When a storm destroys the eco-resort, however, the interconnection of watery and earth worlds proves fatal. Phil wades into the sunken garden, alive with small fish swimming in the grass and, enchanted, picks up one of the fish, which flashes silver in the air. A moment later Phil also flashes and dazzles, consumed by energy. An electricity cable, "writhing like a snake" (120) has fallen into the water and electrocuted him. It is almost as if the lower, watery world had come to claim Phil, as if the meanings below the surface had been realized in actuality, with deadly results. In the snake, the fall and the destroyed garden Edwards deploys the traditional symbols of the loss of paradise.

Similarly the human femur recalls the presence of death in any imagined pastoral: *Et in Arcadia Ego*. When Anna tries to save Phil, her leg is badly gashed, laying open "Bone that had never felt the air" (121). Gunnar dresses her wound and then takes her to a second space, also modelled on the shape of Aristotle's lantern, an underwater chamber some thirty feet beneath the surface, from which he and a chosen few carry out experiments on novel biological communities, discovered close to hydrothermal vents in the ocean floor. Gunnar is fascinated by change. As he explains, in these communities he is not studying fossils but organisms which are still evolving. The work is secret. Most of the group have never gone below the surface to this place where the real meaning of the community lies. Anna is carried away by his vision of the development of new proteins or fuels from the underwater plankton, and imagines him saving the world from hunger and fuel-exhaustion. She, too, experiences rapture of the deep, drawn repeatedly to this underwater pleasure dome. The second globe, hidden below the surface of the usual, features fish circling in their "slow

orbits" above her "like strange moons", and plankton "like stars" (125).
The image underlines the way in which utopia spawns utopia, with ever
more entrancing worlds succeeding each other. Underwritten by Yukiko's
personal fortune, the community's public symbolism conceals the second
space, the haunt of the chosen few, dominated by Gunnar, whose determination suggests someone who will go to the end of the line for his beliefs. In
the event his scientific mission takes precedence for him over his wife and
daughter, over Anna, and over Jonathan, ejected for his inability to forecast
wave strength. Connections are more fragile than Anna realises.

Although Gunnar espouses change and fluidity, the irony is that in her relation with him Anna fulfils the fate prepared for her in the opening incident.
The real snake in the garden turns out to be the traditional one: desire. In the
original incident Anna compared the passing of the regulator, warm in her
mouth from his lips, to an exchange of kisses. Eventually, after a night dive,
she consummates the relationship with Gunnar. It is as if the erotic charge of
the opening incident had finally surfaced and been turned into actuality. The
couple swim to shore and make love half-in and half-out of the water, two
people, moving as one in the shallows of the sea. Gunnar does not, however,
remain with Anna and she understands at once that she will have to leave
the community: "my leaving had been seeded long ago" (130). In the story's
beginning was its end. It was always seeded with the final fatal denouement; it
was itself entelechial, coming back to the point at which it started in an image
of determined circularity rather than connectivity. At the end Anna realises
that the central global symbol also illustrates the ways in which symbol making can backfire. The community had modelled itself on the shell and used it
to symbolise its global mission, as an experimental environmental group. But
it therefore discarded the other symbolic implications of the shell. Sea urchins'
spines are poisonous (106) and they can only be handled when dead. Like the
femur, like Anna's gashed leg, the urchin is a bone that has never seen the air,
until it was dead, beyond change. Anna's perfect world, her little globe, was
actually a skeleton. She ends the story contemplating the urchins:

> Their perfect, hidden bones curved to hold the light, their thorns repel-
> ling, interweaving. So beautiful they were, so strange, *Echinodermata:*
> *Echinoidea*, with a thousand eyes, all blind. (130)

Sea urchins cannot see.

"Aristotle's Lantern" remains a haunting image of possibility. Anna holds
onto a fragile globe which seems to symbolise the globe, seen in a new light
as interdependent, organic and cooperative, suggesting both our intercon-
nectedness and our fragility. Yet just as she could not maintain her hold at
the beginning of the story, so she cannot hang onto it now. The magical settings and incidents in the story imply that change is possible, and other more
satisfying worlds available, but that the drive to realisation is problematic.
Tsvetan Todorov makes a crucial distinction when he argues that utopianism

attempts to bring utopia into the world, and is therefore necessarily despotic, whereas utopias may have many functions, as tools for thinking and modes of criticising society.[16] At the close of the story, Anna is still thinking of "that hidden room, the secret locus of all yearning" (130). In the story the second, underground global space carries the suggestion that behind one utopian space lies another and yet another. The yearning for utopia is the positive force; the attempt at realisation its darker side. As Bill Ashcroft has argued, "Utopias embody desire."[17] Bloch sees utopia as the education of desire, Marcuse speaks of repression in contemporary capitalism as the manipulation of desire. Desire is the essential driving force of the imagination of a different world; yet that very desire ends up being condemned in utopia itself.

> This becomes a characteristic of Utopia: all needs are satisfied by virtue of the limitation of desire, "wants" being contained by their conversion into, and satisfaction of, manageable needs.[18]

There is a paradox therefore in the conflict between the irrepressible desire for utopia itself, and utopia's apparent fulfilment of desire. As a result all realised utopias are degenerate, "to achieve Utopia is to fail to realize the possibilities of Utopia."[19]

In response to this paradox, Edwards develops a technique of pairing stories, unpacking a central symbol in different ways, as a strategy which allows the utopian impulse to be propagated while maintaining a critical dialectic. Two stories consider scientific utopianism, each centred on the discovery of radium. Given what we now know of the consequences of that discovery, it might seem well-nigh impossible for these stories to be anything but dystopic. "A Gleaming in the Darkness" opens with a quotation from Marie Curie's memoir of her husband, recalling how the couple often returned in the evening to their greenhouse-laboratory, to admire their precious products,

> these gleamings, which seemed suspended in the darkness, stirred us with ever new emotion and enchantment.[20]

Eve Curie also describes her mother making these evening visits, to admire radium: "She was to remember forever this evening of glow-worms, of magic." [21] In her day, Marie Curie was heavily idealised as an enormously dedicated seeker of a cure for cancer, and as a progressive, with a positivistic belief in scientific progress. Edwards has described how as a girl she was enthralled by Curie's passion for her work, the extremes she went to, and the fact that she was a woman doing what a woman didn't do. She comments on Curie's faith in science: "One of the sources of her passion for science came from this belief that she was going to change the world for the better."[22] Curie did not live to see Hiroshima. Her life spanned "the scientific age of innocence."[23] Later biographers have sought to peel back the layers of idealisation surrounding Curie, focussing on the dangers of radium.

It became obvious fairly early that radioactive substances caused burns. Lab workers developed necrosis of the hand and one lost a finger.[24] Curie's own fingers were deeply scarred by radio dermatitis.[25] Edwards takes the image of damaged hands as the centre of her tale, and picks up on a historical detail: the fact that at the outbreak of war Marie was left with one technician "and a little charwoman about as high as the table."[26] The story is told from the point of view of the charwoman, Marie Bonvin, a humble domestic who idealises Madame Curie as an image of female freedom. Now however, Marie is dying, her hands (the colour of pig's liver and the texture of bark) burn in their bandages as if the flames of Hiroshima had reached her from half a world away (48). In the story it is implied that although she did not foresee global damage, Madame Curie saw the local damage done to Marie. Their hands touch on three separate occasions. Marie takes her hands in hers to console Curie when a year's experiment goes wrong. On a second occasion Curie holds Marie's hands against the glass of the jars extolling their beauty and the potential for a cure for cancer: "her hands holding mine to the glass were very strong" (49). Finally they meet again, years later, and Curie comments "You have worked too hard. Marie, look at your hands! Your life has been too hard" (54). The comment evades responsibility, for it is not just hard work which has caused her hands to age. Madame Bonvin remains none the less entranced. "Her work exploded with the violence of a thousand suns, but I must tell her that it was not her fault, the way they twisted her creation, tampered with her dreams" (56). Curie provided the vital magic in Marie's ordinary life; she was attracted to the beauty of radium as something "rare and numinous to be fingered in a quiet moment "(51). For her Curie is a magician who can make everything in the room turn blue, yellow or green. The story closes as Marie looks forward to reunion in heaven with Curie, "carrying balm for our hands" (56). Marie Curie's perfectionism, her persistence in developing the latent element seeded in the pitchblende, establishes her as entelechial. But by approaching her through the eyes of Marie Bonvin, Edwards restores a sense of innocence and magic, and is able to indicate the ambivalence of the utopian project.

The companion story, "In the Garden", loosely based upon American history and a rewriting of Hawthorne's "Rappaccini's Daughter", also invents a woman to carry the utopian imaginative freight. In the story Andrew Byar, a steel magnate, experiments in his Pittsburgh garden, pouring radium water onto his orchids, which increase massively in size and beauty.

> What had been ordinary had become something from another world, a place more fertile and profuse, a place of unending plenty. (203)

Encouraged, he drinks the "elixir of life" (20) himself, along with his much younger lover Beatrice, a woman "as pale and slender as the stem of a plant" (204). Born poor in Scotland (and loosely modelled on Andrew Carnegie)

Byar believes in the power of his own will and in science. The year is 1922 and the Curies have just transformed plain earth into something unimagined. "A secret of the universe had been revealed, and a restless world dreamed of transformation." (205). For a brief moment, Beatrice is radiant and Andrew rejuvenated; "Paradise lost, now found" (205). Then, however, they find that they can no longer touch each other. One kiss and their lips burn for hours, and the touch of Beatrice's hand leaves a brand. Death rapidly claims them.

The story explicitly pits imagination against history. Andrew is based on Eben Byers (1880–1932), chairman of an iron company in Pittsburgh, who took "Radithor", radioactive water, as a tonic. Byers thought that he had found the Fountain of Youth and consumed 1400 bottles, three times the acute lethal radiation dose. As the *Wall Street Journal* headline said, "The Radium Water Worked Fine Until His Jaw Came Off."[27] Radium is a bone-seeker and in the event Byers exemplified rotten perfection; his skull rotted. Byers was an extreme case, but as David I. Harvie demonstrates, Madame Curie was not alone in underestimating the dangers of radium, which was seen as a life force. Radium fertilisers were used on plants and radium toothpastes, cocktails, facecreams and even contraceptive jelly were sold. What is striking is that Edwards's story is still able to assert the affirmative power of the utopian imagination, catching a moment of magic and freedom, in the invented character of Beatrice. She is involved in an experiment of her own, consciously pursuing freedom.

> She would embrace every experience; she would discard all preconceptions; she would see every moment as an open door, and she would step through each one wide-eyed without fear. (209)

When they meet for the last time she tells Andrew that she has no regrets. "I was your experiment. And you were part of mine" (220). Unlike Anna, she was "no vessel for another's dreams" (221), no hapless victim, and unlike Hawthorne's Beatrice she shakes off the young man from Padua who is pursuing her, without damaging him. The story closes on her vision of a porous world, shaped anew in every instant, unfixed, volatile, "each atom in constant if invisible motion" (221). While the facts of history suggest an ironic perspective, the revision of Hawthorne's "poison woman" undermines a potent and damaging symbol.

Where these two stories revise a cultural symbol, the first two stories of the collection focus upon the potentially deterministic nature of language. The opening story, "The Great Chain of Being", suggests that there is no "seed" of an ending, no determinism in language; rather that language exploits human beings in the interests of power. The title evokes the transition from tradition to modernity, with the premodern idea of a divinely-ordered great chain in which every creature had its fixed place, giving way in the modern world to the idea that order is created by men. In both this story and its companion "Spring, Mountain, Sea", language is explored as it connects different worlds, as it negotiates between modernity and tradition, and as used by men to dominate women. In "The Great Chain of Being", Eshlaini's father, a man of considerable influence before his country gained independence, is a believer that history repeats itself. Although the mother names the children, the father, "the most eloquent speaker of his generation"(4) later substitutes other names, to reinforce the connection to their ancestors, as if the children were repeating their destinies. Jamaluddin becomes Sayed (his great-uncle who defeated a communist rebellion), one brother is named for a trader, another for a healer, and twin sisters after beautiful twin aunts. The father assumes power over words, naming his children for role models worthy of emulation, coded images of past perfection. Eshlaini's siblings see no problems in this procedure; they have been named for the strong and famous and can afford to believe in the preordained. But all Eshlaini's attempts to attract a name to her (by singing like a poet ancestor for example) prove unavailing.

When her mother gives birth to twins and is on the brink of death, Eshlaini remembers the midwife saying that "if you give life again you will pay with your own life" (3), and takes her words literally, as if words had power to kill. If the twins could cost her mother her life, she could save her by killing them. Interrupted as she prepares to stifle the babies, Eshlaini is instantly rechristened Rohila after a grandmother who attempted to kill her child when suffering from childbirth fever, and was sent away to live out her life caring for relatives. But when her father drives off Eshlaini's suitors, she realises that "This was no divine destiny but my father's will" (10). He is motivated by the desire to be looked after in his old age. She therefore insists that if she is not to marry she must inherit his house. For once, her original name is restored to her; the will has to use her legal name. This small victory prefigures the eventual transfer of power over words to Eshlaini. First her shaky father can no longer write, then cancer eats through his voice box. As he declines, so she flourishes. Her father's withered body is "the dark seed I had discarded" (14) while she has "new, insistent life rising from my skin, hair flowing out like a sea anemone" (16). Ironically she does become Rohila for a moment, angry and vengeful, conditioned into evil by the name he gave her, cruelly tormenting her father with visions of her future without him, desisting only when he mouths once more, her name, Eshlaini.

On her father's death the family try to repossess the house, but the battle is lost from the moment the eldest brother addresses her as Rohila. She replies to him as Jamaluddin, the name her mother gave him, and asserts "My name is Eshlaini" (15). When the house was left to her, the land had been worthless. Now modern development has expanded the city into the jungle and made it priceless. Sold, and demolished for high rises, it makes her a rich woman, who promptly buys a city apartment, throws out her sarongs in favour of crisply tailored clothes and adopts a daughter. The story ends as Eshlaini watches the high rises going up, and thinks of the room prepared for her daughter, pleased with the idea of "my house filling up with the unexpected" (17). She recognises that her legal name, given for a star which her mother saw on the day of her birth, was not destiny but "a bright wish, a continuity of light to light" (17). Now, driving herself to "a place where only the future lies waiting", she is that light. "I have no other destiny. I am Eshlaini and history ends with me" (17).

The story suggests a utopian image of a woman liberated from the iron hand of tradition and patriarchal law into a glowing woman-centred future, by the forces of modernisation. The unnamed country (recognisably Malaysia) appears to have left any socialist tendencies firmly behind in favour of global capitalism. In her final words Eshlaini echoes Fukuyama's evocation of the "end of history". If the story stood alone, the reader might well see Edwards as a happy globalist, writing a paean to progress, masked in a Western feminist rhetoric of the defeat of the evil male word and the return of the silenced mother. But in the second story, "Spring, Mountain, Sea", Edwards turns the tables. In this story a mother clings obstinately to her native language and her children's names, refusing to assimilate to America or to English. Jade Moon, a Korean bride, arrives in small-town America in 1954 with her husband Rob, a skilled translator, who has spent the war in the navy, where instead of seeing active service he intercepted and translated messages. "His war had to do with language, with the nuances of translation" (20). Rob is skilled in fighting with words, and his linguistic perfectionism spills over into the domestic sphere. Jade Moon, however, hates the sound of English and is a very slow learner, insisting that at home he speaks to her and their children only in her own language. Several of Rob's workmates have lost relatives in combat in Japan or Korea and their womenfolk view Jade Moon with incomprehension. Once children arrive, the control of language becomes a battlefield. Jade Moon names her children Spring, Mountain and Sea, holding to the belief that entelechial power resides in the Korean names: spring as renewing strength each year, mountain as a steady rock and the sea as controlled by the moon (the mother), so keeping the child close to home. Rob registers the children as April, Michael and Maria (a particularly poor choice given that his wife cannot pronounce the central consonant.)

Jade Moon's instructor in language, Ellie Jackson, is another perfectionist, described as someone who might have been a missionary in another life "so great was her zeal, so pure was her determination" (24). The house is festooned in name cards–"cupboard","stove", "refrigerator", "table"—and Ellie's maxims swiftly become law. "Use milk to remove ink stains." "Vinegar and newspaper make the glass windows sparkle." (25) Language learning is also acculturation into the domestic role of an American housewife, as cleaner, laundress and cook. Invited to a church social, Jade Moon is firmly instructed to prepare tuna noodle casserole with a potato chip crust. Instead she celebrates her own culture with a huge fish, poached complete with its head and eyes, a dish which predictably revolts the tuna-noodle eaters. By next day the name cards have gone and Jade Moon has rejected assimilation in favour of retaining her own culture and passing it to her children. When Rob accuses her of laziness she reminds him of friends who had a baby in Hong Kong and were horrified when what they assumed was mere babble was revealed to be Chinese—the language of their nanny. They could not speak to their own child. Jade Moon sees language not as a weapon but as an emotional resource, with power to comfort, strengthen or soothe. Her children are hers, "not just yours and not just America's" (31). For Rob her decision is infuriating; he returns home as if to a different world, as if stepping back into the past (30) and finds himself repeating words again and again, louder and louder, with increasing exasperation, as if through the sheer force of repetition he could make his wife understand English.

It is only at the close of the story that he realises his own lack of understanding. When Jade Moon is diagnosed with inoperable cancer, Rob is too stunned to translate the death sentence to her, but she has understood perfectly and startles him "with perfect, lilting English" (36). He remembers suddenly that it was in the spring that he had courted his wife, walking with her to a spot on a mountain, with a view to the sea. His children's names spring into life;

> Spring, Mountain, Sea. The four syllables were suddenly as powerful as a poem. (37)

The children were "seeded" by that meeting place. For all his spoken proficiency Rob had never read Jade Moon's language well; its characters are complicated and appear to conflate language and symbol. He had never thought of the names, as she did, as "three small strokes of language that reconstructed their shared past" (38). Repeating the names he is transported back "sitting on a rocky cliff, gazing at an ocean as wide and full of promise as his future". (38). Jade Moon had not merely named her children to tie them to a past culture but to create an image of futurity, and to celebrate their love. The story closes with Rob telling her, both in his language and in hers, that he has finally understood. The children find him "whispering their old, discarded names again and again—as if, by the sheer force of repetition, he could make her understand." (38). While these two stories suggest the pitfalls of linguistic determinism, therefore, they vary in envisaging the means of transcendence. Eshlaini embraces modernity; Jade Moon strikes a balance between past and present, linking her two cultures. The linguistic quest for perfection threatens the relations between the women and their families; the decision to remain "imperfect" in Jade Moon's case allows her to maintain the connection with her children

It is worth noting at this point that the function of utopia is not always to advocate change and transformation. As Ruth Levitas notes, to say that utopia can produce change is itself a utopian statement. The Land of Cockaigne, for example, is a compensatory fantasy where the skies rain cheeses and larks fly ready-cooked into the mouth.[28] Several of Edwards' stories examine the function of small local utopias which interrupt the daily routine to offer magic and escapism without necessarily having political aspirations. In "The Secrets of a Fire King", for example, the fire-eater is a natural with the rural crowds because he knows the banality of their lives so well, "the dust rising off their endless fields, the flat somber light that filled their homes and churches" (135). He mesmerizes them with his colour and illusion, meeting a need identified by Bloch who saw the circus as "a wishful world of eccentricity and precise dexterity" satisfying desires for more power and satisfaction in ordinary people's daily lives.[29] Two stories concern ordinary people who are not centre stage, each story focussed on the image of a fall. Both concern the juggling compromises of life, the balancing act between dreams and mundane reality, and in more general terms, the centrality of the concept of balance to any rational utopia. "Balance" concerns a troupe of acrobats who perform only at weekends, in the squares of small towns. Francoise and Marc founded the group when their own careers as dancer and gymnast stalled. She is now an instructor and he a plumber, but at weekends they are transformed as "masters of a balancing act" which they have sustained for fourteen years (64). The couple are poised in a moment of equilibrium between the expectations of youth and the quieter life to come. She is a trapeze artist and he a juggler, accomplishing a limited, partial transformation of the world for their weekend audiences. Now, however Francoise has been retired as an instructor and promoted into school management and the balance of their relationship has shifted. Francoise performs on the trapeze, without a net, high above the rooftops, specialising in a manoeuvre in which she appears to slip and plunge straight down, only to catch herself at the last moment, to gasps from the crowd. Marc hates them, understanding that they do not come to see the miracle of balance, but for the possibility that she might fall. For the crowds the possibility of imperfection is what draws them, not the utopian image of balance and dexterity, but the failure. Something in human nature wants disaster, not perfection. Francoise is made up as a clown, with bright pink circles on her cheeks and black lines making sad, exaggerated eyes (58), and she mimes clownishness and falling, even as she is perfectly in control. This time however it is different. Marc remembers their repeated attempts to make love while standing on their heads, an act which requires immense balance, maintaining control even as you lose control (61). On the one occasion they had succeeded Marc had felt himself beginning to fall but had stared into her eyes, steadying himself even as his body moved. The image is of a couple being able to have their desires only by means of a series of checks and balances, cooperating intently. Marc realises however that this time Francoise intends to dive straight down onto the square. "Or to him if he could catch her" (69). The moment comes; the balance shifts and she plummets towards him. The story ends as he lifts his eyes and arms to her, "Hoping that the years of the past could balance them both against this moment." (69). Is she caught or not? The question is left with the reader. Was she already caught by a mundane, compromised existence? Are the days of soaring above that existence now over? And if Marc catches her will she then be caught in a darker sense? Whereas if he fails, will she escape? Francoise can no longer see herself as potentially reaching perfection; she recognises her imperfection and has no desire to continue. The story suggests that the free fall is a more attractive prospect for her than the compromises and tiny shifts and adjustments necessary for a balanced existence.

The companion story, "The Way It Felt to Be Falling" also focusses upon a dive from the sky, and also presents a protagonist mired in a small town, watching planes and skydivers overhead and wishing that she too could escape, like her friend Emmy, currently following The Grateful Dead on tour. Kate is fiercely envious, caught in a small town while overhead she sees the planes tracing their daily paths to places she is losing hope of ever seeing. Kate has to stay because her father has become unbalanced, recession having driven him into depression. "Madness was a graceless descent, the abyss beneath a careless step" (73). The narrator is haunted by the precarious nature of sanity, and the desire for control and order. "I was afraid of falling" (73). Like Francoise she also plummets from the sky, making a parachute jump with her friend Stephen. Stephen, who has made suicide bids before, is also in "the suspended world between sanity and madness" (74). In the event he chickens out of the dive, unlike Kate. He remains in the suspended world, unable to admit that he could not jump, and caught in a limbo without hope. In making the dive Kate takes the plunge, loses control, faces her fears and overcomes them. Paradoxically, in the dive she experiences no sense of descent. All summer she had felt herself "slipping in the quick rush of the world" (82) but now she floats and nothing seems to move, in a different world beyond the ordinary. The fall is not a fall; from now on she will move forward confidently into life. The story ends in bathos; Kate sprains her ankle and returns to a furious mother, who is making wedding cakes to keep the family solvent and wonders how they will pay the costs of the injury. For Kate the money is irrelevant. "Compared to other things, the money aspect is a piece of cake" (86), she says. Gazing at the wedding cakes around them, "confections as fragile and unsubstantial as the dreams that demanded them" (86) the pair dissolve into helpless laughter. Kate realises that although she has a bandaged ankle, the rest of her is strong. "Whatever had plunged my father into silence and Stephen into violence, wouldn't find me" (87). The imperfection and the comic foolishness of her situation are some sort of guarantee of sanity. Francoise mimed the clown, but could not abandon the rotten quest for perfection; Kate makes a wiser choice.

In the final analysis Edwards' conclusion is consonant with that of Burke, who argued that as human beings we would do better to aim for imperfection, counter order and a perception of our own comic foolishness. If we recognise that we are all trying to swallow up and possess the souls of others by means of our symbols we may become more tolerant of each other, and if still fighting with words, perhaps at least do so with some humility. Edwards none the less offers a nuanced and suggestive exploration of the ways in which utopia may function, for good or ill, in the contemporary world, whether as implicitly despotic, liberatory or as a form of social dreaming which offers potentialities beyond the mundane.

3   Fiction and the Unabomber
Susan Choi, *A Person of Interest*

Susan Choi's 2008 novel, *A Person of Interest* begins quite literally with a bang, as a terrorist bomb blows Professor Hendley to bits. Even more shocking is the reaction of his colleague, Lee, in the adjacent office, "Oh, good."[1] Until the explosion Lee had never admitted to himself how much he disliked Hendley, "a raw, never-mined vein of thought in an instant laid bare by the force of explosion" (3). Lee resents Hendley because of his popularity which makes Lee, an aged professor, feel obsolete and unloved. Hendley, a computer whiz kid, has been hired at some cost by the university maths department, whence he proclaims his intention of "midwifing an unprecedented information-technology age that would transform the world as completely as had the industrial revolution" (6). Hendley is worldly, engaged, more likely to publish in a magazine full of ads for "a mysterious item called Play-Station" (6) than in a dusty scholarly journal. Lee, on the other hand, is a lonely Luddite, who watches television on a blizzard-prone Zenith and remains wedded to his Montblanc fountain pen and pads of paper.

It is instructive to juxtapose this opening scene with a quotation from a philosophical critique of technological civilisation.

> The moral code of our society is so demanding that no-one can think, feel and act in a completely moral way. For example, we are not supposed to hate anyone, yet almost everybody hates somebody at some time or other, whether he admits it to himself or not. Some people are so highly socialized that the attempt to feel and act morally imposes a severe burden on them. In order to avoid feelings of guilt, they continually have to deceive themselves about their own motives and find moral explanations for feelings and actions that in reality have a non-moral origin. We use the term "oversocialized" to describe such people.[2]

The passage is quoted from *Industrial Society and its Future*, the manifesto of Ted Kaczynski, otherwise known as the Unabomber, who carried out a series of bomb attacks between 1978 and 1995, targeting universities and airlines, killing three people, and injuring 23 more. Kaczynski was motivated by a utopian desire to end the domination of technology and return to an essentially pastoral world. Like Choi's fictional terrorist, Donald Whitehead, aka the Brain Bomber, Kaczynski was a highly educated mathematical genius, renowned for solving a problem in pure maths which had defeated his colleagues, who landed a plum job at UCLA Berkeley, only to leave after two years and retire to live in self-sufficient isolation in a remote cabin in the Northwest, whence he launched his campaign of terror.[3] Choi's novel is set in the mid-1990s, as the reference to the newly marketed PlayStation (launched in America in 1995) implies. Digital technology is in its infancy. Emma Stiles, the discoverer of Hendley's mortally-wounded body, enjoys the privilege of access to the Internet, a mysterious process which the full-time secretaries do not understand (7); they assume it is some sort of vocational training. The irony cuts two ways here. Lee may appear old fashioned with his pen and paper, but the temporal setting also places Hendley in an ironic perspective. For today's reader, Hendley's two huge computers with their "robotic bleeps" and "primitive honks" (4), and the "strange goose-like yodel" (5) of his dial-up modem, relegate the apparent whiz kid to the obsolescence of yesteryear. The pen is mightier than the dial-up modem.

Choi's irony suggests the implicit rivalry between writer and programmer. Hendley thought that he was going to lead the mouldering world of scholarship into the digital age and saw himself as "revitalizing the dying university" (6). The irony is crashing. Hendley ends up dead and, from the perspective of 2008, also quaintly old fashioned. Shockingly, therefore, the irony of the text appears to align the novelist with the terrorist's own mission, in demolishing the claims of technology, a process assisted by the third person focalisation through Lee, in free indirect discourse. It could be Lee in the 1990s who thinks that PlayStation and Internet are "mysterious" but it is only a later narrator with knowledge of more sophisticated computers who could call the modem "primitive". The narrative spotlight catches Hendley in a beam of irony.

Choi is not of course the first writer to draw attention to the links between writer and terrorist. Margaret Scanlan, for one, has argued for an affinity between the writer and the terrorist, given the Romantic image of the writer as a legislator of mankind, a revolutionary or an outsider, marginal to society. Indeed, some writers (DeLillo, Dostoevsky) envisage terrorists as in some senses their rivals, in fiction which is increasingly pessimistic about the novelist's social power. DeLillo has argued that there is a deep narrative structure to terrorist acts.[4] Critics have connected DeLillo's *Mao II* to his doubts concerning the effectiveness of fiction in a world given over to the electronic media. The protagonist, Bill Gray, worries that the traditional role of authors is giving way to that of terrorists, in that terrorism offers a superior means of achieving a voice.[5] "If the writer has lost the power to influence the social future with his work, then the terrorist has learnt how to use the society of spectacle and images in his favour."[6] The degree to which terrorists influence mass consciousness measures the extent of the novelist's decline as a shaper of sensibility and thought. Scanlan also notes particular cases in which terrorists appear to have drawn upon and exploited novels, including the Unabomber, who was widely thought to have been influenced by Conrad's *The Secret Agent*, with its themes of anarchy, alienation and dehumanisation. Both Conrad's Professor and Kaczynski were brilliant, isolated and ascetic bomb makers.[7]

The Unabomber offers a suggestive example of the literary terrorist in several other respects. All his bombs were sent using Eugene O'Neill $1 stamps, presumably in homage to O'Neill's 1928 play *Dynamo* in which technology figures as a god that will destroy mankind. Kaczynski also played clever word games, and adopted a dominant symbol, wood. His bombs were partly made of wood or disguised as pieces of lumber. One bomb was sent inside a book published by Arbor House, a company using a tree leaf as a trademark. His third victim was Percy Wood, who lived in Lake Forest; his tenth lived in Ann Arbor; his fifteenth on Aspen Drive; the sixteenth worked for the California Forestry Association and the bomb was sent from a fictitious wood-working company in Oakland. Kaczynski wrote to the *San Francisco Chronicle* as "Isaac Wood of Wood Street, Woodlake", and at one point supplied a social security number which turned out to be that of a convict, who had been tattooed "pure wood." In Choi's novel the first letter from the bomber to Lee is sent from Maple Lane, Woodmont, the second from Ailanthus Circle, Lumberton, and reference is made to a previous bombing involving an academic at UCLA who picked up a piece of wood and lost several fingers. It is a macabre moment when Lee's friend Fasano comments, "Knock wood, so far no one's dead" (74). While the Unabomber's symbolic system initially suggested an environmentalist eco-terrorist, it was in fact a literary reference, familiar to any reader of Chaucer. In Old English to be "wood" is to be mad or angry. Kaczynski was certainly very angry and also extremely well-read, with a cabin full of books, augmented by heavy use of his local library. Choi's Brain Bomber is similarly literary, also befriends the local librarian, and sprinkles his utterances with literary quotations. Whitehead is described as the leader of Lee's cohort of graduate students, most of whom are goldenly handsome, and brooding in the Byronic vein, wearing studiedly Romantic garb. For the Byrons, as Lee christens them, introverted disconnection from society is a badge of genius; Whitehead is merely the most extreme example of their assumed Romantic alienation.

Fairly obviously, a novel about a terrorist must discuss or dramatize their motivating ideas, and risks lending the terrorist the oxygen of publicity. Again, the Unabomber case is at the sharp end of the spectrum. In 1995 Kaczynski demanded that his 35,000 word manifesto be published by a major newspaper, offering to end his campaign if the *New York Times* or *Washington Post* would print it. (If only the less respectable *Penthouse* printed it he reserved the right to plant one more bomb.) As he wrote in the manifesto, using a fictional "we",

If we had never done anything violent and had submitted the present writings to a publisher, they probably would not have been accepted. . . . In order to get our message before the public with some chance of making a lasting impression, we have had to kill people.[8]

A storm of protest erupted, centred on the morality of publishing under duress the work of a killer. But following the intervention of Janet Reno, the Attorney General, his publishing strategy worked. The *Times* and the *Post* went ahead in the hope that somebody would recognise the killer's distinctive writing style. And indeed somebody did, Kaczynski's brother, who after protracted soul-searching contacted the authorities. Stylistic analysis of his letters revealed his guilt. Ironically, given that Kaczynski deplored the weakened family ties of the modern world and the dominance of society, his brother felt more responsibility to society than to him.[9] The news media which he had courted also hastened his arrest; they got wind of the FBI stakeout and gave them 24 hours grace before they planned to break the story. Kaczynski was seized in his cabin and eventually sentenced to life in prison.

The reason that the authorities took so long to capture Kaczynski may be ascribed to the pathologising of the terrorist, who was seen in psychological terms, thus displacing the focus from the political and social causes of violence to private or personal concerns. The FBI assumed a psychological motive (jealousy of an academic colleague, for example) rather than that the Unabomber was killing to promote his ideas. Lee makes a similar mistake, assuming that the bomber is professionally jealous of a more successful academic. As he comments, baffled by the notion of a series of attacks on academics, "Who would want to kill us? We're only professors. We don't do anything" (12). But actually Kaczynski chose his victims, including computer specialists, a geneticist, and a company executive, for the ideas which they represented. As his biographer Allston Chase comments,

For him, they assumed the ontological status of characters in a novel.[10]

So how does a novelist compete with a rival who has designed his campaign around literary models, symbolism, language and characterisations? As I shall argue, Choi artfully inhabits the bomber's symbols, and takes them over, layering them with alternative narrative meanings in a palimpsestic narration. Writing in the spirit of Marin, Choi generates meanings from the interplay of various spaces, and from a narrative structure which exploits the absence of a stable narratorial ground. Events are doubled across dual time schemes and characters also doubled, forming shadows to each other, disrupting one-dimensional representations. Choi also makes a clear distinction between terrorist and writer in her plot, and does not endorse the idea of an affinity between fellow outsiders. In the novel, the betrayal is not by a brother. The terrorist is identified by a poet, with whom he had corresponded. At first the poet follows the Brain Bomber story with anarchic glee, but when he reads the manifesto he feels as if "a specter of his poet's invention had materialized" (321), as if one of his characters had come to life. Far from feeling kinship with Whitehead as a Byronic outsider, the poet is terrified that he too will become a target, and calls the police. When Lee lures the bomber out of his cabin so that he can be captured, a character bearing the name of Jim Morrison, the archetypal countercultural rebel, lead singer of The Doors, and focus for a Romantic cult, is the FBI agent who makes the arrest.

Choi, however, does portray the sinister power of the state, against which the marginalised outsider is pitted, complicating the plot by combining most of the major elements of the Unabomber case with a second historical source, the case of an innocent victim of state persecution. At the risk of a minor digression it is important to underline how this case is employed (in somewhat altered form) to expand the frame of reference of the novel, away from ethnic issues, in order to focus on issues of socialisation and technologised emotion. Where the Unabomber case appears to confirm the necessity for state vigilance and surveillance, the second source puts state power under the microscope, particularly in relation to the effective suspension of civil liberties in a federal investigation with associated trial by media. In 1999 Wen Ho Lee, a Taiwanese-American scientist who worked for the Los Alamos national laboratories was falsely accused of passing nuclear secrets to the People's Republic of China. He endured 278 days in gaol, eventually pleaded guilty to one charge of not storing his computer files correctly, was sentenced to 278 days, and immediately walked free. Both the judge and President Bill Clinton apologised to him. Like Choi's Lee, Wen Ho Lee saw the story leaked to the *New York Times*, which published assertions as if they were facts.[11] His life became a media circus; reporters, FBI agents, TV satellite trucks and photographers camped on his doorstep and trampled over his neighbours' gardens. His house was ransacked, his phone bugged and he was trailed everywhere by up to a dozen FBI agents in five or six cars, all of which is exactly as happens in Choi's novel. In one significant respect, however, Choi's story differs from her source. In the novel relatively little is made of Lee's ethnicity. Choi never specifies Lee's place of origin. In interview she said that she had deliberately selected a generic surname, and when she was unable to find a similarly generic forename, decided not to supply one.[12] He is merely Professor Lee, and could be from Taiwan, China, Japan, Malaysia or Korea. The reader only knows that he spoke Japanese as a child, and has memories of living through a violent civil war. When an FBI agent fishes for his identity with Japanese phrases and discussion of Asian food, he is non-committal (136). As a student, stopped by American police as a potential Communist agent, he points out that he speaks no Chinese language, and hates Communists for what they did to his family (144). His ethnic identity remains unspecified.

It is tempting to see this post-ethnic impetus as being in tune with Kaczynski's arguments. One of the groups whom the modern individual is not supposed to hate, according to the Unabomber's manifesto, is the ethnic minority. Kaczynski argued that the modern focus on minority rights was a diversion from tackling the real enemy, the industrial-technological system: "in the struggle against the system ethnic distinctions are of no importance."[13] The post-ethnic presentation is also a major deviation from Choi's historical source. In Choi's novel only one incident suggests a racial motivation on the part of the FBI. Lee is subjected to a lie-detector test, which he passes, only to be told that the results have been reinterpreted on the grounds that Asians cannot produce reliable results. According to the agent, they lack the Judeo-Christian ethical orientation and have a relative notion of truth (200). As a result he cannot polygraph Asians, Chinese, Japanese, Malaysians, Indonesians or Koreans. Nor can he get reliable results from Pakistanis, Indians, Bangladeshis or natives of the Middle East. All Arabs are impossible, as are Hassidic Jews. The Taiwanese are "a maybe" (200). Polygraph testing is now discredited and considered as pretty much akin to belief in the tooth fairy.[14] However, when Wen Ho Lee was accused he was given a polygraph test by the FBI, told that he had passed, given three more tests, then told that the results had been reinterpreted and that he had failed them all.[15] But unlike the case of Choi's Lee, that of Wen Ho Lee swiftly became an ethnic issue. He received hate mail claiming that no Chinese should work in American laboratories, as they were more loyal to China than to America (doubly ironic given that he was not Chinese and had survived the Mainland Chinese invasion of Taiwan, with attendant massacres). There were waves of protests across the US with several groups suggesting that his arrest was driven by his ethnicity.[16] As a result of his experiences Wen Ho Lee was politicised and in his own account of his ordeal argues that "Chinese American and Asian American people have to stand up." "If you don't get involved, whatever you have can be taken away from you."[17] His politicisation occurred despite community and family solidarity: his daughter had campaigned vigorously for him, her fifth grade teacher had offered her house as bail-security, and his neighbours stood by him, hosting a huge celebration when he was released, an example, in his own words, of "America at its best".[18] In contrast, in Choi's novel America does not get off nearly so lightly. Lee's daughter is absent, his neighbours and colleagues shun him, a brick is thrown through his window and his mailbox vandalised.

In contrast to her source material, Choi only allows Lee's ethnicity to emerge in the denouement of the novel. Some twenty pages from the end, as the FBI prepare to storm the snowbound cabin, he remembers that the Communist soldiers had worn white cotton clothes in the winter and crawled through the snow while invading his country (333). The reference is to the Chinese invasion across the snow of the Korean winter in 1950, also referred to in Choi's *The Foreign Student*.[19] The alert reader finds out who Lee once was—Korean—only once his story has been told and he has been established, not as a victim, but as a hero, the foreign-born American who has saved his country from a home-grown terrorist. It is also at this point in the novel that Lee discovers the true identity of the bomber, his former colleague Donald Whitehead not, as he had thought, Lewis Gaither whose wife Aileen he stole many years before. Lee had needed Gaither's villainy to excuse his own ignoble acts. Just as the Unabomber created characters to embody his ideas so Lee, unable to admit his hatred for Gaither, has cast him in the character of the bomber out of guilt over his own previous actions, which led to the loss of Aileen's son, abducted by Gaither and his new wife, Ruth. The issue is not ethnic at all. The Brain Bomber is American through and through, as was the Unabomber. To strengthen her major point Choi uses the Wen Ho Lee material to cast the United States in a less than affirmative light, and to focus on the home grown nature of terror. As a student at Harvard Kaczynski was the victim of CIA-sponsored experiments in interrogation techniques, which his biographer argues were instrumental in making him into a bomber, and from which he draws the moral that "Terrorism is as much a product of our own history, ideas and values as those of other people.[20] Lee is a transnational figure in a globalised and technologised world, rather than a representative of any one ethnic group.

Thus, in contrast to Wen Ho Lee, Choi's Lee's experience of interrogation by polygraph focuses on technology and socialisation rather than ethnicity. When Lee undergoes the lie detector test and appears to have passed, he feels relief in being "verified by a machine" (185). In its rubber grip he experiences a sedative effect as if he had "outflanked his emotions" (184). The machine allows him to demonstrate his completely moral nature, his total absence of wrongdoing, and he feels "clean and reborn" (186). The polygraph relies on skin conductivity, heart rate and breathing; any surge of emotion will register as deception. As such it is a microcosm of an over-mechanised society in which affect is technologised and processed, with any inappropriate response—indeed any strong response at all—seen as a sign of guilt. Just by sitting the test, Lee becomes a suspect person in the eyes of his colleagues, and realises the theatricality of innocence in playing one's role in society, the necessity not merely to be moral but to look the part, to be "in character" and enact his innocence to the social audience.

Choi was drawn to the Unabomber case partly because her father had been a graduate student with Kaczynski at the University of Michigan. When she read the manifesto she commented that it was "not garbage. It's interesting".[21] This is hardly surprising, perhaps. After an initial flurry of attention the manifesto faded swiftly from view, probably because most of its ideas were so familiar.[22] As Timothy Luke comments, Kaczynski took his place in a long line of American oddballs, beginning with Thoreau, who have moved into shacks on the edge of civilisation and penned jeremiads against society's oppression.[23] Millions of Americans share at some level

Kaczynski's utopian desire to end the domination of technology, the alienation of human beings from nature and the loss of small family-centred communities. Kaczynski drew eclectically on a variety of thinkers, cherry-picking ideas which suited his own technophobia. The manifesto particularly reflects Jacques Ellul's understanding of technology as not merely machinery but as a category of knowledge, so that behavioural psychology, bureaucracy or political lobbying may be understood as "technologies". One of the Unabomber's victims was the executive of a public relations firm, chosen because its business was seen as the development of techniques for the manipulation of people's attitudes and emotions.[24] Kaczynski saw "human dignity and freedom bleeding away into pre-processed modes of subjectivity."[25] Oversocialisation (by which he appears to mean social conformity achieved by propaganda, image and emotion control, education, or surveillance) had denied individuals the freedom to control their own lives. His was an agency panic in the face of increased state power.

Kaczynski also drew on E.F. Schumacher ("small is beautiful") and Leopold Kohr, for notions of ecology of scale, favouring the recollectivisation of human beings in small communities. Kaczynski's core philosophy was a form of cultural primitivism, condemning bigness (big business, government or science) as destructive of local cultures. He argued that where once technology served us we now serve technology, so that the modern industrial-technological system reduces people to cogs in a social machine, running on rails laid down by government. Science and technology provide government with the tools to control billions of people. TNCs move people and factories from one country to another because they can use planes, phones, computers and satellites. Therefore (in his argument) the only way to shrink such institutions was to take away their tools of technology. Kaczynski was not arguing for a change of government or a political revolution, but for the overthrow of the economic and technological bases of modern society, effectively for the end of globalisation. In his view the system was not grounded in ideology but on technical necessity. Although he appeared to defend small-scale technology as against organization-technology, the system could not be easily broken down into small communities with the "good" parts of technology separated from the "bad". As an anarchist his aim therefore was to create social instability and usher in a time of trouble and uncertainty which would magically achieve the destruction of technology. (The irony of using sophisticated bomb technology to achieve his aims appears to have been lost on him.) Similarly he wanted to destroy large-scale systems such as public utilities, computer networks and highway systems, yet used the postal system and the Greyhound bus network to deliver his bombs. The positive ideal which he proposed was that of a return to "wild nature", those aspects of nature which are beyond human management, independent of human imagination and free from human interference.[26] As Cynthia Ozick noted, "His dream was of a green and pleasant land liberated from the curse of technological proliferation."[27] While at times sounding as if his project was not far removed from bombing America back to the Stone Age, the ideal appears to be that of the American frontier, with people in tune to a large extent with nature, and pursuing individual freedom in small groups.

In some respects Choi takes the Unabomber's ideas seriously. One example which the Unabomber offers is that of the freedom of walking where one will, as opposed to the modern use of the car, which means that we have to follow the rules of the road (as a pedestrian or a driver); we can only go where roads go; and in most of America, we have to have a car to be able to function at all. In Choi's novel Lee escapes from media surveillance by following his old jogging paths, slipping back into his house through the tall pines of his boundary and remaining undetected because none of the hostile neighbours camped on his doorstep with the media assume he can possibly be there—because his car is not there. At several points in the novel Lee escapes from social control into parks or woods, and images of trees and woods are frequently associated with him, revising their more sinister association with the bomber. Choi takes the bomber's symbol and reverses its aspect, just as in the denouement she replaces the letters from the bomber with a letter which reintegrates family and social networks, as opposed to emphasising a narrative of estrangement. In the third part of the novel walking comes close to salvation for Gaither's son, a committed hiker who discovers his true self in a forest. In the outcome, knowledge of who he is depends upon his awareness of the age at which he first walked freely by himself.

In addition "oversocialisation" is a constant theme in the novel, which sets up a dynamic opposition between natural, authentic emotion and over-socialised pretence. After the bombing Lee feels so guilty at his initial reaction that he puts on a terrific show of grief. Coming out of the hospital he steps into a thoroughly unnatural scene, in which the tulips glow a livid white as if "blasted by rays of the moon", their shadows so crisp they look "razored" (12). This blasted environment is the result of the harsh, bluish lights of the news cameras. Engulfed in a stroboscopic crowd, Lee is interviewed apparently blazing with rage, describing Hendley as one of the great thinkers of the day, a man of the future (13). Afterwards, watching himself on television, he feels as if seeing "a stranger perform a harsh version of him" (14). As a result of his outburst, however, his newly discovered dislike for Hendley is so well-concealed from his colleagues, that he is soon also "able to conceal from himself his own poor sentiments" (15). Lee's performance, however, is not sustainable for long, and he attracts suspicion because he is incapable of maintaining a social mask. He fails to attend Hendley's funeral or to meet grief-counsellors, or to participate in the University's corporately managed grief-fest, a mourning machine ferociously satirised by Choi. When Lee arrives for Monday class ready to counsel his students, it is to discover that the University has replaced any individual speeches with a corporately authored script, to be read to all classes at the same time. Individual utterance has been replaced by an official text designed to control and manage emotion—anathema to any creative writer. Public relations appear to have triumphed. Meanwhile scores of grief-counsellors are holding "talk-outs" and "one on one" meetings with students. Because Hendley died late on a Friday, the machinery (and it is described as machinery) has been set in motion over the weekend, the committees swiftly cobbled together over the "telephone tree",

> the news relayed—no time for tears—Friday night, no time for dissent—
> Saturday, its components amazingly hauled into place on Sunday. (78)

While the bombing shuts down the University's computers, it turns on a sophisticated social machinery. The Grief Plan offers a technology for managing affect, produced by bureaucracy, and with a corporate text. Lee's own voice has been suppressed in favour of an official discourse. His mind moves to a November day when he saw students clustered in similar groups on campus, the day Kennedy was shot. Today's students seem less traumatized than "elevated by the sense of a drama in which they played roles" (83), a thoroughly distasteful spectacle of staged grief. Hendley is not after all J.F.K. and the college's official solemnization is both self-important and sanctimonious. It is however effectively compulsory to participate in the machinery, and act in character, as Lee discovers to his cost.

So far, the novel might well seem to engage positively with some of the Unabomber's points, demonstrating the danger of oversocialisation, the salvatory role of nature, the horrors of technology (whether computers, polygraph or behavioural psychology) and the alienation of the lonely individual. (Lee, twice-divorced, lives alone and appears estranged from his only daughter.) Things are however rather more complicated than that, as the method of the novel demonstrates, particularly its mode of narration. Choi divides the novel into three parts, in each of which discrete self-contained chapters move between past and present. The impression is less of traumatic fragmentation than of fragments being juxtaposed meaningfully so that a whole story can be put back together. The bomb has exposed "long-buried strata" (76) in Lee's emotional landscape, primarily the history of his first marriage. For several weeks Lee almost forgets about Hendley, lost in memories of Aileen,

> with so many of the artifacts of Lee's own life catapulted aloft, with the
> arbitrary detritus of this era and that, of chapters heretofore held apart,
> now suspended together in space, and demanding Lee gaze on them. (76)

While the image suggests a freeze frame of a bomb blast it also implies a narrative of his life which will now be reconnected, its chapters no longer held apart, but becoming a connected story. Events in the mid-1990s alternate with memories of some thirty years before. At least half of the novel appears therefore to have nothing to do with the terrorist plot, particularly in Part Three where the point of view undergoes a tectonic shift from Lee to Aileen's lost son, introduced without warning into the narrative. The novel thus insists on the primacy of narrative in reconnecting Lee to his emotions, and putting back together a shattered whole. Far from seeing the writer as the double or rival of the destructive terrorist, Choi reasserts the primacy of writing as a creative force in meeting the challenge of a technologised world. Paul Harris has argued that in the globalized world the human need for stability becomes more acute, and narrative becomes more essential as a means to tune worldly discourse into a coherent resonance, to help make sense of the world. "Narrative ultimately becomes a tuning into the world which rediscovers and re-establishes our place, our home in it."[28] In *A Person of Interest* Choi constructs a narrative which re-establishes a place in the world for Lee, and for Aileen's son. At the close of the novel, Lee is astonished to realise that his life has been as normal and varied and full as Whitehead's has been narrow and empty. He has been a "person of interest", a rounded character. Whitehead was only a person of interest in the sense that he became a suspect. Terrorists do not create, they merely destroy, a banal point to make, perhaps, but one which underlies Choi's novel in which the forces of creation—biological in the shape of Aileen's children—constantly tug the reader back towards the recognition of the emptiness of the terrorist mission. This emphasis on human creativity as her value field allows Choi also to avoid the narrative problem of contesting ideas which, in themselves, may have something to recommend them, and which could be opposed only in detailed analysis, rather than in dramatic narrative terms. There is little to quarrel with in many of the Unabomber's ideas—the quarrel is with the violent means which he adopted to propagate them.

Choi focusses on the issue of writing through the opposition of different letters, destructive and creative. Lee is unjustly suspected of being the bomber himself when his mail is screened by the police, who detect a letter which he had not mentioned receiving. The letter is illegibly signed, and Lee assumes it is from Aileen's betrayed husband, concealing it from the investigators, because he is mortified that his only piece of personal mail is a letter full of hatred. Lee is swift to parse the letter in terms of alienation and outsiderhood. The letter-writer refers to a photograph of Lee in the press and comments, "'Princely', I believe, was the word sometimes used around campus for you" (140). Lee is enraged; he resents his status as a "you" who is not part of "some great campus we" (140). His sensitivity to grammatical person is acute. In response to the letter Lee tries to phone Gaither but the directory cannot find any number for him, and he draws out his Montblanc, reduced to hand writing a reply to the letter, a message which also fails to get through; the address is false. Clutching the letter, he is appalled (just like the Unabomber) by the way in which the postal system has kept going regardless of the bombing. "Its vast, branching, impersonal systematicity" suddenly revolts him (40). The letter has got through, however, to the reader of the novel who has read both the original and Lee's reply in full. In the novel the process of reading is deliberately highlighted by the presence of the fictional reader (Lee) between the letter and the reader, calling attention to the writer's ability to create a finer emotional truth.

Aileen's letter describing her emotions on the birth of her son and during his first weeks of life, hand-delivered to Lee, stands as a counter-letter to the bomber's. Importantly, her letter interrupts the dominant narrative mode of the novel, free indirect discourse, with her unchecked first person narrative. In the novel, the narrator is in a relation of wavering empathy and irony in relation to Lee, precisely because of the use of free indirect discourse. In relation to Aileen's letter, for example, the reader learns that

> These were sentiments Lee wasn't convinced a wife would share with her husband; why would Aileen want to share them with him? And such outsize, almost lunatic, fervor for her child. (124)

While the first clause reports from the outside (third person) viewpoint, the second is a rendering of Lee's own question (without any phrase such as "he wondered" or "he asked himself"). And the emotional tone of the third, almost an exclamation, is clearly the childless Lee's personal view of love for a child as lunatic. As Franco Moretti has commented, the "Style indirect libre" is a style that clicks with the modern process of socialisation; it leaves the individual voice a certain freedom while permeating it with the imperial stance of the narrator, turning subjective into objective.[29] In classic nineteenth century novels (Austen for example) it lends itself to irony, producing a voice somewhere between character and narrator, a socialized voice with the inner voice colonized by social commonplaces. (Compare "These were sentiments. . . . " (124) with the opening sentence of Austen's *Pride and Prejudice* "It is a truth universally acknowledged that a single man in possession of a good fortune, must be in want of a wife.") Free indirect discourse offers a position of "implicit and almost invisible social mediation."[30] The voice of the character is checked and regulated by social discourse. But it also allows for a blend of empathy and irony, allowing personal idioms and a distinct individual tone along with the narrator's detachment. Often an emotional phrase sparks the style into being. "Signs of emotion function as signs of self reference."[31] They are signals of a personal situation, and a recognisable personal style. There is nothing remotely socialised in Lee's third clause, in which he condemns a mother as a maniac for loving her child. Choi exploits this shifting objective and subjective style in order to move between past and present, exposing the false socialisations and the personal evasions of the past, and allowing Lee a voice of his own. As readers, therefore, we are both with—and against—Lee.

Ostensibly the title of the novel refers to Lee, who is named by the FBI as a "person of interest" to their investigation. But it also refers to the manner of its narration: between first and third person there is a person of considerable narrative interest. In legal terminology a person of interest is somebody who is relevant to a judicial investigation, who can come under third party surveillance but who is not actually accused as a suspect.[32] The person of interest has come to the attention of the authorities, is under a degree of surveillance; and may be closely observed and questioned, but has not lost his liberty. Similarly Lee is not always directly in the sights of the narrator but enjoys a measure of first person freedom, escaping from social definition. Style indirect libre (as Cohn notes) is a highly kinetic style, drawing the reader in and out of the character, and veering between sympathy and irony, amplifying emotional notes, but throwing into ironic relief all false notes struck by the figural mind.[33] Here, the text weaves in and out of Lee's mind, alternately fusing and separating external action and inner reality, facts and reflections. Grammatical person is therefore at the centre of the meaning of the novel. In similar fashion the structure of the novel alternates between subjective and objective frames of reference to restore a whole sense of the past. The events surrounding the bombing alternate with memories of sexual love and Aileen's developing pregnancy, with an emphasis on the contrast between natural emotion and technologized affect.

Choi also demolishes the Romantic image of the pro-nature terrorist by exploiting that most emblematic of Romantic poetic strategies, the pathetic fallacy, with its attribution of human emotions to nature, using the technique ironically to indicate that there can be no wild nature beyond the human imagination. Nature is permeated with Lee's imaginings and his emotional projections. Aileen and Lee first meet at an evangelical cookout, with prayers and square dancing, linked to the preceding scene in the present by the motif of tulips. Although the cookout is supposed to be a pleasant excursion into nature, the weather is cold and windy and the wind-lashed tulips are described as "flinging themselves supplicatingly" on the ground, suggesting penitents "prostrating themselves in abased ecstasy" (20). The connection which Lee makes between guilt, religion and ecstasy is proleptic. Previously Lee had envisaged Gaither's wife as probably dowdy, plump and clad in plaid skirts and support hose, but when he meets her there is a brisk reassessment. Aileen is shatteringly beautiful, completely bored, and makes not the slightest attempt to look at all interested in the event or in Lee. Lee is plainly pole-axed. The landscape suddenly looks to him less penitential and more like "a rumpled bedsheet" (22). He is so intent on Aileen that Ruth has to tell him that he can get out. "The car's stopped" (23). The reader sees clearly that Lee's is no pre-processed subjectivity. The backdrop of oversocialised evangelical platitudes contrasts with the directness of the couple's exchanges. Given that her husband travels every Sunday to services at a church some 90 minutes away, the timing of Aileen's invitation to Lee to come over for coffee (Sunday morning at nine-thirty) tells him all he needs to know. The description of their fevered coupling (leaving slime, semen and uprooted hair all over her living-room carpet) appears to underline the "wild nature" of their relationship. Nature, however, has a surprise for Aileen, who discovers that she is already pregnant with Gaither's child and reverts to convention, ending the affair. Even wilder spring weather then erupts, bringing three feet of spring snow, blasting the burgeoning spring. Here, Choi's evocation of the pathetic fallacy has a specific political resonance. Imagistically the snow has a clear connection to political violence, as the novel moves to Lee's original encounter with Donald Whitehead, which occurs in a markedly literary context. Whitehead stops to talk to Lee, because he sees that Lee is reading *Spring Snow*, by the Japanese novelist Yukio Mishima. As a romantic writer and anti-leftist revolutionary Mishima is probably the most obvious modern example of the writer as would-be revolutionary. His attempt to stage a nationalist coup in 1970 failed and was immediately followed by his public suicide by *seppuku*.

In contrast to Romantic notions of wild nature, the campus setting is established as impersonal and mechanised. Lee's office had originally been in a natural setting with floor to ceiling windows so that grass appeared to grow right up to the pane. The new facility is constructed around an enormous computer centre, with an enclosed atrium full of leaf-shedding, shivering ficus trees under arctic fluorescents. Access to this anti-human edifice involves swipe card technology; Lee is frequently lost or excluded. The only view of the trees outside is through an elevated octagonal window which appears to him to frame their limbs "frozen in postures of horror" (39). Lee, however, has a coping strategy. He had previously noted that despite the many painful memories which the town holds for him their effect is mitigated by the fact that each place in the town is variously overlaid with so many different memories, in a "palimpsest world" (38), like a manuscript where traces of past writing have been only partially erased, and can be glimpsed below the overwritten surface. Writing is never quite erased. Similarly Lee hangs onto his Montblanc on the grounds that ink keeps one's errors on record. The youth and the modern technology of the office building is unhelpful. "Not enough had transpired here for the palimpsest theory to work" (39). As a result, for many of his colleagues the bomb has blown a permanent hole in their sense of the place. Lee, however, uses memory against memory, overlaying the bombing with his past and with a more complicated narrative, generating other meanings from the interplay of narrative spaces.

A subtext runs though the novel in which vapid or pre-processed messages contrast with the expression of authentic emotions. Back at home after the bombing, Lee finds on the answerphone only stock messages from old colleagues long forgotten, or neighbours whom he hardly knows, their tone of concerned inquiry a mask for nosiness or *schadenfreude*. There is no message from his daughter Esther. Esther has opted out of the social world and into nature, as an environmental volunteer helping to feed eagle chicks, endangered because for some unknown reason the parent birds cannot care for them. Her identification with these abandoned offspring suggests a commitment to nature as a retreat from human engagement, motivated on some subliminal level by awareness that her father had been instrumental in the loss of Aileen's son. Lee recognises that most of her messages were essentially prophylactic, designed to fend off any substantial emotional exchange. The question lingers—can there be a true message for Lee—or are machines merely talking to machines? The exception is a call from a real friend, his old colleague Fasano, who is so keen to talk to him and so useless with answering machines that he has to send more than one message. Fasano goes beyond the social script and dominates the machine.

When Lee is transported back in memory to Aileen's account of the moment when she revealed their affair to her husband, the emphasis on empty adherence to social scripts is continued. Tulips again link the scene to Lee's present. Aileen had been a keen gardener, finding that gardening returned to her some measure of the self-control and independence which her marriage had destroyed. Blooming in her pregnancy, an image of natural creativity, she steps into her garden, sees the castrated stalks where her husband has cut off the flowered tulips' stems and leaves, and realises at once that she must leave him. The resolution is strengthened when Gaither insists on a visit to his parents, who had previously ignored Aileen completely. Throughout their marriage Gaither had maintained a dumb show of family devotion, sending his parents platitudinous letters and generally receiving only the occasional seasonal card with a pre-printed message in return. When Aileen reveals her adultery Gaither slaps her hard into the wall. Aileen's reaction mirrors that of Lee to the bomb blast: "Good, she thought. Good, it's real" (63). Like Lee's relation to Hendley, Aileen's relationship to her husband suddenly appears in its true colours, unmediated by conventional morality or public appearance. Part One of the novel ends with Lee's memory of this event, presented as an alternative "big bang", creative rather than destructive. Lee recalls how he had felt that as Aileen spoke he saw "clouds of dust whirling in space, asteroids coalescing, the hot lump of a planet accreting more mass. The unthinkable force of Creation" (54). Just as memories of Aileen's pregnancy run in parallel to the process of Hendley's dying, so the creative force pulling things together runs in dynamic tension with the force of the bomb blast which tore things apart. The layered narration, memories overlaying other memories and the present, offers a palimpsestic remedy against the terrorist's power to alter place forever.

In order to complete the process of revising the Romantic notion of nature, the novel moves from the Romantic to the Gothic register. Fleeing from the grief-fest, Lee enters Mashtamowtahpa Park, named for a pre-Columbian people, and makes his way to the Wagon Wheel restaurant, a western-themed bar, made of weathered boards like a cabin, and featuring an old brand of beer ("Black Label") served not in the modern can but in the old-fashioned brown bottle. Lee's engagement with his past is however in no sense the same as the Unabomber's primitivism, nor does Choi endorse nostalgia. The setting emphasises the obsolescence of earlier technology and the results of that decline on a previously thriving economy. Lee notes how the freight trains which once criss-crossed the town, and which for him symbolised the grandeur of America, have gone. In the past the park had a miniature freight train ride for children which Esther had adored, but now the location in the Rust Belt means that most of the town's youth have also departed, and the part of the park which once housed the children's activities has also gone, its tall pines replaced by klieg lights and Astroturf. Lee registers it as a "diminished landscape" (92). Implicitly, the scene suggests that abandoning modern technology would not restore society to health but turn it into an economic and human graveyard. Far from offering a nostalgic location, the bar suggests a visit to the Underworld. Dim candles make little impression on the interior darkness (93), there is a smell of mildew, and a pervasive chill. The Gothic subtext is reinforced when to Lee's horror he is accosted by a vision of his dead wife "raised healthy and young from the grave" (94). With a start he realises that the uncanny stranger is merely Hendley's girlfriend Rachel who bears a resemblance to Aileen. Rachel is accompanied by "two more ghosts" (95), a severely melancholic young woman clad entirely in black and a man dressed in "fake lumberjack" (96) gear who seems also to resemble Hendley. "Wild nature"—the cabin in the woods so evocative of the Unabomber—is not merely an anachronism but a place of death. On leaving the restaurant Lee opens his mail, only to find his letter to Gaither returned to sender. Gaither, unknown to him, has been dead for 12 years. Lee has been trying to communicate with the dead.

In a second excursus into nature, Lee makes an early morning visit to the state park. In this particular park the convention is to ignore other joggers, leaving each other to "fragile illusions of wilderness" (152). Alone, Lee feels for a moment as if in "an actual Eden" (152). The scene is remarkable for its absence of technology, of electrical wires (152) and at this early hour, of any aeroplanes. When he returns home to mow his lawn, however, he encounters the machine with a vengeance. As he is mowing he notes a neighbour's toddler escaping from control and his mind moves, prompted by the handle of the mower, to the years he spent pushing Esther in her stroller, a happy and well-respected father in a harmonious small community. Suddenly he comes back to earth at a terrible noise, the handle leaping from his hands. For a moment he is in both past and present. "There was a double instant, Esther's small compact weight torn from him. He was practically fainting on top of the mower" (164). In fact he has merely been stopped by a piece of wood, a branch which he has run over, and which almost flings him onto the blades. It is as if wood blew Esther up and out of his arms. The lawn mower had been bought to mow the lawn at the house to which Lee had insisted on moving, after a neighbour's dog had bitten Esther. He suddenly remembers declaring that "The welfare of a child is more important than anything else." To which Aileen had replied, "I guess that depends on which child it is" (164). Now Lee realises that his previous happy state depended entirely on the absence of Aileen's first child. To Lee, the abduction was "a miracle" (164) an unpleasant loose end from the past conveniently tied off. The symbolism here links the destructive branch, the potentially damaged child torn from the parent, Esther, Aileen's son, technology and nature. Lee's true feelings emerge, "Was he crying? . . . He felt a strange misery, very much like remorse, as if in running over the branch he had injured someone" (164). It is as if the Unabomber's bomb (in the guise of wood) had finally reached Lee and revealed his errors. Over-laying one memory in the palimpsest may restore Lee to a precarious bal-ance, but other memories also come up violently through the surface. The lawn mower is now a rusted, gasping contraption with a "deathbed rep-ertoire" of labored drones, scummed with the "dead sod of ages" (160). Death haunts the scene, already emblematic in its image of grass cut and withered, as Choi runs a gothic subtext under the surface of pastoral and Arcadian images.

Now Lee remembers the events leading to the loss of Aileen's son. Aileen had not performed the role of "fit mother" with enough zeal and lost her son because she admitted committing adultery. A divorce court would have tried her and found her wanting on those grounds alone. She was under-, not oversocialized, not nearly conventional enough. In the present Lee goes through what Aileen did and learns what it is to be unable to perform one's innocence appropriately. In the past Lee had not helped Aileen. His com-ment on the moment when Aileen discovered her son gone is chilling. "Lee had known then that the battle was won" (132), because Aileen sobbed alone. "She did not bring her grief to her husband. She had realized she shouldn't" (132). Her grief was already subject to careful policing. After the polygraph test the two stories of past and present come together. The memory of Esther had been triggered by the sight of a young mother, a neighbour, chasing after her toddler. Now that mother reappears on his doorstep, threatening him not to go near her two young children (217). It is as if Aileen, who also had two children, but never caught up with one of them, had reappeared from the dead to confront him. Guilt returns to haunt him, and he finally faces up to the deceptions of his past.

When a second letter arrives, enclosing a page of his thesis, Lee checks the library copy and finds the Bomber's contact details in place of the missing page. An apparently impersonal communication—a page of mathematical symbols—carries the most personal of messages, a message which only Lee can read. What might appear to the uninitiated as a letter entirely devoid of personal emotion triggers a memory of his happiness with Aileen. Lee remembers Aileen laboriously typing each page of symbols three times, the thesis growing along with her pregnancy, and he links together her terrible mechanical toil with memories of their past happiness, in a period of shared creativity. Anyone seeing the page of thesis would see only abstract imper-sonal symbols, but to Lee it opens out an entire past chapter of his life.

At this point in the novel the balance shifts decisively between narra-tive persons of interest with a major change of narrative focalisation. Part Three suddenly introduces a new character, through whom the story is refocalised, in third person narration, Gaither's son John, now rechristened

Mark. Writing may itself be considered as a form of technology, manipulating readers' responses. Choi therefore takes care to interrupt the process
and defamilarise the characters and their perspectives, forcibly reminding
us that we are reading a book, a work of imagination. As she said,

> just when Mark discovers that everything he's ever been familiar with,
> everything he's ever believed about himself, is false, that he doesn't even
> know who he is—the reader is subjected to the same experience. Every-
> thing the reader has come to be familiar with about the book—Lee's
> consciousness, Lee's perspective, is swept away in a stroke. The reader
> has to start fresh like Mark, and has to start fresh *with* Mark.[34]

The stable ground of narration is swept away from under the reader's feet
and we have to reconstruct the story of Mark's life, just as he does himself, from hints and clues. Choi deliberately leads us astray, creating a red
herring in which Mark seems to be a candidate for the role of bomber.
Mark functions as an entirely innocent double to the Unabomber. Like the
Unabomber he follows a life of careerless subsistence survival (251), living
free of most technology in a small cabin in the mountains. He has a vexed
history (drugs, a short term in prison), his disturbed youth implicitly the
result of his disrupted background, "angry at he knew not what" (248).
Like the Unabomber he has a warm relationship with the town librarian,
who keeps him supplied with books. He also finds salvation in wild nature,
hiking in solitude. Walking is a key clue. The alert reader will already have
noted Esther's baby shoes in Lee's desk, his memories of her walking at
fourteen months and his neighbour's toddler also walking for the first time
at the same age—and running away from his mother. Mark's memory of
making a similar dash for freedom, supposedly at ten months, is clearly
wrongly-dated. Mark also shares the bomber's impatience with socialised
creeds. His rejection of religion is the result of the demand that he share his
feelings with others and put his innermost self on display (272). The basis
of his close friendship with Gene, another hiker, is that Gene never expects
to be repaid in disclosures, and self-revelations (272). But reticence can go
too far. When Mark discovers that Gene has two children whom he has
never mentioned, he feels an inexplicable sense of betrayal. Aileen also had
two children and the reader knows that Aileen and Lee never mentioned
her son. Mark's sense of betrayal is the product of buried memories. Where
Lee is too self-centred (and grammatically focalised as such) Mark leads
an impersonal existence, hardly aware of his true self at all. Choi said in
interview that she introduced Mark to give a sense of someone looking at
Lee as opposed to the relentless self-scrutiny of the latter.[35] Mark is himself
like a third person narrator, coolly observing events. His major pastime is
photography: "he wanted to formalize memory" (258), a desire presum-
ably connected to the absence of proofs of his own identity and past, which
is slowly dawning on him. Mark gives the impression of someone who is

always at a distance, always behind the camera, rather than in its focus, as Lee has been. When Mark sees a photo of Lee, for example, he immediately notes that he looks suspicious, his eyes concealed under a hat, and understands the motives of the unseen photographer (265). In bringing the lost child and the terrorist together in this fashion as doubles, Choi also brings Lee into sharper focus. Where Lee willingly fled home and family, to a new life in America, Mark has had exile and a change of identity thrust upon him. Mark would fit the profile of the bomber much better than Lee—he is solitary, alienated from society, and might reasonably be expected to bear a grudge. But it is Lee who has been scrutinised as a possible suspect. Where the Unabomber treated his victims as one-dimensional characters, embodying one idea, Choi allows characters to be porous, sharing aspects in an ambiguous fashion, engineering a slew of reciprocity. In interview Choi argued that it was important to grasp the recognizable, human motives driving monstrous behaviour.

> We have to acknowledge the continuities between ourselves and these so-called monsters or we'll never understand or ameliorate that kind of behaviour.[36]

Writing off the 9/11 hijackers as monsters was a mistake, in her view, since demonization was likely to create more of them. In *A Person of Interest* characters shadow and double each other, establishing common continuities, and the reader reads one character through knowledge of another. Characters offer parallels and strike variations on each other: Rachel and Aileen, Mark and Whitehead, Lee and Whitehead, Esther and Mark. Lee cannot understand, for example, why Aileen, dying, tolerated the presence of Esther's band of delinquent, misfit teenagers, whereas the reader sees that this "circle of waifs" (301) is some sort of compensation, in numbers at least, for the absence of one particular motherless, delinquent child, her son. Doubling has a reparative function, assuaging loss.

Importantly, Mark finds out the truth of his past not only by walking and thinking about walking, but also by narrating while walking, finding a stable ground for his identity in narration. His realisation that the story of his past is completely unreliable takes place in an environment quite foreign to the various Christian Missionary posts in which he spent his youth, a grove in the wood, described as an arcade or mosque of old trees, their base "a verdant prayer rug", the overall impression that of a temple (273). The clearing appears to him to mingle past with present. The altitude means that the mountain laurel (faded at lower altitudes) is now in bloom, as if Mark had gone back in time to May when it bloomed originally (261). Mark realises that he is in full emotional crisis and solves his problem by narration. He addresses the story of the mysterious last few weeks—the doubts about his identity, the police visit questioning his knowledge of his childhood, the discovery that his father knew Lee—to the long-dead Gene.

Like Lee with his lawn mower/stroller, Mark is now in two places at once, and two times at once, "with Gene both before him and lost to him." (276). Gene does not solve the conundrum: he merely says (in Mark's imagination) that all parents are mysteries to their children. The point is not that Gene is some sort of spirit guide but that the process of narration finally produces meaning out of events, making things hang together rather than blowing them apart. Climactically Mark is led to recall a childhood memory of an argument between Ruth and her mother, who cries out, revealingly, "And what about his mother?" (278).

And what about Mark's mother? At the close of the novel Lee re-reads Aileen's letter. Aileen begins composing the letter in her mind from the moment she goes into labour, and notes that everything that happens in the next few weeks "had been slightly dilated by the echo of her internal narration" (115). The letter is a form of creative writing which accompanies the birth of John. It is important to note the word "dilated": events have been expanded and made more meaningful by her own internal account of them as they are occurring. She is in a sense experiencing them as if they were simultaneously being narrated. "Dilate" suggests both anatomical expansion (here, the cervix) and the verbal. To dilate on a topic is to speak at length, expand, flesh out the details. When Aileen actually comes to write, she writes with great speed, "as if simply transcribing something already printed" (115). The text has already been fully created in her mind. Lee, however, originally receives the letter at a point when he thinks they have separated forever and he reads it with unease. As an uncensored transcript of her most private thoughts, it looks like a diary; he has to flip back to be sure that it is addressed to him (124). It is so entirely a first person account that it seems as if Aileen is talking to herself—yet she clearly assumes that he is the ideal reader. Lee shuts it away in his desk. Yet he keeps the letter, and is deeply moved when the FBI give it back to him. Agent Morrison confiscates it as evidence but then decides that it is unimportant (340). But of course the letter is massively important. Lee realises now that it is a "slow revelation." He had never read it properly before: "he'd only glared fearfully at the words through a mesh of defences" (352). Now he falls into a trance of enjoyment, reading and re-reading. And the reader shares this experience with Lee, reading passages over his shoulder—the description of her son's eyelid, and her belief in the importance of writing down these experiences which otherwise her son will never know. The letter is an education in reading, restoring Aileen's unsocialised private self to Lee. It "conveyed her to him, thoroughly, without any constraint" (352). At the close of the novel Lee passes it to another reader, her son, and restores his mother to him. This is a letter which is all about freedom and creativity—Aileen's son, new to this world, something she has created—and creative writing, the free, unregulated expression of her thoughts, writing which is identified with the power to create, not to destroy. In the succession of readers (Aileen to Lee to Mark to the reader of the novel) Choi creates a small community deeply engaged with creative "letters" (with literature in modern parlance), rejecting the idea that literature cannot act as a counterweight to the messages of the destructive terrorist, or the pre-processed mechanical utterances of the oversocialised.

4 Blowback
André Dubus III, *House of Sand and Fog*

One area in which the relationship between utopia and terror is particularly acute is what has been termed "human rights imperialism," when an empire intervenes in the affairs of another country, justifying its intervention by its humanitarian and liberationist mission. Political or military interventions then figure as rescue missions on behalf of the abused or persecuted. Samuel Moyn has argued that there is a clear connection between the modern, international human rights movement and utopia. Human rights involves an agenda for improving the world and bringing about a new one in which the individual enjoys international protection. Indeed Moyn argues that the movement emerges in response to the bankruptcy of other utopian movements, particularly the radicalism of the 1960s and the collapse of socialism. The discourse of rights is easily appropriated, however. When in 1968 the UN declared "International Human Rights Year" and hosted a conference in Tehran, the Shah, a dictator, opened the proceedings by crediting his ancient countrymen with the invention of human rights, proclaiming that the tradition of the Emperor Cyrus, a thousand years before, was now continued in his own dynasty's respect for moral principle.[1] Jean Bricmont provides a detailed analysis of the selective use of "human rights" as a pretext for old-fashioned imperialism.[2] Women are often a useful pretext for the spear-carriers for the belief that the West has a providential right to intervene wherever in the world it wants, in the belief that Western ideals are universal. Fighting against Islamic terrorism then becomes a means of saving Muslim women from the evil of their men: Laura Bush famously justified the US invasion of Afghanistan as an opportunity to liberate Afghani women from the gender hierarchies of the Taliban.[3] This is a tactic which is a continuation of a similar strategy employed by the British in India (the campaign against sati) and China (the campaign against footbinding) and memorably characterised by Gayatri Spivak as "white men saving brown women from brown men". [4] In *House of Sand and Fog* André Dubus examines the question of American intervention in the first of two novels which focus on the American sense of a sacred rescue mission, each focussed upon apparently vulnerable women.

Since Seymour Hersh published an article in the *New Yorker* in April 2006, exposing an apparent Pentagon plan to attack Iran, an attack in which for the first time since Hiroshima the use of nuclear weapons was contemplated, Iran has become a focus of American attention.[5] It was not always thus. As Gary Sick observes, before the Iranian hostage crisis, Iran hardly even evoked a stereotype for the United States citizen, not even in the way China, Egypt or India did.[6] At best, as Persia, it might suggest cats, carpets and caviar. American awareness of Iran was characterised by a combination of ignorance and wholesale amnesia. For Hamid Dabashi the invasion plan raised the question "of hegemony and Empire—one with or without the other." Did the American empire have a hegemonic project or ideological agenda? Or was it just making a mess all over the world?[7] Recent debates have focussed keenly on this question of the degree to which the American state knows what it is doing and consciously pursues Imperialist aims. For Niall Ferguson it is an empire which dare not speak its name, an "imperialism of anti-imperialism", posing as liberationist.[8] Hardt and Negri simply portray American domination as corresponding with economic domination.[9] In his Empire trilogy (*Blowback, Nemesis,* and *The Sorrows of Empire*) Chalmers Johnson equates empire with militarism, based upon American armed forces stationed in foreign countries, whether in an advisory and support capacity, or in the 737 US bases in some 130 countries which he counted in 2006, and described as "a planet-spanning baseworld"of foreign enclaves which function as parasitical neo-colonies completely beyond the jurisdiction of the occupied nation.[10] For Johnson, most US imperialism operates as a "stealth imperialism" well-below the sightlines of the American public.[11] American ignorance about their country's operations also explains why attacks on Americans are greeted with cries of shock and outrage. In his analysis Johnson adopts the term "blowback", first invented by officials of the CIA to refer to

> the unintended consequences of policies that were kept secret from the American people. What the daily press report as the malign acts of "terrorists" or "drug lords" or "rogue states" or "illegal arms merchants" often turn out to be blowback from earlier American operations.[12]

Examples would include the 1988 Lockerbie bombing, blowback from the 1986 Reagan administration raid on Libya which killed Gaddafi's step-daughter; or the epidemic of cocaine usage in US cities fuelled by central and Southern Americans whom the CIA or the Pentagon had supported in Nicaragua. (The Contras made deals to sell cocaine in the US to buy arms and supplies.) Because we live in an increasingly interconnected, globalised system, we are all living in a blowback world, though the time lags between events, and the distancing effects of geographical displacements, tend to erase the causative links. "The unintended consequences of American policies and acts in country X are a bomb at an American embassy in country Y or a dead American in country Z."[13] In these circumstances it is easy for memory to falter—or to be erased. Dabashi argues that the

US propaganda machinery is contingent on a systematic loss of collective memory, as if America really had moved, in Francis Fukuyama's formulation, beyond history.[14]

In this connection Iran brings the issue of what Americans know into sharp focus, as the controversy over Azar Nafisi's memoir, *Reading Lolita in Tehran*, indicates. Memoirs by and about Iranian women have become exceptionally popular in America, with at least ten mass-market titles published in the last decade.[15] For Gillian Whitlock such memoirs are "soft weapons", used to buttress aggressive Western intervention in other countries. Life narratives of this type, emphasising the oppression of Muslim women, play to Western traditions of benevolence, masking privilege, reifying dominant social relations and naturalizing the neo-liberal discourse of the free circulation of ideas, goods and peoples in global networks of exchange.[16] (Whitlock gleefully notes the participation of Nafisi in a marketing campaign for Audi automobiles. For the promoters Nafisi was fashionably cool: "Azar is to literature what Audi is to cars."[17]) An Iranian commentator similarly argues that memoir-writers are deeply enmeshed in the politics of rendering Iran from a transnational perspective, making Iranians "Other" in a neo-Orientalist discourse, authored by American-identified women.[18] Hamid Dabashi portrays Nafisi as a comprador intellectual, functioning as a feigned "native observer", claiming a fake authority and authenticity.[19] In his view, her book supports the US agenda for Iran, particularly by propagating a view of Islam as violent and abusive to women. This is not the place to discuss in detail the controversy over Nafisi's portrayal of Iran, ably tackled by Fatehmeh Keshavarz and John Carlos Rowe, respectively.[20] It is worth noting however that Nafisi's own text is amnesiac. In a lengthy, and largely pro-American, discussion of the modern history of Iran she never mentions the CIA coup of 1953, which reinstated the Shah in power.

André Dubus's novel, *House of Sand and Fog* (1999) makes an important counterbalance to Nafisi and her fellow memorialists, engaging with the issues for which "blowback" will serve as shorthand, exploring how the forgotten past returns to plague an ignorant American and how "human rights imperialism", particularly the use of gendered horrors to legitimate Western domination, manages to compound the damage. Where memoirs risk functioning as a means of making Iran other to America, *House of Sand and Fog* pursues a narrative strategy which makes Iranians into Americans—and Americans into Iranians. In its themes and techniques the novel establishes the intersection of distance and knowledge as its key concern. *House of Sand and Fog* is the first American bestseller centred on a Muslim protagonist; it was a finalist for the National Book Award, enthusiastically adopted by Oprah, made into a major film, and has some two million copies in print. As Donna Seaman commented, it depicts "a microcosmic conflict of profound cultural implications".[21] The novel imports a wealthy Iranian refugee family to California to do battle with a working class Italian-American woman over their rival claims to their own place in America, a house. Kathy Lazaro, a recovering cocaine addict, with no connections to, or understanding of American oil-politics in the Middle East, loses her house through a bureaucratic error to Massood Behrani, formerly a colonel in the Shah's Iran. Behrani and his traditional Muslim wife are pitted against the sexy, self-indulgent Kathy, and her policeman lover, Lester. The city has sent a tax bill to the wrong place, evicts Kathy for non-payment and auctions the house at a knockdown price. When the error is discovered the Colonel agrees to sell the house back, but only at full market value. Fairly obviously there are sizable issues at play in the fight to the death which follows, as a downwardly mobile "old" immigrant confronts the upward mobility of the new immigrant. Kathy, a domestic cleaner who inherited the house from her father, is only a slip away from the underclass, living in a recognisably blue collar America of truck stops, diners, cheap motels and country and western music. The Colonel almost appears to be living in a different country entirely, in a city made up of recent immigrants, as he drives through Japan Town, past Spanish-speaking areas and Iraqi and Nicaraguan businesses.

Kathy's Kafkaesque nightmare seems entirely undeserved. She thought the mistake had been rectified, has ignored the letters from the tax officials, and doesn't know that her house is about to be repossessed. Throughout, she is characterised by ignorance. She repeatedly describes the Behranis as "Arabs", talking "Arabic or Israeli" and names them variously as Bahroony, Behmini and Barmeeny.[22] She has about as much awareness of Iran as she has of the origins of her cocaine supply. It is beyond her to envisage that her life as an ordinary American might be affected because America supported a corrupt and torturing regime. The Colonel, however, sees himself as a victim of events; he buys the house in all innocence as an opportunity to follow American ideals and climb up the property ladder. Confronted by Kathy, he feels "accused of a crime I did not commit" (135). The suspicion lingers, however, that as a member of the Iranian military, he may have been complicit in other crimes which were committed. The novel takes considerable risks in the way it sets up this conflict. Does a rapacious Oriental dispossess an American of her lawful inheritance? Or has Kathy a false sense of her entitlement? Is the Colonel (hardworking, disciplined and a firm believer in the American dream) the true heir to America? Is Kathy an unfortunate victim? Or a messy, self-indulgent woman, dissipating everything her father worked for in a cokestorm, a representative of the soft underbelly of a decadent America? Or was that cokestorm itself also the result of American support of corrupt foreign regimes? To what extent are the protagonists innocent—or ignorant? And is their absence of knowledge culpable and in some senses intentional?

Dubus's plot is carefully designed to emphasise the long history of American involvement in Iran. The Behranis flee Iran one week after the fall of the Shah (January, 1979) and reach America with $280,000. The Iranian

Islamic Revolution of 1979 came as a complete surprise to Americans. It was only in November 1978 that US foreign policy experts began to see that the Shah was faltering.[23] (It is usually seen as one of the CIA's greatest predictive failures.)[24] The violent Anti-Americanism which followed, the storming of the US embassy with 52 Americans held hostage for fourteen months, was an even greater shock to a public which thought they were rather well-liked in Iran. What Americans did not "know" was the long term effect of the 1953 CIA-sponsored coup which removed Mossadeq, an elected leader, to protect US access to Iranian oil. Most analysts agree that America intervened in 1953 largely out of ignorance, in the mistaken belief, fed to them by the British, that Mossadeq, a conservative, was turning towards Communism. Effectively Eisenhower removed a moderately democratic government to install a repressive dictatorship. In 1953 the Shah fled at the first sign of trouble, and returned only with US support. In 1979 the Shah entered America on 22 October and as a result on 4 November the Tehran embassy was overrun. Iranians remembered that the US had previously returned the Shah to his throne and they feared a repetition. The 1979 revolution was in many respects blowback from the 1953 coup.

It is no accident that the Colonel is in the air force, and previously bought F16s from the Americans, nor that he retains the trappings of wealth, nor that he has gravitated to San Francisco, home of Lockheed and Boeing. As an air force officer he has benefited disproportionately from American largesse. The Shah's reign was characterised by militarism and excess. In the period between 1953 and 1957 alone, the US provided $500 million to Iran, one quarter of it earmarked for the military.[25] The Shah's defence budget was never less than twenty-three per cent of the general budget. American aid and technological assistance also established the secret police, SAVAK, answering directly to the Shah, run by men with military backgrounds and regulated only by military tribunals. Interrogation, torture and imprisonment without trial were so commonplace that in 1974 Amnesty International described Iran as having the worst human rights record in the world.[26] The Shah's principal aide for military procurement was an air force general; the Shah took a keen interest in the air force, even in the appointment of middle-ranking officers. (The Colonel is pictured with the Shah in a photograph prominently displayed in the living room.) Writing before the revolution, Robert Graham noted that

> By virtue of their role as defenders of the throne—not of the realm—the Officer corps has become a'privileged class. Their pay and fringe benefits put NATO to shame, including the provision of villas, domestic personnel, low taxes on luxury goods and holiday compounds.[27]

Effectively Iran was a US military base, policing the gulf for America. Successive Presidents allowed an enormous arms build-up, and sent in technical personnel to support sophisticated weaponry. Modernisation on the

Western model was marked by excess, memorably condemned by Khomeini as "Westoxification". The Persepolis celebrations of 2,500 years of monarchy, in October 1971, cost $100 million, with French chefs from Maxims serving up dishes of Breast of Peacock on Limoges porecelain. (At this point Tehran still lacked a sewage system.) In *House of Sand and Fog* Kathy does not lose her house to an invading "Other" but to an American citizen, the product of American past policies. Behrani buys the house with money which can only be American in origin.

Given Dubus's Marxist training it is tempting to see Behrani's refusal to sell the house back at less than its full market value as a neat demonstration that "property is theft", and that capitalist economics underwrite the final disaster. But Kathy's outrage is also reminiscent of the Western reaction to the Iranians when Mossadeq nationalised the Anglo-Iranian oil company, and demanded a fair market price from the West, instead of the notional sixteen per cent which had previously been paid.[28] The Colonel wants a fair price for his assets and a legal profit. He has shored up American access to cheap oil, and in some respects has a claim to a rightful share in the economy. At the risk of stating the obvious, Dubus continually emphasises the American reliance on cheap gasoline. The novel opens with an emblematic scene in which the Colonel, along with Panamanian, Vietnamese and Chinese workers, toils in the hot sun on the southbound lanes of Route 101. The Colonel has become one of the "garbage soldiers" (17), spearing refuse for the Highways department, a soldier of lesser rank but still part of the infrastructure of an oil-based economy. On the way home he admires the mansions of Pacific Heights with their Porsches, Jaguars and Lamborghinis, "the cars of the old Tehran" (20), where he had himself enjoyed the use of a huge Mercedes equipped with TV, telephone and bar. Even now he drives a Buick Regal, carefully stowed in the garage of a luxury hotel, to conceal his servile day job from his fellow exiles. Four nights a week he works in a convenience store, attached to a gas station. Kathy never connects the Colonel to her own home. Yet when she loses it she tells Lester wryly that she is "staying at the Bonneville" (85), in other words living in her car, one of the larger gas-guzzlers, given to her by her brother, an auto-dealer. (When she tells him that her husband has left her, he merely asks, "Did he take the Pontiac?" 197.) Kathy's father bought the house from the profits of a delivery business; she remembers long hours in his van. Dispossessed, she relies on gas station restrooms and spends her time in aimless driving. Later, as her sense of dispossession becomes more acute, she acquires some hardware (Lester carelessly supplies her with his gun) and drunkenly holds up a gas station to get fuel to attack and burn out the Behranis—a violent American stealing some one else's oil.

If both Kathy and the Colonel embody the operation of American petropolicies, the role of shoring up a dictatorship by force falls to Lester, a field-training officer in the local police. Earlier in the novel the Colonel remembered an encounter with a young Iranian policeman, a Savaki, who told him that the way to interrogate "subversives" was to focus on their children. "Make a subversive watch his little one lose a hand or arm and they will tell you everything" (61). In an attempt to make the Colonel give the house back, Lester (minus his badge but in uniform) visits the Colonel and tells him, "You have a family. I'd be thinking more about them if I were you" (168). Behrani makes the connection immediately to the possibility that "America has its officials who operate over the law" (170), "dark men in suits, Savakis" (170). Effectively the apparent "Others" have swapped places. Formerly American power was masked behind SAVAK; now the masks are removed. Lester is a Savaki; the American steals oil by force; the Colonel's rank and power are stripped away to reveal a dirty soldier, keeping Americans on the road.

Narrative method enforces the underlying connections between the apparently oppositional characters. Dubus divides the novel into two parts. In the first, events centre upon responsibility; "Not knowing" drives the plot, and becomes an effect of the narrative method, which confronts the reader with a corrective perspective. Part One is alternately narrated by the Colonel in first person and present tense, and Kathy, also in first person, but in the past. The sequential arrangement of events (first the Colonel, then Kathy, with her narrative looping back over events which the reader has already witnessed first hand) places Kathy in the position of the unaware American. In Section 16, for example, covering Wednesday and Thursday, Kathy celebrates what she believes is the imminent return of her house.[29] But the reader has already reached Friday with the Colonel, and knows that following the lawyer's advice on Thursday, he is not going to give it back. Kathy is the person who does not know, whereas the reader is often superior in knowledge and watches a naïve American who is clearly about to come to grief. Kathy's use of the past tense suggests a desire to distance herself from involvement in events, which she narrates as fixed in time and unchangeable. In contrast the Colonel's present places reader and character "in" events simultaneously. We share his narrative space, without any of the distancing effects of a time lag, whereas we look back on Kathy as if in a past arena. Temporal distance reverses spatial distance. Iran is right in our lap; the American is operating at a distance. The two individual narratives at first encourage an oppositional reading—as if the reader were weighing up a balance sheet of rights and wrongs, Kathy versus the Colonel. Kathy's brother believes in resolving a problem by the balance-sheet method: "On one side of the page you got your costs and on the other side your benefits. All you do is mark which one is which, then you weigh one side against the other and you get your decision" (84). Kathy, however, is not very good at telling a plus from a minus, a benefit from a cost. Nor is her opposition to the Colonel so clear-cut. Slowly parallelism operates to bring them closer together, and to make sense of the one through reference to the other. The novel thus demonstrates that the "I" has no story of its own which is not also the story of a relation or set of relations. As Judith Butler puts it,

"When the I seeks to give an account of itself, it can start with itself, but it will find that this self is already implicated in a social temporality that exceeds its own capacities for narration."[30]

Throughout the first part of the novel a series of parallel events remind the reader that responsibility is shared, that ignorance is not innocence, and that "not knowing" causes disaster. Americans become Iranians imagistically, just as Iranians became Americans. The plot erases the distance between the two by bringing the results of foreign policies into the domestic sphere. Evicted, Kathy is advised to keep her distance and avoid returning to her former home. As Gerald Turkel notes, when the law takes control of a dispute, procedural and spatial boundaries are established to control and direct the conflict in ways that limit the direct expression of animosity.[31] Not here, however: Kathy steadily breaks down the distance, accosting the Colonel's workmen, haranguing potential buyers, entering the house to plead with his wife and finally staging a suicide attempt on the doorstep, until she is back in her own bedroom. She invades the house to force an awareness of his error on the Colonel, and to demand reparation. Throughout, she is motivated by the desire to conceal the truth from her family. They do not know that her husband has left her, nor that she has lost the family inheritance. Similarly the Colonel's children do not know that he is slaving in menial jobs, to keep up appearances so that his daughter Soraya can make a suitable marriage. He withholds the true situation from his wife, Nadi, who does not know that the house was auctioned in error. "Not knowing" is the engine of the plot, and of the novel's exploration of individual responsibility.

The parallels also establish that it is not difference which unleashes violence but sameness under the skin. Parallel events occur in successive units of narration with events in the Colonel's life mirrored in Kathy's account. In the fifth section, for example, Behrani recalls Nadi's accusation that they were forced to flee (and are now on a death list) "because of you, you and your SAVAK friends" (57). Behrani denies any responsibility for SAVAK: "I purchased fighter jets. I was not with SAVAK" (58). Recalling, however, the encounter with the torturer (American-trained), he becomes uncomfortable. He "did not like to be reminded of the secret police", the role of America, or that "this was the manner in which our king retained his throne and our way of life" (62). The Colonel met the torturer at his friend General Pourat's house, at a highly ceremonialised drinking party where the oldest man ritually serves the vodka to the younger ones, regulating their consumption and implicitly keeping their excesses under control. The traditional way of life depends however upon more sinister controls; the authority of the older man is only a politer version of a repressive dictatorship. From the account of this group meeting, the novel moves immediately to Kathy recalling her inability to control her drinking and drug use. She attends the group meetings of a rehabilitation programme, Rational Recovery, which emphasises that irrational behaviour and beliefs can be overcome by the use of our reason.[32] In Rational Recovery the addict creates a personification of the compulsive thoughts tempting him to drink: the Beast (65). The Beast is actually seductive and internal, but Kathy is encouraged by the programme to see it as an occupying force, an "Other" and alien threat, rather than the result of her own weakness. Once externalised, it can be attacked. Kathy actually prefers Alcoholics Anonymous, which is based on the idea that our behaviour is caused by circumstances over which we have no control. RR insists on personal accountability; AA on surrendering all responsibility to a higher power. Predictably, Kathy loves it, especially the group meetings with everyone "telling their stories and backing each other up, nobody any wiser and more together than anyone else" (65). In telling her own story, Kathy presents herself as a powerless victim, pushed around by the state authorities and under alien occupation. As the Colonel takes over her house, so the Beast takes over Kathy. The Colonel on the other hand sees through the apparently benign controls of the Iranian male hierarchy to the punitive reality at its centre. The parallel memories offer an oblique comment on the novel itself, as the reader switches between the disciplined Colonel and the powerless Kathy, giving their rival accounts of themselves.

From drink to sex: the following sequence expands the parallelism between the two, through parallel erotic encounters. Nadi invites the Colonel to her room (a fairly rare occurrence for him); Kathy makes love with Lester. Earlier the Colonel had reproached his wife for her hypocrisy over SAVAK. "She never complained of the maids and soldiers she used for the upkeep of our home . . . or of our bungalow there overlooking the Caspian" (58). Nor did she object when they were automatically taken to the front of the cinema line, despite the fear visible in the manager's eyes. Now, freed from the need to keep up appearances, "free of our own masquerade, our own lies" (81), the Colonel feels once again like the young man on his wedding night. Sex eliminates time and distance, restoring an innocent past. Similarly Kathy, in bed with Lester, feels "sixteen all over again." (94). In the patrol car with Lester, however, she notices the fear of the other drivers, all of them moderating their speed and avoiding eye contact—just like the cinema manager in Iran. Two formal social occasions follow: Kathy and Lester go out on a proper date, for dinner at the Hyatt. The Behranis host a party for Soraya on her return from her honeymoon. Both situations appear to offer a clearer view through the previous fog of lies: the Behranis entertain on their "Widow's walk" with a vista to the ocean; the Hyatt features a revolving restaurant with a clear view of the landscape in the round. The Colonel explains the situation with the house to his son; Lester decides to tell his wife everything and end "this masquerade ball I've been at for years" (121). But their disclosures are only partial. Kathy tells Lester that drinking was her husband's problem, not hers, and promptly falls off the wagon. Lester's "not knowing" that she has real problems with alcohol is a major contributory factor to the final disaster. Kathy also edits her past to focus only on herself as a young girl, to avoid mentioning her first husband, divorce, rehab and suicide attempts. Similarly Soraya, horrified at finding her parents in a small bungalow and desperate to keep up appearances in front of her mother-in-law, spends the party reminiscing about her life as a young girl in Tehran, enjoying parties and calls from the Shah. The Colonel has not told Nadi his problems because he wants her cheerful and innocent as a child, and has maintained "this mask for my children" (164), never explaining their difficult financial situation. Assuming a false responsibility for his women, treating them as irresponsible children, is ultimately destructive. His lack of candour with Soraya poisons their relationship. Nadi retreats from him into the music of Googoosh, a music "of romantics ignorant of any history but their own" (213).[33] Kathy is so unwilling to reveal the truth to her mother that all communication between them breaks down.

The parallels establish a resemblance between the apparent opposites and draw them together across their narrative separations, before the plot erupts into the violence of Part Two. At the mid-point of the novel a tenuous resolution is reached with Kathy once more back in her own bedroom, sheltered by the Behranis who have saved her life. Implicitly the novel makes the point that the recognition of guilty responsibility is more likely to produce a solution than forcible intervention and the re-occupation of the moral high ground. The reader absorbs both narratives, sees the parallels and erases the apparent distance between them to establish a shared position. In the words of one reviewer, "the hope for a home that is free of the stranger, a home that is all mine, and not also partly yours, is an illusion built on the most unsteady ground."[34]

The tragedy of the novel is initiated with a change in narrative focalisation. In Part Two Lester suddenly emerges as the focaliser of the story, in third person and past tense, a third party erupting into the narrative, upsetting a precarious balance and taking charge of events. Feeling neglected by Kathy and "shut out" (268), not knowing about her drinking problems, he smashes into the kitchen, in the mistaken belief that she needs rescuing, and goes on to hold the Behranis hostage to force the return of the house. Lester's intervention, motivated by his desire to protect Kathy against "brown men" triggers comprehensive disaster. By the close of the novel the Colonel, his wife and son are dead, Lester's family has broken apart, and he and Kathy are facing lengthy jail terms. Part One sets up an initial opposition over the disputed territory, but eventually associates Kathy and the Colonel, both American citizens, both complicit, both learning to recognise a degree of responsibility. Part Two demonstrates the dangers of premature intervention on the basis of situational ignorance. Whatever the difficulties of resolving the dispute over the house, it is Lester's intervention which seals everyone's doom. He is the logical extension of the Colonel's desire to protect women, viewed as innocent children who are not fully responsible for their actions. In political terms he is the outsider who interferes in the domestic affairs of others, out of mistaken idealism. Ironically, he is an

American naïve idealist, who becomes an Iranian-hostage taker (as opposed to an Iranian hostage-taker). The sudden access to Lester's thoughts is a surprise to the reader and in narrative terms plays with notions of "inside" and "outside", domestic and foreign. As readers we listen to the voices of Kathy and the Colonel, but in Lester's case an authority is in charge of our access to him, in the shape of an omniscient narrator. With Lester, authority enters the text.

In the novel, Dubus uses the image of domestic violence to draw the political moral, substituting the domestic microcosm for the political macrocosm. A classic image of the kind of "barbarity" that the West deplores is offered by the fate of the Colonel's cousin, Jasmeen. When she has an affair with a married American oil executive, her father locks her up, beats her repeatedly (and also beats her mother for good measure). When his son hears market talk of "the Behrani family, of the shame their kaseef (dirty) daughter had brought upon their heads" (151) he forces his father to act to avenge their disgrace. The father drags Jasmeen out by the hair, barefoot, bruised and in her nightdress, and shoots her dead. Everything in this anecdote conspires to present the dangers of brown men to their women. The target is not the American seducer but the woman. The killer is not just the father but the family males in collaboration. Afterwards, "None of her brothers or uncles would take revenge on Jasmeen's killer" (152). The abuse is collective, serial (repeated beatings) and involves more than one woman. The Colonel however dissociates himself from the event. "I hated my uncle . . . The hurting of women I have not approved of" (153). Though he drags Kathy away from the house, bruising her, he rejects further violence. "I am not my uncle from Tabriz" (186). When he discovers Kathy (now also having an affair with a married man) in a suicide attempt, he suddenly remembers "my long dead cousin, Jasmeen" (214) and, overcome by tenderness, takes her into the house. Watching Kathy sleep, he wonders if now, perhaps, she will be able to acknowledge "who her real enemy has become" (218). The sequence of events establishes the Colonel as a flawed individual but in the end a man who is a rescuer, not someone to be rescued from. As he remembers Jasmeen, he recalls again the Savaki torturer and acknowledges that he had not made a sufficient moral stand (218).In the final analysis the enemy is not the Beast within Kathy, or the apparent alien "Other", now inside her house, but Lester. Lester's very first intervention provokes domestic violence. When Lester originally threatens the family, a panicky Nadi upbraids the Colonel who slaps her. Contemplating the moment he feels as if "it belongs not to my family but another" (169). Lester would not have gone to visit the Colonel, if not for his own family problems. Just as Kathy waited in her car to shout at the Colonel, so Lester's wife Carol waited outside police headquarters in her car, "shouting and crying. Hitting me" (155). Earlier in the novel Lester discussed the inadequacies of the domestic violence laws. In California, no matter which spouse initiates the violence, the police have to take both in (161).

Responsibility is shared. However large the husband or slight the wife, if she defends herself she will be arrested (162). One husband repeatedly beats his wife, who dare not bring charges; they appear in public, arm in arm, "like it was nobody's business" (111). In response Lester takes the law into his own hands, planting drugs on the erring husband, to give the wife the opportunity to escape. Kathy's response is telling. She questions Lester's right to do this, wondering if the wife liked being the powerless victim. And why, she wonders, does Lester need "to wear this cape and mask" (113)? Lester's illegal intervention in an affair which was not his business is part and parcel of his American idealism.

Lester does know something of Iran and he uses that knowledge to threaten the Colonel. Lester's wife has volunteered at different points for a variety of causes, Palestinians for Self-Rule, South African Alliance to end Apartheid, the Coalition against Intervention and Oppression. Lester first meets her when she is working a political leaflet table, protesting against multinational corporate interventionism. She immediately lectures Lester at length on Nicaragua, El Salvador and (in a garbled soundbite) "the CIA killing the elected leader of Iran in 1953 for oil fields for the Rockefellers" (238). She goes on and on, until suddenly "she began to run out of gas" (238) and they head for a hamburger joint. Carol's dream is to travel to the battle zones of the world "to capture the truth of American imperialism" (238)—to intervene against intervention. Lester was attracted to her all-purpose mall radicalism: "it was her conviction he had proposed to" (237). Like her, he "had no idea what he wanted to do, but whatever it was, he wanted it to be good, he wanted to do good" (238). Thwarted by his young family from entering a larger political arena, he carries on the crusade at home. He joins the police because he sees a poster of a young cop standing between a man and a woman with the slogan "World Peace begins at Home", beside the hotline number for victims of domestic abuse. Lester is motivated by fear of his own weakness, in a newly transnational world. In his adolescence he had been repeatedly bullied as the only Anglo in a Texas school. Lester's girlfriend, Charita, was Latina, and he recalls how her brother Pablo had pushed Lester away from her, grabbing her by the hair and hauling her off. Lester did nothing to stop him. The incident is a mirror image of the Jasmeen story—though here brown men are protecting brown women against white men. For Lester it is one of many events in his life in which he fears that "one day someone would see just how unfit and weak he really was" (229). In his worst dreams he is surrounded by crowds of those he has arrested, ganging up on him as all his actions come home to roost. Just as Lester adopts the role of crusader, without realising that it is internal weakness which is the real problem, so America is prepared to go to war on behalf of its idealistic self-image.

In Lester, Dubus satirises the American need to be clean, innocent, to act as the self-appointed moral policeman of the world, and as the guardian of other nations' women. Lester wants "not only to clean up everybody else's act, but to make the world safe again by doing so" (235), to set the world to rights once and for all. Homeless, Kathy and Lester retire briefly to an isolated cabin on a lake, a neglected fish camp, where they immediately engage in an absolute orgy of cleaning and scrubbing. The suggestion is of a return to an earlier, pure America, of poverty without power. The lake is fed by an underground spring and evokes Lester's wonder at being back at "the source of something" (139). Kathy bathes in the Purisima River and feels "cleansed to the bone" (157). For a moment the cabin suggests an uncompromised America without oil or empire: the cabin is at some distance from the road, inaccessible to cars and has no electricity or mains drainage. The idyll is short lived, however. Surfacing with a hangover, Kathy longs for mango juice, a shower, air-conditioning and an aspirin. She goes off to get drunk and steal gas, and Lester pursues her to the house.

The road to hell is paved with good intentions. The final disaster is caused by Lester's "protective" interventionism, accelerated by the characters "not knowing" the true facts of their situation, and concealing weakness behind a show of strength. The Colonel's young son Esmail, used as "human collateral" (310) by Lester, is shot dead because Lester concealed from him the fact that the gun he seized was not loaded. Lester recognises that Esmail would have put the gun down had he known, "But Lester had denied him the truth" (347) out of fear. Nadi dies because the Colonel wants to protect her from knowing that her son is dead; he suffocates her. He also does not want her to know that he had ordered Esmail to keep the gun pointed at Lester. Since he gave that order in Farsi, he takes that fact to his grave. He does face the truth about his past, "For our excess we lost everything" (329) but can't resist leaving a last message for Soraya telling her not to take less than $100,000 for the house. The Colonel dies by his own hand but only after he has reassumed the external trappings of power, donning his air force uniform before putting a plastic bag over his head. As he dies, hearing the roaring of F16s in his ears, "the plastic becomes iron" (339) against his face; he is once more a man behind a mask. Lester, as a policeman in jail, is an outsider on the inside and once his time in protective custody expires, his fate at the hands of the inmates can be imagined.

But what of the woman at the centre of the story? Kathy, half strangled by the Colonel, survives, temporarily voiceless from her injuries. Because she is mute, her fellow inmates christen her "Remote". Kathy uses silence to maintain the distance between herself and everyone else; she is glad to have a glass screen between her and her family when they visit. She is "safely out of their reach in every way" (362). Even when her voice recovers she remains silent, "relieved I didn't have a voice" (361). She has become a parodic version of one of the voiceless, brutalised, silenced women on behalf of whom so much rhetoric has been expended in the discourse of human rights. For the reader, however, who does have access to her voice, she can never be an innocent victim. In jail she rejects her lawyer's plan to plead diminished responsibility in the aftermath of her suicide attempt, reiterating that she does not want to look as if she were not responsible for the kidnapping (360). Significantly it is at this point that Kathy abandons the past tense and moves into the present (357) placing the reader right beside her in a position of shared knowledge.

House of Sand and Fog was published in 1999, before the enormous "blowback" of the 9/11 attacks. Four years later it was adapted for the cinema.[35] Just how far the average American was envisaged as capable of accepting the savage irony of the novel's ending may be gauged from the treatment of the two central characters. In the movie, the scales are weighted heavily against the Colonel. In the novel the opening scene introduces him as a hardworking labourer for the American dream, toiling with other immigrants on the highway. On screen he first appears as the father of the bride at Soraya's extravagantly-staged wedding. Later it is strongly implied that he has Savaki connections. On the other hand Kathy's cocaine use is suppressed; she does not hold up a gas station; and at the close she gets off scot-free. Indeed it is Kathy who features as would-be rescuer, attempting in the final scene to save Behrani by artificial resuscitation. When she fails, she curls up at his feet in foetal position, a helpless child-woman. As a result, the film maintains the image which the novel has completely discredited and protects its American audience against a full recognition of the damage done in their name. The reason for the changes between novel and film may be partly ascribable to the 9/11 attacks. Feelings were raw when the film was made and a terrible knowledge had been forced upon the nation. As we shall see, however, in the next chapter, the helpless child-woman reappeared centre-stage, in the aftermath of the attacks.

5 Falling Woman
André Dubus III, *The Garden of Last Days*

In the light of later events, *House of Sand and Fog* has assumed a prophetic quality. Dubus's subsequent novel, *The Garden of Last Days* (2008) focusses upon the reported encounter between a Florida stripper and one of the 9/11 hijackers, on the eve of his deadly mission. April Marie Connors, stage name Spring, encounters Bassam al-Jizani in the Puma Club for Men, where he pays her for two hours of private dancing and stripping in the club's Champagne Room. Gender politics are the central focus, as American and Islamic rescue missions collide. While the hijacker, eyes set upon an Islamic paradise, lectures April on the evils of her degenerate Western life as a commodified sex object, AJ Carey, a construction worker, ejected by a bouncer for touching a dancer, finds April's three year old child Franny wandering at the back of the club, and carries her off in the belief that he is rescuing her. On this one occasion April has brought Franny into the club dressing room, because her usual babysitter, her landlady Jean, is in hospital. Several reviewers commented upon the irrelevance of AJ to the 9/11 subject matter. Janet Maslin in the *New York Times* could not decide whether Dubus had managed "to deepen or clutter the story with AJ."[1] Anthony Giardina, in the *Washington Post*, thought that the novel took "a very odd turn" when Dubus virtually handed the story over to AJ, and that it was "a relief when Dubus gets back to Bassam."[2] AJ's story, however, is central to Dubus's argument concerning 9/11.

After 9/11 the commonest reaction among writers was to argue that the event could not be written about, resisted language or lay outside literary paradigms. Jay McInerney and Bret Easton Ellis agreed on 9/11 itself that they could not go back to the novels they had been writing.[3] Martin Amis wrote that "After a couple of hours at their desks on September 12, 2001, all the writers on earth were reluctantly considering a change of occupation."[4] In Dubus's novel the narrative time scheme begins on Tuesday 6 September reaching the 11th on page 517, followed by a brief epilogue, some seven years later, of a dozen pages. Although related in the past tense, the precise dating and attention to time, and the way in which Dubus sinks the reader into the characters' thought processes, foster an effect of immediacy, of the past as present. The attack on the towers is not presented or described; April (at the beach) is unaware of it until late afternoon, when she banks the hijacker's money. For the reader however the novel moves inexorably towards it. Bassam's identity is not in doubt from his first appearance. A composite figure, one of the hijackers of American Airlines Flight 11 from Boston to Los Angeles, Bassam is part of the al-Qaida cell headed by Mohamed Atta (described in the novel as "the Egyptian"[5]), who takes flying lessons in Florida, and has been trained to kill.[6] In this novel, unlike *House of Sand and Fog*, not knowing has become an excess of knowledge. This time we know only too well how the terrorist plot will end.

In writing a "prequel" to 9/11, Dubus therefore creates a sense that the story of 9/11 was in some way already known, had already been told. Little attention is paid in the novel to the aftermath of 9/11 precisely because the novel casts the reaction to the event in terms of a regression to the past, a pre-existent pattern which was there before the towers fell and informed responses afterwards. In this connection the "rescue" of Franny is the crucial element in the plot. In the novel two utopian spaces are revealed as holding terror at their centre, the striptopia of the Puma Club, with Bassam at its spatial centre, the Champagne Room and the garden of the title, lovingly tended in her last days by retiree Jean, but also the location of her panic attacks. It is Jean's sudden terror in the garden (mistaken for a heart attack) which sets the plot in motion. Jean's garden evokes images of the New World as paradise, with its luxuriant fruit and blossoms, its eternally flourishing evergreens and cerulean Miltonic enclosing walls, but at the centre of the garden is an attack of terror, an image which points to a specific reading of American history. When Franny is discovered to be missing April goes utterly to pieces:

> the floor seemed to drop away and she was falling, falling into dark and empty sky. (206)

The image of April as Falling Woman explicitly links Franny's disappearance to the 9/11 attacks. Susan Faludi has argued that the reaction of the United States to 9/11 involved reverting to an original terror dream, embodied in the Puritan captivity narratives, of frail white womanhood (later a virginal child-woman) abducted by Native Americans and then heroically rescued by white males. In the example of Franny, Dubus gives us the absolute epitome of innocence (a three year old girl in pink pyjamas), embodying helplessness and the need for protection. He also nudges the reader towards recognition of all female vulnerability, interrupting the AJ plot with flashbacks to two violent rapes, of April, and of the aptly named Virginia, AJ's mother. April's drink was drugged, Virginia was physically overpowered in the workplace; both women are unambiguously innocent victims. Following Franny's disappearance the police interview everyone in the club. With a terrorist right under their noses, however, they focus entirely on Franny. Dubus's point here echoes Faludi's argument that America did just the same after 9/11. The monumental non-sequitur of the rescue plot (which occupies more than half of the novel and takes over from the story of the hijacker for some two hundred pages) echoes the way in which America, in using the attacks as the basis for waging war in Iraq, embarked on an entirely irrelevant course of action after 9/11.

Faludi's argument bears careful consideration. In *The Terror Dream* she describes her surprise shortly after 9/11 when she was approached by interviewers about the so-called end of feminism. The irony of responding to a terrorist attack by heralding feminism's demise, given the Islamic terrorists' conservative views on the place of women, was not lost on her. Yet reaction to 9/11 appeared to exacerbate anti-feminist trends, with feminism almost envisaged as treasonable by right-wing commentators. In the *National Review* John O'Sullivan (15 October 2001) accused feminists of taking the side of medieval Islamists as opposed to ordinary American men.

> They feel more comfortable in such superior company than alongside a hard-hat construction worker.[7]

Significantly, in Dubus's novel AJ, the construction worker, is thrown out of the club while Bassam spends time with April. The suggestion was also advanced in the media that a feminized nation, its men taught from childhood that violence was wrong, had gone soft and lacked the will to fight, so that radical Islamists had exploited a perceived weakness. Jerry Falwell, for example, claimed that by altering traditional roles, feminists had

> caused God to lift the veil of protection which has allowed no one to attack America on our soil since 1812.[8]

Controversially, however, Faludi argued that America had been attacked repeatedly prior to 1812, and that the American foundational drama was a prolonged exposure to murderous homeland incursions by dark-skinned, non-Christian combatants, complying with no accepted Western rules of engagement, and attacking civilian targets on America's own soil: Native Americans. September 11 was not unimaginable or inconceivable; it embodied the characteristic and formative American ordeal. Contemporary Americans' ancestors had already fought a long war on terror, chronicled in the Puritan captivity narratives, the first stories that America told itself, and the story which—with ironic revisions—Dubus retells. After 9/11 Faludi noted a recursus in American culture to images of the Western, and a resurgence of a John Wayne type of masculinity, particularly evoking his role as Ethan Edwards in *The Searchers*, rescuing his abducted niece, Debbie, from the Comanches. Turner Broadcasting devoted all its programming at Christmas 2001 to re-runs of Wayne films. The first post-9/11 supper of the War Cabinet at Camp David was a Wild West menu, featuring buffalo meat, an augury of things to come. Robert Kaplan later said that the war on terror was "back to the days of fighting the Indians" and "really about taming the frontier".[9] When Hollywood was called upon to support the war on terror, Chuck Workman's film, *The Spirit of America* (airing in mid-December 2001), began and ended with the opening scenes from *The Searchers*. Workman saw Wayne as a quintessential US hero because

> He's a rescuer. When he rescues the girl, that's what the movie is all about.[10]

Although most of the victims of 9/11 (by a ratio of three to one) were male, orphaned girls and "9/11 widows" were a major media focus, along with an emphasis on a restored "femininity". Lipstick sales were gleefully reported as up by twelve per cent after 9/11, single women were supposedly rushing to the altar, "security moms" were giving up work to stay home with their children. What was an attack on an urban workplace representative of global capitalism and American power was rewritten as an attack on the domestic circle. The return to domesticity and to the shelter of the protective male was loudly (if entirely erroneously) trumpeted in the media. For Faludi one case study was illuminating: the Jessica Lynch story. Lynch, a serving soldier, hospitalised in Iraq in April 2003 following a motor accident, was portrayed in the media as a helpless white woman, snatched from the jaws of evil by heroic US soldiers, rescued by helicopter (with a US flag on her chest) from terrible maltreatment (in some reports torture and sexual abuse) at the hands of her captors. The story was later discredited. Lynch herself named her friend Lori Ann Piestewa as the soldier who deserved to be seen as a hero, and called her own baby daughter Dakota Ann (Piestewa's middle name preceded by the Sioux word for friend). Piestewa was a Hopi Indian who died of her injuries. But the media had no time for a Native American heroine, preferring to concentrate on Lynch, propagating an image of her in her childhood as a tiny blonde waif who loved pink dresses and Barbie dolls. For Faludi the story demonstrated America's enslavement to a retrograde narrative.

> The unimaginable assault on our home soil was, in fact, anything but unimaginable. The anxieties it awakened reside deep in our cultural memory. And the myth we deployed to keep those anxieties buried is one we've been constructing for more than three hundred years.[11]

Faludi focusses upon the gap between actual events and their subsequent narration, whether in the contemporary or the colonial period, as evidenced in the way in which the early captivity narratives were revised in later years in order to exacerbate the image of female helplessness. Early resourceful captives fended for themselves (Hannah Duston), struck bargains with their captors (Mary Rowlandson) or even decided they preferred their captors to their rescuers (Cynthia Ann Parker.) Later stories substitute dependent child-women. Faludi's account of Hannah Duston has a special resonance in connection with Dubus, and offers a classic example of the ways in which a woman was progressively demonised (notoriously by Nathaniel Hawthorne), her agency undermined in favour of valorising masculinity (in this case that of her less-than-heroic husband). The rescue myth responds to a perceived male failure to protect women and children. Duston's home in Haverhill was attacked by the Abenaki on 15 March 1697. Her husband fled, leaving Hannah to the Indians, who promptly brained her new-born daughter and abducted her. On 30 March Hannah and two other captives arose in the night and butchered their captors with hatchets. Hannah despatched nine of the twelve (the victims included six children), fled, but then returned to scalp all ten victims in order to claim the £50 scalp bounty offered by the Massachusetts legislature. A statue of her was erected in 1874 on Contoocook Island (scene of the killings), thirty-five feet high, clutching a raised tomahawk and a bouquet of scalps, and another, somewhat less alarming, in Haverhill in 1879, portraying her pre-slaughter, minus scalps and with tomahawk merely at the ready. She remains a controversial figure in Haverhill. When in 2006 a town booster group proposed using her as the town brand to attract tourists there was a predictable furore, with Native American groups denouncing her as a murderess. S.J. Reidhead, however, a distant descendant, wrote in his blog on 11 September 2006, that

> Hannah was the victim of a terrorist attack back on March 15, 1697. What was done to her by the Abenaki Indians, if done today by Islamic militants would be called terror. [12]

Dubus spent his childhood and adolescence in and around Haverhill and is well-acquainted with Hannah Duston. As his 2011 memoir, *Townie*, demonstrates, he is no admirer of the "rescue" myth, largely because he was such an enthusiastic subscriber to it in the past. In his account of his childhood in Haverhill Dubus situates himself as an ineffectual and cowardly young male in contradistinction to Hannah. Characterising his childhood as a relentless series of attacks by the local hoodlums of the depressed mill towns of the Merrimack valley, he describes himself being beaten up, bullied, chased and terrorised, his brother ditto, his sister raped. As a child he was a great fan of Clint Eastwood Westerns, and various vigilante-avenger movies, from Buford Pusser, cleaning up a whole town in *Walking Tall*, to Charles Bronson's *Death Wish* movies, and Eastwood as Dirty Harry.

> When I thought of the word *man*, I could only think of those who could defend themselves and those they loved.[13]

The young Dubus imagined himself beating up everyone who had bullied him or his family, "I saw myself doing it to anyone, everyone".[14] Shortly afterwards he evokes the statue of Hannah Duston in Haverhill, and describes how she killed and scalped her captors.[15] After a final childhood humiliation at the hands of a local bully (chased off by his sick mother wielding a bough) Dubus has an epiphany and undergoes a conversion to violence,[16] taking up boxing and becoming a young man who picks fights relentlessly, often supposedly on behalf of abused women. When he learns that his sister has suffered domestic abuse he recalls again "the statue of Hannah Duston and her raised hatchet"[17] and later mentions driving past it, just before he tells the story of his old friend Cleary, who was chased and stabbed to death by the wife he had repeatedly beaten up.[18] Where the early ineffectual Dubus contrasts with the ferocious Duston, then evolving into Dubus-as-rescuer, the final incarnation recognises that violence is no solution. After beating up a lout who has terrorised a woman at Miami Airport, Dubus registers the contradictory look in the eyes of bystanders, mingling respect and fear: "the look that Clint Eastwood got aimed at him in the *Dirty Harry* films."[19] He realises that his behaviour was self-serving, gratifying his own pride and his injured sense of masculinity.

> Don't think you did any of this for her because you didn't. You did it for you. And you need to stop.[20]

The memoir closes with a scene in which Dubus protects an entire party of thirty-five sleeping schoolgirls from rowdies on a train—but in this case he uses the force of persuasion and reasoned argument rather than his fists. *Townie* is a compelling study of male violence in its own right; it also offers a comprehensive deconstruction of the alibi of rescue. Similarly in his novel, Dubus delineates the ways in which his own fantasy of being a warrior rescuing women was also that of America.

The fate of AJ bears out the moral. AJ believes himself to be entirely blameless, a rescuer, saving a neglected child from the Sodom and Gomorrah of a strip club: "he'd taken Franny to protect her from men at the club. To *protect* her" (401). But the police construe the event as an abduction, and AJ is sent down for a lengthy jail sentence. Because AJ is seen as a wife beater, the judge is particularly unforgiving. AJ has dreams of fishing and hunting with his son, Cole, being able to "lounge around like naked warriors. And no women. No goddamned women" (109). But following a court ruling after an episode of domestic abuse, AJ has been denied contact with his son until he takes an anger management course. He appears to offer a classic example of a man's natural aggression being denied by women, his manhood weakened and condemned, his emotions managed by the state, while feckless working mothers get off scot-free. His protest is heartfelt:

> They don't let me see my son and she brings her baby to the fuckn' *Puma* club? (363)

AJ's identity as rescuer, however, comes unfixed. Reviewers located a problem with Faludi's account, in that she does not ask who was terrorising whom in Colonial America, which was not of course the settlers' homeland, but an imperialist colony.[21] In *Townie* Dubus recalls a film which made a particular impression on him, which tells the other side of the story: *Billy Jack*, in which a Native American whose wife has been raped and murdered by white racists tracks down the culprits and beats them to death with killer martial-arts kicks and punches. In the novel, Dubus calls attention to the ambiguous nature of "rescue" by associating AJ with the history of conquest. His long night-drive with Franny takes him through the historic district of Bradenton, past the old stone courthouse that went back "to the time of the Seminoles and Spaniards" (225) and the ruins of Braden's Castle, which he describes as "overrun by the Seminoles" (226) and burned to the ground. Planning to stage a fake accident to extort compensation from Caporelli, his employer

> it was Caporelli Sr. AJ thought of, *his* castle falling, AJ the wily Seminole about to take a piece of it. (227)

AJ has moved from rescuer to abductor, and in the process become the other, the threat. The link to Bassam reinforces the parallel. In a gas station Bassam sees an old woman who reminds him of his mother. Her skin is as dark as his, but her overall advertises the "Miccosukee Indian resort" (328), run by a branch of the Seminoles. In addition, AJ's grasp on history is poor. Braden Castle, built as a fortress in 1850 *was* attacked during the Third Seminole War in 1856, but the settlers repelled the Seminoles, then tracked them down and killed them. (The castle burned much later in 1903.) AJ's history suits a myth of white victims in need of rescue from malevolent others, but Dubus turns him into one of those Others, abducting Franny, and the references invoke a history of conquest and white aggression. When AJ leaves Franny, locked in a car in a stranger's garage, there is a real risk that she could die in the heat before anyone finds her. When he decides to alert the authorities anonymously to her location, he finds a tourist phone cabin but the phone is missing, and standing under its thatched roof like those of "the old Seminoles'" (348), he abandons Franny to her fate. Franny is only rescued because AJ's prints are on April's car. As a result of the restraining order sworn out by his wife, Deena, they are also on the police record. Indirectly it is Deena, a woman who stands up against her abuser, who is responsible for Franny's rescue, not her husband. The fake nature of the rescue myth is also underlined when AJ digs himself into a hole beneath his excavating machine to stage an industrial accident. As he lies there waiting to be rescued himself, from an accident that never was, he wonders if a piece of sharp metal is "the broken tip of a de Soto sword" (364), evoking the conquistador who landed at Bradenton in 1539, reinforcing the sense that America was not a homeland but a place of conquest and that the "rescue" narrative is a fake. When the rescue party appear, they turn out to be the police who arrest him.

Like all revisionary narratives, the novel employs a risky strategy, offering the possibility of being read as itself a retrograde narrative of rugged masculinity, fiendish Others and helpless womanhood. But the fates of the other characters also underline the irrelevancy to 9/11 of the retrograde narrative of rescue. April, a working Mom who neglects her daughter, only gets Franny back after she has proved her worth as a mother and home-maker to a social worker. Ironically the state is much more exercised to police her domesticity than to investigate the hours she spent with Bassam. The FBI interview is cursory and unthreatening; the child protective investigator's interrogation and her inspection of April's cupboards, bedrooms and bathroom is relentlessly thorough. A frenzy of dusting, vacuuming and tidying, plus prominent display of Franny's pink backpack and Barbies, pays off with the return of her child, and April gives up stripping, returns to her mother's house, and at the close is about to marry. As a result, in redomesticating April, the American state implicitly acts on the Islamist agenda for women. Indeed it has an unlikely ally, in Bassam. It is Bassam's blood money which allows April to buy out her mother and own her own home. Lonnie gives up his job as a bouncer in the Puma Club and goes off to die on his third tour of duty in an irrelevant American war. Jean returns to her garden, panic over, at least for the present. By retelling a revised version of the rescue story, Dubus empties it of its power, underlines its irrelevance, and clears the space for his own narrative of 9/11, set in the strip club.

With images of America as new world, paradise or utopia replaced by a terror dream, it appears that the terrorist has gained a monopoly on the idea of paradise. The relationship between utopianism and fundamentalism is complex, including both content (visions of the good life) and structural paradigm (both stem from discontent with the now, and mount a challenge to the contemporary world). Many Islamic groups dream of establishing an Islamic state ruled by Sharia law; Osama Bin Laden's videotapes and speeches offer both a critical take on Western values and a vision of an Islamic state to come. Lucy Sargisson has argued that the particular kind of utopianism which drives religious fundamentalism is perfectionist, an authoritarian utopianism based on the notion of one truth, "the truth".[22] Bassam is utopian in this respect, demanding that April tell him the truth. In the club he pays her a small fortune to reveal her real name and to allow him to touch the scar from her Caesarean, thus fixing her "true" identity as first and foremost that of April-a-mother, not Spring-a-dancer. Bassam believes in an Islamic paradise, Jannah, also a garden of last days, but his belief makes him into a ruthless killer. Although Dubus rehearses most of the motivations which have been ascribed to the terrorists in an attempt to explain the attraction of a suicide mission (resentment at the presence of US bases in Saudi Arabia, young male unemployment, the encounter between tradition and modernity, the economic inability to marry and loyalty to a band of brothers) it is the image of paradisal rescue which recurs most strongly as Bassam's motivation. Throughout the mission Bassam remains wedded to the image of Jannah, and the belief that by becoming a *shahid*, a martyr, he will make a place in paradise for some seventy family members

(489) thus rescuing his unbelieving brothers, who adore American music, drink Pepsi, smoke Marlboros and wear baseball caps, from eternal damnation. He looks forward with great anticipation to being in Jannah (469, 488) and dwells on the prospect of reunion in heaven with his dead brother Khalid, killed when racing his American car (92). Dubus, however, never lets the reader forget that Bassam is a trained killer; he repeatedly thinks how easy it would be to kill, to thrust a blade into an American throat (114, 251, 379, 437, 451). Bassam is the other side of the rescue myth, the John Wayne hero as killer and woman-hater. In *The Searchers* Ethan Edwards is also a hardened killer, a veteran of the Civil War and the renegade actions afterwards, who almost slaughters his niece when he catches up with her, because of his racist beliefs. For Edwards Debbie is polluted by her abductor and husband, the Comanche chief, Scar. Sex is a wound, a pollution, just as Bassam sees April's scar as evidence of corruption. However much Bassam is tempted by them, American women are characterised as those who would "pull him between their legs straight to the eternal fire" (25). The opening scene of the novel in which April veers off the straight-and-narrow to do an illicit U-turn into the Puma Club, and spills burning coffee between her thighs, prefigures Bassam's view, forthrightly expressed, that April is a transgressor who will burn in hell. He looks forward to sitting in paradise, full of joy "as he watches these whores fall from the bridge into the flames. As he watches them fall" (463). April again figures as Falling Woman, this time from the narrow bridge into the Islamic heaven, down into Jahannam, hell. Utopia and dystopia tend to accompany each other. Heaven needs hell to ensure its attraction. Bassam needs April to burn; he does not merely need a sense of his own imminent entry into paradise. To strengthen his resistance he imagines April's Caesarean scar "not as if it had been cut and healed but burned, like the skin of the burned. He made himself see her entire body that way" (260). For Bassam, the club is dystopian, an image of America as sex- and money-mad, the image which motivates his mission. Although himself very imperfect, he is on a quest for perfection.

So what is Bassam (masquerading as "Mike") doing in a strip club? The plot is based on fact.[23] There were reports of the hijackers spending time in such clubs, the Cheetah in San Diego for example, and the Pink Pony in Florida, and the Sarasota branch of the FBI did interview a woman who had danced for them.[24] As in the novel where the group enter the club for the first time because they fear they are being followed (23), the cells may have chosen to meet in such clubs as a cover for their activities. (Nobody expects to meet an Islamic jihadist in a strip club). Muslim commentators emphasised that true believers would not go to strip clubs, drink alcohol or kill, and that Islam is not synonymous with terrorism. But the reports (including, as in the novel, the purchase of prostitutes) met a psychic need in America to discredit the piety and authenticity of the hijackers. From the ordinary American point of view their participation in "terrorist stag parties" demonstrated that they were not genuinely motivated by religion, but fakes, wallowing in the culture they had come to destroy, not authentic political activists but demonic killers.[25] However, by placing the terrorist in the strip club Dubus does not calls into question his authenticity as a believer. Rather he focusses on authenticity itself as a key concept and problematizes it, in order to highlight the value of fiction—itself a form of fakery—rather than the notion of one killer truth. When April and Bassam meet in the Champagne room they perform a double masquerade, a battle between two role-players. Is Spring a fake? Or April? Mike? Or Bassam? Or are all these identities in some ways "true"? American and Islamic visions of paradise yield place to a utopian location which exposes the myth of a single authentic truth. Locating the terrorist in the strip club allows Dubus to consider the utopian nature of terrorism as much as the terror at the heart of the American New World. The inauthenticity of the club becomes an ironic frame for the truth-based nature of Bassam's utopianism.

Dubus used a Guggenheim grant to carry out research on clubs in Florida, and conducted interviews with individual dancers. The novel is also informed by recent sociological research, paying particular attention to the management of time and of emotion, which establishes the club as a utopian location. First and foremost the strip club functions both as a satire on the staging of conventional femininity, and as a site which exposes the capitalist practices which were the terrorists' actual targets. To restate the obvious, the World Trade Center housed the headquarters of a host of international businesses and corporations, plus the offices of some governmental bodies, and was a building that symbolised American economic power. The nude dancer is a perfect image of the free enterprise economy. She is not a paid employee of the club, but pays it club fees to be allowed to perform. She makes her money from tips, and she herself has to tip the barman, bouncers, DJ and house Mom. April remarks, "The act was never where the money was." (33). The money is in the private sector, performing private dances. In the club the client buys the dancer's time; time is quite literally money.

In characterising the Puma club as a utopian location, several key elements are worth highlighting. The term "striptopia" was coined by Michael Uebel in a discussion of the utopic nature of the clubs. On entering a club, he writes

> one becomes conscious of entering an almost magical domain, where a temporary reprieve from the protocols of everyday life can be expected.[26]

Uebel, of course, writes as a customer; April enters the club through the back door and the stench of rancid Fryolator oil and garbage cans. In Uebel's view the explosion of gentlemen's clubs from the 1980s onwards in America is related to a defensive, restive manhood, and to men who needed to demonstrate and reaffirm their masculinity. Sociological analysts have argued that strip clubs of this type are designed to separate customers from the real world and induct them into a fantasy space. In particular they are carefully organised so that the experience of time is different to "objective" time. Customers buy dancers' time, for "one-on-one" dances, in a dimly lit VIP lounge, where the dancer strips to the background music in front of the seated customer, but still in view of the other customers, or in the Champagne room, beyond the public gaze. Dancers' time is measured by music, and the stage rotation is also tracked by the songs. Since songs vary in length, time appears less rigid, not standardized; the time spent in the club is separated from clock time, and gives a sense that "time is not important." The public space thus offers an illusion of a different time, in a repetitive fantasy, as the rota repeats through the night. In the novel there is a dynamic tension between this fantasy time and the reader's awareness of real time, of the clock ticking towards 9/11; and also between the timeless world of the customers and the intensely calibrated time of the working dancer. If called, a dancer must be on stage in two songs, and generally naked by the end of her own second song. In the Puma club April can tell when she will next be on stage because she can hear a song finishing in the background. On arrival she hears Renée's song and realises that Renée is already shedding her icicle costume, and that she is "less than two numbers from having to be on stage herself" (18). AJ, outside the club, knows from the music that Sadie is on stage (184). Lonnie notes that a song is "in its last measures, which meant Spring was naked and collecting folded bills" (41). Then "Retro's gown was off as her second number began" (43). The rota is interrupted only if a performer is bought out and goes into the Champagne room. Money has the ability to transform time: April is mesmerised by the huge sums Bassam has given her, calculating that she has made "six, seven, eight weeks pay" (199) in the two hours she has spent there. When she is first in the Champagne room, she keeps one ear on the rotation, from the end of Renée's number (80) through Retro's act (84) and Sadie's final song (104), but then hears a hard rock song which she does not recognise. "She'd lost her bearings in the rotation"(105). April has lost control of real time, and as a result she does not check on her daughter, who wanders off. Fantasy time becomes a source of danger.

Indeed, for the reader, with the benefit of hindsight, the hands of the ticking clock are moving inexorably towards 9/11. Bassam punctures the illusion of the club with reminders of his own timetable, which undercuts the repetitive utopian fantasy on offer in the club. When April warns him at the end of the first hour that "Your time is almost up," (106) the reader recognises the deeper truth of the observation. April can think of time only in terms of money; he has paid for only one hour at this point. But for Bassam these are his last days; he has only five more to live. When he points out that the bouncer patrols the Champagne room at only fifteen minute intervals, too infrequently to offer protection from a potentially violent client, April (blissfully unaware of just how violent her client will turn out to be) argues that he is there to make sure an offender will be caught. Bassam (his thoughts on the suicide mission) responds that "there will be no catching"

(106). "You think that he is here for protecting you, but he is not" (175). Ominously he highlights the power of the suicide bomber: "He only has power if I care what happens to me" (175). April is not protected at all by the bouncers; just as in the American rescue myth there is no real protection for women at the heart of the fantasy. April has an illusion of invulnerability when she dances, feeling that "this was her show, that *she* controlled *them* and always would" (21). Uebel argues that despite its nudity, the stripper's body is vitrified, a location of self-closure, and self-pleasure. The pasties, garters, gloves, thongs, make-up, boots, breast implants, shaved pubis and fake tan are a kind of second skin of mass cultural signifiers, a vitrification of the body, a protective envelope sealing the body in signs.[27] The Puma club rotation includes Renée the Ice Queen, in white eyeliner, long white gloves and with pasties with foot long silver threads attached (74), Sadie in cowboy boots and hat and Retro in red leather. But once out of rotation, April can no longer feel that she is merely an anonymous cog in a machine "just one working part of a huge and necessary machine" (81). Bassam makes her feel embarrassed, not styled as nude but merely "naked" (107).

As the mechanical imagery of wheels turning, bearings, rotation and cogs suggests, the Puma Club's workers are not so different from workers in any other place of business. The club is a site where time is money, shifts and routines are observed, and physical labour is performed. Emotional labour is also a key element in the analysis. The action in the club foregrounds issues of authenticity, both the authenticity or otherwise of the hijacker, and the inauthenticity of the American dream, corrupted by the power of money. Fairly obviously, strip clubs appear to market stereotypical images of women. But April's first dance does not conform to this kind of stereotyping. Late clocking in, and with no time to get into costume, she strips in her own street clothes, uncomfortably aware that

> when she got her jeans off, it'd be *her* underwear she pulled down for them. Not Spring's but April's. (21)

Even worse, the problems of removing blue jeans over high heels turn out to be insurmountable; she ends up barefoot (strictly against health rules) and loses her balance, coming down hard on one foot, out of time to the music. At this point she is April, not Spring, and seems to be not quite inside the illusion, not fully in character, slightly out of sync with club time. Lonnie is relieved when she next appears to see that "Spring seemed to be back on her game" (63), in blouse and cotton skirt, soliciting private one-on-ones, smiling "like she was your best friend's sister you'd always wanted and this was the night she was coming to tell you she'd always wanted you too" (39). Her smile, he thinks, "never looked phony" (39). In this opening April's role is established as that of the girl next door, the friend's sister, not the sultry or exotic *femme fatale*. In her blue jeans she looks genuine, natural. In the club men repeatedly ask her for her real name, but April never obliges, sneering inwardly: "Like his twenty bucks entitled him to that" (64). In the club she is Spring, outside April, her night self rigorously separated from the day identity as mother, in an extreme example of the self-division and alienation enforced by the separation of home and workplace. In this she is entirely typical of nude dancers. Gabrielle Egan reports that most dancers describe themselves as having separate selves (dancer self, outside self) distancing their "real" self from the stigma of the sex industry.[28] They report problems if the dancer self leaks into life outside (just as April is horrified when recognised by a client in a restaurant) or conversely when other selves (mother, for example) drift into the club, as here. Just as the club forbids physical contact between clients and dancers, the dancers establish boundaries between the separate spheres of their day and night selves. They have assumed characters which are as inauthentic as that of "Mike". Affect is being managed on both sides. The hijacker, a member of a close-knit band, schooled by military training to conquer fear and channel aggression, repeatedly demonstrates his close feelings for his "brothers" in arms, his affect closely tailored to his mission. "Brothers. I have such a love for you. I have such a love," (444) he declares to Imad and Tariq on the eve of the attacks. The dancer is also engineering emotion, though for economic rather than political ends. The novel demonstrates Dubus's understanding of the true nature of the clubs, which are not selling sex, so much as emotion, often closely akin to domesticity (the friend's sister), in carefully regulated performances of what sociologists have characterised as "bounded authenticity."[29] The term (as defined by Elizabeth Bernstein) describes the sale and purchase of authentic emotional connection, and has been understood as a common phenomenon of late capitalism, involving as it does a merger between private and public, an extended service industry and a preference for the neatly bounded commodity over the messy diffuseness of non-market exchange. In the service industries, emotional authenticity is incorporated explicitly into the economic contract. The classic account of commercialised feeling (a study of smiling air stewardesses) by Arlie Russell Hochschild demonstrated the ways in which workers tried to feel the "right" feeling for the job, and to induce the "right" feeling in customers. Bassam's name means "for smiling" (202) though April comments that he does not actually smile very much. He, however, remembers American workers as perpetually smiling, from Kelly his gym trainer, to Cliff in the gas station, Gloria the realtor, restaurant waitresses, the stewardess on the flight to Boston (380), and the hotel receptionist in Boston smiling brightly with "the tightness of a business transaction across her features" (501). He even learns to perform emotional labour himself and return the business smile "as if he has pressed a button inside himself, and when she looks away, his smile diminishes at once" (380). April's raw pain and terrified screams when Franny goes missing none the less cut right through his defences; her cries "were difficult for him to bear" (282). April's cries remind him of his mother's screams over her dead son, Khalid, soon to be repeated over him.

His mother also performed the appropriate feelings in public at Khalid's funeral, but afterwards expressed raw, unprocessed emotion, just as April does—and just as many other bereaved Americans will do as a result of Bassam's mission. In the novel while April counterfeits empathy for her clients, Bassam finds that he has to force himself to repress it. Far from portraying him as someone who hates Americans, Dubus underlines his attraction to them, not merely sexually, but also in everyday interactions. He has to struggle to objectify them and maintain his hatred. In a horrible irony, as he boards the fatal plane in Boston, an airline employee invites him to "Have a nice day, sir" (511).

For AJ, like Bassam, April also has only one identity: "Spring. One of the coldest bitches at the Puma", "a pro" (192), unlike his favoured dancer, Marianne. AJ is ejected from the club because he confuses a commodified exchange for a real emotional relationship and attempts to hold Marianne's hand. Lonnie characterises AJ as a "lone dog", like another of the club regulars, Gordon, who has spent $50,000 on Wendy in the Champagne room. "That was the trouble right there. A lone dog fell in love" (42). AJ has spent weeks paying Marianne for one to one talks, with her full encouragement. Lonnie watches her nodding her head "with feigned interest" (43). The club also has a rescue scenario at its centre. The Puma Club for men demonstrates just how easily America buys into a fantasy in which women are protected in order to perform emotional labour to bolster the male sense of masculinity. Lonnie's job is to prevent the clients touching the girls. A man who adores fighting, he is an institutionalised version of the John Wayne rescuer. Marianne's role is to act as the "real" girlfriend. Tonight, AJ sees her smile as "warm and friendly like always. Then it got fake." (76). He realises that although he has been spending $100 a night on her, she "never once meant it when she said she'd meet him somewhere else" (76) or that "he was the only one" (77). When AJ is ejected and his wrist broken, she merely "rested one hand on her hip, and held out the other to get paid" (44).

It may seem that AJ is simply a naïve fool, but as Katherine Frank has established his behaviour is absolutely typical of strip club regulars.[30] Frank studied lap-dancing clubs in detail, as a participant observer. (She stripped, herself.) Analysing the behaviour of regulars she argues that the experience reflected a quest for an authentic experience in a world where everyday experience has become artificial, overmediated. Frank noted how often regulars asked a girl for her real name, sought out some sort of authentic relation to the dancer, used romantic terminology ("dates") or offered advice and friendship. Regulars also claimed to be able to see through staged performances (girls who were just there to make money) as opposed to the dancers who convinced them of real emotional connection (as if "that smile is just for me"). Lonnie characterises this customer illusion sardonically as he watches April undressing for her "twenty dollar one and only "(63). Men paid most to the dancers who convinced them of authentic engagement. A dancer telling a man her name, for example, was considered as proof that the man was not just the average customer but that she really liked him. Frank commented that

> I, and many other dancers I knew, would reveal our real names strategically to just those customers who needed to feel they were different or special.[31]

When April reveals her real name she confirms Bassam in a truth-based utopia where he calls the shots; she merely sees it as a commercial transaction, in which he is seeking the bounded authenticity of the striptopia. For a dancer, divulging "private" information (often in fact fictional) kept the men interested. Finding out things about a dancer made the experience seem more genuine and more individualised. In this respect "realness" was often more highly valued than what was actually real. The men enjoyed the fictional relationship, because it did not involve real commitments. A dancer who was too real, too graphic, like the unnamed new girl performing in the Puma club (69) and showing "the pink", would not necessarily be successful. Nervousness or awkwardness in performance, however, could signal that a dancer was more genuine, more like a real girl, and the same was true of mistakes (sometimes carefully crafted) or of the masquerade of being a new girl. Frank, for example, had problems getting out of a bathing suit in five-inch heels, and got more tips as a result. Lack of professionalism implied to men that the girls were not skilled at manipulating them or their money, that they were not actually working. Frank quotes Roland Barthes's view that amateur strippers are often more erotic than professionals, whose icy technique can be a barrier, as opposed to

> gauche steps, unsatisfactory dancing, girls constantly threatened by immobility, and above all by a "technical" awkwardness (the resistance of briefs, dress or bra) which gives to the gestures of unveiling an unexpected importance, denying the woman the alibi of art and the refuge of being an object.[32]

But as Frank comments, the girls know how to trade on that, a point which does not seem to have occurred to Barthes. The action of the novel begins on "Thirsty Thursday", and some of the girls are wearing business suits and blouses, with their hair up. Thursday is a night when office workers will pay well to see the girls take off the same clothes which their co-workers wear in the workplace. As Frank noted,

> If I wear full underpants instead of a thong, the customers think I just walked in off the street.[33]

April does just that; offering an image of the amateur in her own underwear, making mistakes on stage, as opposed to the vitrified nudity-as-armour of Renée in her pasties or Retro in red leather. In the club, what the girls are often paid most for is the performance of emotional labour—rather like flight attendants, or waiters, or other workers in the service economy, smiling continually and offering a simulacrum of real interest in the client, the illusion of authenticity.[34] As Gabrielle Egan observes, however, when regulars realised that they could not have a relationship outside the club, they sometimes wept, raged, fought and got barred from the club. "A dancer's job is to frustrate".[35] It is AJ's disappointment which triggers the performance of the rescue narrative. But his disappointment is not merely sexual. Working every hour there is to support his family, struggling to create a home, he is confronted with a wife who finds him much less interesting than the TV soap stars she follows all day in her stay-at-home boredom:

> actors better-looking than he'd ever be . . . carrying on in bedrooms bigger than their whole house. (122)

Frustrated, AJ lashes out, is thrown out of the house, and ends up in the Puma Club. The club offers a fake paradise which does not deliver on its promises, just as America teases with a fake image of emotional and economic plenitude, and, when the disappointed rebel, quells them with violence. Lonnie is constantly alert to the possibility of "pockets" opening up in the crowd, areas where trouble is starting. Violence is always about to erupt, to be suppressed. After 9/11 he feels as if the whole club had erupted into pockets, "Yet there was nowhere for him to go, no one to defend" (513).

Dubus tells an old story—the oldest American story of captivity and rescue—but he also tells a new story, of an America caught in consumer fantasy and commercialised feelings. Corrupted by the power of money, its baulked utopianism feeds repetitive, retrograde fictions, which obscure the truth of its workers' lives. It was the symbol of this America—a fantasy of plenitude and power—which was attacked on 9/11. In *Townie*, when his sister was abused by her husband, Dubus was taken aback when his father promptly wrote a story about it. Although proud of the story ("Leslie in California") in which his father wrote deeply and poetically from a woman's point of view, he was also profoundly ashamed since his sister's husband remained unpunished, merely fictionalised. "How did it help my sister? What *good* did this do?"[36] Similarly, in the aftermath of the attacks, writers saw 9/11 as going beyond fiction, as "too true" to be represented, as if there would be something cheap or fake in fictionalising it. Dubus, however, demonstrates that America lives by fictions and fantasies, not facts, and that the way to write about 9/11 is to engage with its fakery and to contest the stories a culture tells, with other stories, rather than to reject fiction itself. His is a fictive utopianism in which fiction creates different roles, models alternatives, and undermines "one truth" narratives.

6   Pictures from a Revolution
Dalia Sofer, *The Septembers of Shiraz*

Where Dubus focussed on Muslims in America, Dalia Sofer considers the effect of Islamic terror on a minority, Iranian Jews, interrogating the role of art in relation to terror, as unleashed by different visions of utopia. *The Septembers of Shiraz* opens with a striking juxtaposition. In September 1981 Isaac Amin, a wealthy Jewish gemologist, is arrested by revolutionary guards at his desk in Tehran, where his calendar stands open at a glossy photograph of the tomb of Hāfez in Shiraz, subtitled *City of Poets and Roses.*[1] Shortly afterwards, blindfolded, he is transferred to the notorious Evin prison. With his eyes "submerged in blackness" (8), he is embarrassed by the comments of passers-by in the street. "Deprived of his vision, he has forgotten that others can still see" (9). The juxtaposition of colour and poetry on the one hand, darkness and deprivation on the other is emblematic of the dynamic set up in the novel between a colourful past world of cultural glory, and the contemporary Islamic republic, depicted in terms of greyness and brutality, apparently a contrast between a bygone Golden Age and a degenerate present. From the perspective of the Iranian regime, however, the past is a degenerate state, and the Islamic Republic constitutes a utopian project, to restore Islamic purity.

Western critics have been slow to recognise non-Western forms of utopia. Krishan Kumar is magisterial in his pronouncement that "utopia is *not* universal. It appears only in societies with the classical and Christian heritage, that is, only in the West."[2] Yet, as Jacqueline Dutton has argued, most cultures have foundation myths of some sort of Golden Age, whether Hellenistic, Sumerian (Dilmun), Judeo-Christian (Eden), Hindu (the reign of Rama), or indigenous Australian (the Dreaming).[3] The period considered by most Muslims to be the Golden Age of Islam begins with the first gathering of the Prophet and his followers in Mecca. The *hijra* (pilgrimage) of 633 marks the beginning of the Muslim calendar and the beginning of the Medinan regime or First Caliphate. It is the restoration of the purity of this regime which inspires Muslim fundamentalist movements, a restoration which takes on utopian dimensions, offering a model to be re-enacted through political and social action. The period is remembered as the Golden Age of pure Islam, when because

Muslims practised their faith perfectly, divine blessings rained down upon them.[4]

Frederic Jameson has underlined the extent to which utopia may be a response to and a defence against historical processes in which older institutions and cultural practices are being destroyed.[5] The structure of More's Utopia for example bears a close resemblance to that of the monastery, an institution which was facing wholesale dissolution during the reign of Henry VIII. Secularisation and modernisation in Iran, globalisation in the present, all give the spur to utopian projects. The utopianism that inspired the Islamic revolution of 1979, while partly the product of Marxism, also had its roots in the ideal Islamic social system promulgated by Navvab Safavi, executed in 1955, a thinker with whom Ayatollah Khomeini reputedly had a strong affinity. By formulating a detailed plan for an Islamic utopia, Safavi helped to establish the vision for a popular social movement which led to the Islamization of the Iranian revolution. Savafi's ninety-page pamphlet, *Barnameh-ye Enqelabi-ye Fada'ian-e Eslam* (*The Revolutionary Programme of Fada'ian-e Eslam*, 1950) sets out a programme based upon modesty, benevolence, chastity and abstinence from drinking, illegitimate sexual activities and corruption. While the monarchy is not threatened and there is no formal theocratic model, most elements of the plan foreshadow the Islamic regime. There is to be complete segregation of the sexes in education, and the universities come in for particularly sharp criticism, anticipating Khomeini's Cultural Revolution thirty years later. The issue of the sexual provocation of women is a prime concern. The containment of sexuality and the presence of women in public are central elements of reform in *Barnameh*.[6] Women's appearance in public without the *hijab* is condemned as sexually provocative and the plan is for the police to enforce its wearing. The press is not to be allowed to publish sexually provocative images; cinemas and theatres are to be closed; music banned and replaced by chanting from the Qur'an; alcohol and gambling suppressed; and the religious allegiance of the nation reflected in clothes worn in public. (European ties and hats will be illegal.) The pamphlet also prescribes amputation of the hand for a thief, whippings for fornicators and capital punishment for repeat offenders. While Savafi's social utopia has been described as unimaginative and based upon a simplistic notion of Islamic theology and ethics, with little understanding of history, society or economics,[7] its key features have been highly influential, particularly in the populist-utopian character of the Islamic revolutionary movement, and the imagined reinstatement of a Golden Age of unadulterated religious purity.

Others, however, have their own conceptions of Golden Ages. As the image of the tomb of Hāfez suggests, the evocation of a glorious past can be tailored to quite various political purposes. In the novel Isaac is a highly representative figure. Under the Qajar dynasty (1797–1925) the Jews of Iran had faced a variety of discriminatory measures, but under the Pahlavi regime they prospered, and Isaac is no exception, rising from poverty to riches. The reigns of the two Pahlavi Shahs were a Golden Age for Iranian Jews, as discriminatory laws were repealed, Jews were able to serve in the military, attend state schools, and live outside the Jewish quarter. Rapid modernisation during the Shah's White Revolution (1963–79) created enormous opportunities, and the urban Jewish community participated fully in a booming economy. While the regime deployed art to evoke the cultural glories of the pre-Islamic past, the Jews could also look back to the reign of Cyrus, who freed the Jews from capitivity and whose edict for the rebuilding of the Temple in Jerusalem is usually seen as ushering in a Golden Age for the Jews. The Pahlavis projected an image of continuity between the present and the pre-Islamic past, emphasising secular and nationalist pursuits, values and symbols, such as Persian art and music. While retaining Jewish identity, the Jews wanted to be perceived as Iranian and assimilated to this culture, identifying with nationalist aspirations and values. They saw themselves, after all, as denizens of Iranian territories for 2,700 years since the Assyrian exile. Judaism is the oldest minority religion in Iran. Many Iranian Jews thus emphasised the majestic distant past as an integral part of Jewish history.[8] Isaac is the only child in his family to bear a Jewish name; his younger siblings' names are Iranian, Shahla and Javad. This new national identity based on the Aryan race of ancient Iran posed some problems in the Nazi period, with newspaper propaganda trumpeting the supposed common Aryan origin of Germans and Persians, but effectively the Jews moved from the ghetto to the upper middle class in one generation. In 1968 the Iranian Jewish community was the wealthiest such community in Asia and Africa. In 1976, they numbered some 62,000, the largest Jewish community in Asia and Africa (with the exception of South Africa). In 1979 it all ended. The Islamic Revolution triggered a mass exodus of some two million Iranians to the United States, with the result that there are now more Iranian Jews in Los Angeles (popularly known as "Tehrangeles") than in Iran (35000 and 25000 respectively). About 85% of Iran's Jews have fled since 1979. In one neighbourhood in Tehran the Jewish population fell from 7,000 in 1979 to 70 in 1999.[9] Sofer remembers lining up at school to chant "Death to America. Death to Israel."[10] As Roya Hakakian notes, "The Islamic republic undid an ancient history and made us extinct."[11]

A generation later, the result is an outpouring of memoirs and novels, many by women. Perhaps unsurprisingly, almost all of these writers are possessed by an overwhelming urge to retrieve, celebrate and memorialise the lost past. Gina Nahai, for example, typifies the tendency to look back to a past that is disappearing, a magic past. Nahai immigrated to America aged sixteen and has published four novels, three on Iranian themes.[12] To her surprise when she began to research her first novel she found that there was almost no written historical record of the Jews of Iran; the only history (three volumes in Farsi) was out of print.[13] As a result she spent seven years interviewing Iranians in America, where there is now an impressive archive collected under the aegis of the American Jewish Oral History Project in

Los Angeles, and a modern history.[14] The archival impulse is strong in Nahai's fiction. *Cry of the Peacock* (1991) sets the story of a Jewish woman in twentieth century Iran against a backdrop of Iranian history from 1796 to 1982. *Moonlight on the Avenue of Faith* (1999) adopts fairy tales and magic in order to explore the political transition from the Jewish ghetto in Tehran in 1938 to city life in 1956, exile in America and, in a flight of feathered fantasy, a bird's eye view of Iran in the 1980s, torn apart by war. Moonlight, a light that is only seen in darkness, becomes a metaphor for a fragile hope. In the novel the attempt to break the curse of the past (a line of doomed women) clashes with the realisation that escape will also mean the end of family history.[15] The idea of a ransacked and betrayed past features in the plot, where characters in the house on the Avenue of Faith are beset by robber ghosts, stealing the treasures of the past. Less magically they eventually turn out to be the owner herself, liquidating her assets to secure her financial future. *Caspian Rain* (2007) focusses on a Jewish family during the Shah's last years, confronted by an avenging ghost from the ghetto past which they are attempting to deny in their upward social ascent. Situated somewhere between magic and history Nahai's fiction interrogates the history and politics of a lost world, at times revelling in the past, at times underlining the perils of memorialisation, and attempting to escape its haunting presence. The exceptional popularity in America of memoirs by and about Iranian women extends also to Jewish American memoirs, such as *Journey from the Land of No: A Girlhood Caught in Revolutionary Iran* by Roya Hakakian (2004), and Ferideh Goldin, *Wedding Song* (2003).[16] Indeed the list is expanding.[17]

The Jewish experience of modern Iran is an ambivalent one. If the Pahlavis were good for the Jews, they were not so good for everybody else. The glories of the Hāfez mausoleum may resonate with the Shah's encouragement of pride in a pre-Islamic past as part of the nationalist agenda, but Isaac's blindfold is also emblematic. In order to prosper, as he comes to realise, he had to turn a blind eye to the abuses of the regime and to its excesses. In 1981, in contrast to the highly coloured official version of the past, Isaac's daughter Shirin sees Tehran as "the black city" (243), "black and permeable, filled with holes through which people fall and disappear" (241). To his family Isaac has simply disappeared into a black hole. The reader, however, is not spared the details of his torture, merely for being a Jew with a rich lifestyle and family in Israel. (Judaism and Zionism tend to be conflated in Iranian political rhetoric.[18]) The novel was carefully researched, drawing on Sofer's father's imprisonment, prison memoirs, and her family's own escape (sixteen hours on horseback and six on foot to cross the Turkish border[19]). Sofer even obtained an audio recording of an interrogation and torture session.[20]

In her novel Sofer paints a picture of the Jews of Iran, which offers a critique of the archival and memorial, and an interrogation of the relation between art and terror, through the method of ekphrasis—the evocation in the verbal text of a series of visual images. Primarily she sets up a dialectic between images of the colourful past and those of a darker present, though the opposition is not in any sense simplistic. Firstly, Sofer depicts the Shah's emphasis on pre-Islamic art as a reaction against a colonial past. Isaac's sister Shahla has married Keyvan, whose father, a minister under the Shah, has already fled. Shahla, however, cannot bear to leave behind her collection of rococo furniture and a home crammed with priceless antiques. Keyvan's grandfather was a court painter to the Qajar king, Nasir al-Din Shah, whose portrait, painted by the grandfather in 1892, looks down from the wall as Shahla is served tea and cakes on a fine European porcelain service, also a gift from the Shah. (For Isaac's wife Farnaz, the French madeleines trigger a political rather than a Proustian insight, as an image of the country's aspirations, its desire for cosmopolitanism and its delusions of grandeur.) Nasir al-Din was thoroughly Europeanised, the first Iranian to be photographed and himself a noted painter and photographer. For Shahla, the painting alone is reason enough to stay (55). She can't let go of a cultural capital which will be worthless elsewhere. Keyvan's career as a professor of art history is heavily dependent on his lineage; nobody would care for his opinions on art if it were not for his last name. Keyvan, however, is now less certain of the value of art; he fears arrest. "How will this painting—and all the pages I've written about it in all those useless art magazines—help me in jail?" (55). The scene is immediately followed by a description of Isaac in jail, cigarette-burned and suffering, watching his cellmate Mehdi carving in wood. Mehdi is attempting to make a clog for his daughter, without much success. He throws it down, exasperated, "Enough artistic expression for today" (64). Though poorly executed and of no commercial value, Isaac sees in the wooden shape the clean intentions of its maker, and his hope for reunion with his child. The clog is some sort of argument for the <u>intrinsic value of the artistic impulse, even in times of terror.</u> Isaac's mind moves to Farnaz, as attached to her possessions as Shahla, and similarly refusing to leave Iran. For him, a certain warmth has gone out of her, "leaving her face beautiful but flat, like one of her prized paintings" (67). Sofer's novel appears to make no bones here of the way in which the materialism of the Jews has overtaken their culture. Isaac works with valuable jewels but has not set enough value on his family; Farnaz and Shahla are slaves to their possessions.

Where the Qajar painting appears to indict materialism and Eurocentrism, pre-Islamic art offers a different perspective. Isaac's family is eventually torn apart by the revolution and even Shahla and Javad escape ahead of him. In order to launder the cash paid to the people-smugglers, Farnaz has to pretend to buy a miniature from an antique dealer, just in case the government should ask her what she has spent $10,000 on. Like Shahla the dealer is possessed by his art-objects, "a slave to my relics" (215), which evoke the pre-Islamic past: a jug predating the Mongol invasion, Achaemenian jewels and silver tables engraved with figures of Cyrus and Darius, "relics of an age long gone but to which people cling like proud but destitute heirs to a dead tycoon" (215).When the dealer produces the miniature, it is described as a painting of a palace,

> one prince slaying another before the eyes of many viziers and court-
> iers, the scene drenched in sparkling reds, blues, and greens, with gold
> woven throughout. (216)

The dealer describes it as taken from a book, the Tahmasbi *Shahnameh*, Ferdowski's *Book of Kings*. Ferdowski's epic poem (pre-Islamic), writ-ten in the tenth century in classical Persian, became Iran's national epic, with many different illustrated versions. The Tahmasbi is a particularly fine example with some 250 miniatures, painted by the best artists of the period. Like all Iranian miniatures, they are marked by extreme subtlety of colour, using colour clusters to lead the eye, with perhaps a dozen hues of the same colour in a single picture.[21] In the Pahlavi era the *Shahnameh* was exploited to promote a nationalistic agenda; Farnaz remembers her son Parviz performing scenes from it at school, though under the Islamic regime it is no longer taught. The miniature also carries a further nationalistic charge. As the dealer explains, in 1962 an American collector bought it and ripped out the pages to sell them individually, some to a New York museum and some to collectors. The book evoked here is known as the *Hough-ton Shahnameh,* sold by Edmond de Rothschild to Arthur Houghton, the president of the Corning glass works, who promptly began dismantling and selling it. Some pages were displayed at the Metropolitan Museum of Art in New York, to which he donated, to reduce his tax liability. Houghton offered others unsuccessfully to the Shah in 1976 for $20 million, and then auctioned them. In 2006 one page made $1.7 million.[22] When the Metro-politan Museum published a book reproducing some of the illustrations in 1972, the *Shahnameh* was exploited for propaganda purposes. In the foreword, the Iranian ambassador to the United States claimed that, by publishing it, the Metropolitan had honoured the 2500th anniversary of the founding of the Persian Empire by Cyrus the Great, and thus also the first declaration of human rights.

> Such books assist greatly in bringing about an even closer relationship
> between the people of Iran and the United States, two peoples dedi-
> cated to the principles of freedom, morality, and tolerance set forth by
> Cyrus the Great so many years ago. [23]

For Farnaz, contemplating "the orphaned leaf, its counterparts spread around the globe" (217) the miniature becomes "the embodiment of loss" (218). When she flees she takes it with her, thinking of it as "a lost child" (322). The leaves of the book have been spread around the globe in a manu-script diaspora, some to museums, others, as she imagines, reposing in the cabinet of some European or American collector "his acquisition filling him with pride not unlike that of a nineteenth century colonialist in search of a piece of the Orient" (217). The miniature offers an image of American materialism, despoiling a culture of its treasures, in an imperial or Orientalist-inflected greed, which converts the art object into dollars, dismantling and destroying it. Without American petrodollars, the family, the book and the culture would not have been torn apart. It is a neat analogy—but there is more to the picture than that. It also indicts the Islamic regime.

Farnaz describes the picture in some detail:

> the thin, precise lines, the red and gold of a courtesan's robe, the indigo mosaic of the floor, where the slain king sits, his sword and shield by his side. (217)

The description is precise enough to identify the image as folio 36 verso of the *Houghton Shahnameh*, which depicts the hero Faridun striking down Zahhak with an ox-headed mace, itself a supreme moment of liberation in Iranian history. This is the climax of the first cycle of the *Shahnameh*, the moment when Iran is delivered from 1,000 years of tyranny suffered under Zahhak whose name conjures up the idea of tyranny to any Iranian. Zahhak oppressed the people because Iblis (Satan) had kissed him on the shoulders, causing a serpent to spring from each, demanding a daily diet of human brains. Thus Iblis planned to exterminate mankind. [24] The Shahnameh has as one of its core themes the tribulations which Iran endures over the millennia at the hands of both wicked kings and foreign foes. Zahhak comes from Arabia. Transferred from its original book to Sofer's novel the painting suggests that the Islamic regime is just one more foreign-inspired force hijacking Iran.

Farnaz is powerfully drawn to the picture as a deeply moving visual experience, a golden image of a heroic Iranian past, in which the richness and the courtly setting appeal to her nostalgia for the glories of the Shah's court, and also perhaps for tolerance and the freedom of women. The painting shows the daughters of Jamshid freed from tyranny by Faridun, and also depicts a courtesan. Indeed, in the midst of smiting Zahhaq, Faridun's eye has wandered towards a woman at the side of the picture. [25] In 1996 Sothebys in London sold this picture for £419,500 ($634,300). [26] The painting, then, can be read in diametrically opposed ways—as an image of a culture torn apart and scattered, the people of the book who are now in exile; as the result of Western materialism and greed; or as an image of the continuity of Arab domination of Iran. At the dealer's, Farnaz mentions Isaac's collection of antique daggers and his favourite, a Mongol sword with a gold leaf handle. When Isaac finally buys his way out of prison with his entire life savings, the revolutionary guards seize upon the sword. Isaac remarks on its aesthetic values, and engraved workmanship. "The workmanship? How about the functionality?" (254) counters the guard, resting the tip on Farnaz's neck. When he carries off the extorted savings, the sword goes too, placing the guard as one more in a line of tyrants wielding the sword over Iran, and forcing the state of property onto Iranian works of art. Terror seems to take little account of art.

So much for the glories of the past. In contrast to the lavish colour of the *Shahnameh*, contemporary Iran majors on monochrome, notoriously in the domination in the western press of images of the black veil.[27] Iran's most celebrated photographer Abbas, chose to work in black and white, and is openly acknowledged by Sofer as an inspiration for the novel (340), which evokes his images at several points. His book *Iran Diary*, also opens with images of the tomb of Hāfez, and the subtitle "Terre des poètes" (land of poets) though in monochrome and featuring picnicking families as the major focus.[28] Throughout the novel, black and white photographs are evoked and it is tempting to see Sofer as lamenting an inclusive, colourful past which has been replaced by monochrome, at least for women, veiled, devoid of makeup and denied full access to culture. In the streets shampoo ads and movie posters have given way to murals of clerics. On the other hand these images appear to offer a corrective to the spectacular and extravagant Pahlavi past. Monochrome is often seen as a kind of resistance to the saturation of the world by colour, in a crowded modern visual marketplace. As Paul Grainge notes,

> The visuality of monochrome seemed to efface its own relation to the sphere of capitalist simulations, sustaining the illusion that it was somehow removed from the market culture in which it was necessarily produced.[29]

As a young man, Isaac had been a keen photographer and had always used black and white, preferring the mystery of grey scale to the nakedness of colour, believing it to be "more archival, better suited to memory" (237). Arguably he also likes it because it seems less implicated in the life in which he is making a fortune. As he gets wealthier, and loses some of the affective connection to his family, he changes to colour, "his prints, unlike his life, become more and more saturated, filled like a canvas with splashes of longing" (237). As the *Shahnameh* demonstrates, cultural memory is a central part of how a nation is defined. Black and white can be seen as legitimating certain sorts of experience, converting the past from news to history and from surface spectacle to truth, bringing in associations with the archival, documentary realism, veracity and permanence. Paul Grainge notes that in the 1990s monochrome became a fashionable media choice (as in *Schindler's List, Forrest Gump,* and Armani advertisements.) But in Iran, black and white is not a style choice. In jail Isaac feels that his world has actually become black and white, consisting of filthy snow, gray cement walls and the ashen tinge of his own skin. He comes to think of colour as something fantastic. (236). Ironically too, the apparent archival permanence of his photos is an illusion. The photographs become a danger to his family. In a memorable scene, Farnaz and her daughter Shirin rip up every photo which shows anything remotely incriminating—sunbathers, ice-skaters, a woman in a skimpy dress, friends who have now been executed.

Abbas's photos of Iran chronicle the transformation of revolution into Islamic Republic. Several of his photos (which appeared on the front covers of *Time,* and *Stern* among others) became iconic, notably that of Ayatollah Khomeini, strikingly photographed to exploit the high contrast between white beard and black shawl, the left eye partly hidden in the shadows. As one commentator wondered,

> What is this eye hiding? What is going to happen next? Is he in the dark like everybody else as to what is to come, or does he have an inkling of it which he withholds?[30]

Abbas also believed in the archival quality of monochrome.[31] When threatened by mobs, he always said that he was photographing "just for history", a ploy which was surprisingly successful.[32] None the less, as a result of his first book, the photo-essay *Iran, la revolution confisquée* Abbas became *camera non grata* in Iran and went into exile for seventeen years.[33] His photos often operate by ironic juxtaposition: a shantytown followed by the Shah's lavish Persepolis celebrations, or a lone veiled woman on the edges of an all-male demonstration, excluded already from the revolution. Others juxtapose tradition and modernity: two men at prayer with an oil refinery standing in the direction of Mecca, for example. As we shall see, juxtapositions of this type also inform Sofer's narrative method. Three photos by Abbas are explicitly evoked in the novel. At one point Farnaz remembers her son's history lesson, on the French Revolution and the Terror, with images of heads on poles, and reflects that this is a story now coming to life around her. Only a few months ago she had witnessed the charred body of a prostitute placed on a stretcher and paraded down the street, surrounded by a chanting, euphoric mob (69). Having set the woman's body on fire the mob appear oblivious to the fact that pieces are falling off her. Farnaz continues:

> And had she not seen photographs of the Shah's ministers in a morgue, Naked, like mice in a testing laboratory, an experiment gone bad. (69)

Both images feature in *Iran Diary*. The first is the result of a mob, supposedly inspired by "the purifying fire of Islam" burning down the brothel area of Tehran.[34] The burned prostitute stands in strong contrast to the red and gold courtesan of the miniature, and offers an unambiguous image of a woman punished for sexual freedom. The image of the ministers suggests a social experiment which has backfired as an imposed, premature modernisation creates a traditionalist backlash. There are also unhappy associations with the infliction of pain on living beings in the pursuit of truth: scientific or interrogatory.[35] At another point in the novel Farnaz notes her in-laws' doorknocker, the hand of Fatimah, an Islamic talisman which was a gift from their neighbours. Immediately afterwards she is confronted with an image of bloody handprints on walls—again an Abbas image—signifying willingness for martyrdom. The caption reads "blood calls out for revenge."[36] Previous cooperation between different religious groups has given way to violence. The image migrates from the Islamic sphere to the Judaic and the revolutionary. Where the Shahnameh, torn apart by its purchaser, is only a metaphor for a dismembered people, the Abbas images focus upon actual bodily damage—the dismembered prostitute, the corpses, the bloody hands.

Illustrations may be black and white but Sofer's narrative is anything but. One memory explores how images mean, what they can tell us about our lives, and how they may be read in different ways, in this case in relation not to the past but the future. In Seville, on holiday, Isaac had forced Farnaz to attend a bullfight, overriding her protests about the brutality of the spectacle. Like any good tourist he intends to see the sights, ticking off the traditions of the past, even the brutal ones. In return, she insists that he visit a fortune-teller where he is alarmed to see that the cards he draws depict a stooped man dressed in black, and a figure in medieval armour on a white horse, along with a magician. The cards described include the five of cups, traditionally the card of loss, and number thirteen, the death card, which appear to indicate a "black future" (237). The clairvoyant, however, argues that the meanings of the images are not so obvious. Traditionally the five of cups suggests that although the cup of happiness has been overturned, the presence of two full cups in the background implies a need for a major restructuring of one's life, and future happiness. The death card may merely indicate the death of the old life, and the magician (sometimes shown as the cobbler) the danger of taking possession of the world but losing the soul.[37] In the preceding episode Farnaz had been accosted by a cobbler, returning Isaac's shoes to her. The implication is that damage may be repaired, images re-read, just as Isaac's lashed feet will eventually fit back into the shoes, and the brutality of the past need not go on into the future.

Sofer's strategy is to complicate any easy condemnation of any one side—Jewish or Muslim, Americanised or traditional—by a series of juxtaposed iconic images. But what of the narrative method? Like the miniature, Abbas's photos were once part of a book but have now been placed in a different book, which makes its own analysis of events, neither glorifying the past nor condoning its abuses. The dismembered images of different Iranian pasts have been put back together, reconnected by language. By placing the images in a different narrative context, Sofer's technique taps into the essential dynamic of ekphrasis—where the image is always dominated in the end by the word. The poetry of Hāfez is quoted in the novel by Jews, Muslims, Royalists and revolutionaries, capping each other's quotations, united by the power of language (101). In the novel the story is told in 47 short snapshot episodes, from four different viewpoints: Isaac, Farnaz, Shirin and her brother Parviz, a student in America lodged with a Hassidic family in Crown Heights in Brooklyn. These alternating narrative sections cast an ironic light on the claims of any one culture, often by means of subtle juxtapositions and parallels. Sofer's strategy is in some ways a risky one in relation to the Hassidic group, emphasising features common to both Jewish and Muslim fundamentalists. As a young man Isaac identified America with freedom and indulgence. He remembers how in September 1942 he lost his virginity with an American woman, whom he met with a group of American soldiers, stationed with other Allies in Iran to transport supplies to Russia. "Neutral" but pro-German Iran had been invaded. Singing Sinatra songs, drunk on arrack, Isaac succumbs to the charms of Irene McKinley from Galveston, though the night of passion is followed by summary dismissal; no men are allowed in her army quarters. Isaac does not protest. She "was helping the global force against the Reich" (34). The image of American seductive power is clearly foregrounded; though it is an occupying force America is identified with political and sexual liberation.

The following scene moves to Parviz, also a young man, but in an America of stark contrasts. In his architecture class Parviz is looking at photographic slides, "bright images of Californian homes" (37) with atriums, and vast expanses of glass. To him they seem "simple and sunny and cheerful, carrying within the uncomplicated lines the promise of docile decades" spent in the same town, street and house (37). His fellow students, spellbound by the images, are the products of just such homes. Parviz, however, is not exactly living the dream. His parental allowance interrupted, he is lodging in the damp, cockroach-ridden basement of Zalman Mendelson. It is a world of greyness; his television has such poor reception that there are often no images at all, or at best figures horribly distorted as in an amusement park mirror maze. All he can see of the world is feet passing in the street above. Desperately lonely, Parviz in America experiences the same solitude as his jailed father, also in a cockroach-ridden basement, also surrounded by horribly twisted bodies, also with a view only of passing feet in the corridor above (193). In the prison Isaac has a false family thrust upon him. In Iran everyone has to be addressed as father, brother, sister and so on. "The revolution, like all others, wished to turn its citizens into one big family" (12). In America Parviz had answered an advertisement: "Kind, loving family renting basement room" (41). The Mendelsons are in fact a kind family "but they are not his" (41), and the sound of their children running about overhead merely intensifies his loneliness—just as Isaac hears the torturer's child running overhead in the prison. Sofer's exploration of the ways in which religion can bring comfort or be divisive is steeped in irony. Isaac is imprisoned by the regime because of his religion, though Isaac has always been a secular Jew, observing few holidays and dismissing Hassids as "beardies" (41). Parviz, on the other hand, is not Jewish enough in America for the Mendelsons, who police his friendship with their daughter Rachel very closely. While quite clearly the ultra-orthodox Mendelsons are not the equivalent of the torturers in Iran, they function to complicate any clear-cut condemnation of religious orthodoxy and to undermine any easy dichotomy between Iran and America as regarding religious tolerance and inclusiveness. Zalman is treated sympathetically; his community have already got one Iranian refugee back on his feet (Broukhim, the florist), and are subsidising Parviz in exchange for a few hours work in a hat shop. Yet they are also ultra-orthodox, sexually repressive and proselytising. When a customer comes into Broukhim's shop and is advised to buy a peace lily, on the grounds that "like a lover, it's easy to please" (326), the angry reaction by the pious woman to this harmless joke speaks volumes for the possibility of peaceful coexistence with others. The Mendelsons regularly host Hassidic "emissaries", Jews who travel to other locations (often at some risk) to support a beleaguered Jewish community.[38] Unlike other Hassidic groups which advise members to separate themselves from worldly temptations, the Chabad form of Judaism, located in Crown Heights, emphasises outreach to non-religious Jews. Sofer takes a satiric view of one such emissary, whose mother enters the hat shop to equip her son, "an accomplished boy of 18 who has already found himself a wife and is on his way to save the Jews of Los Angeles" (273). Predictably a normal hat size is far too small for this prodigious young man. Zalman's father, like Isaac, had also been imprisoned just for being Jewish (in Leningrad) and is captured in a grim photograph, unsmiling, because all his teeth were knocked out in prison. In his youth Zalman had been an emissary to Morocco. Parviz discovers in the basement a photograph of a Muslim girl, and a letter from Zalman's father, angrily calling him home. As Zalman later says, he gave up the girl he loved because "I look at myself not as an individual, but as a piece of a whole" (312). Though he sacrificed a temporary happiness, he now has eight children and confidently expects that in three generations he will have brought a thousand observant Jews into the world: "that's the only way for us to make up for the extermination of our people" (313). As a result, Zalman sees no future for Parviz with Rachel. Parviz objects, "You can't force spirituality on someone." "You can, I am proof of it," counters Zalman (312).

Rachel, almost as modestly dressed as an Iranian woman, and forbidden any physical contact with the male, is persistently identified with nature, not with culture. She works in the florists and would like to study botany, but her roots in Hassidism will prevent this. The closest the young couple get to culture is a walk to Shakespeare's tree (supposedly a graft from his garden). Parviz has lost his roots; he can't be grafted back into flourishing orthodoxy; Rachel's roots tie her to a future as a mother. In the following section, Isaac thinks of his children as proof of his faith in the world, "like a landscaper who plants an oak tree knowing that it will not be fully grown in his lifetime—but that it will grow" (197). The reflection is occasioned by the sound of the torturer's child upstairs. Mohsen had been tortured under the Shah, and did not think he could ever have children. His child is "his miracle child, the badge of his faith" (210). His orthodoxy, like the Mendelsons', is the product of suffering, pain and death. In Brooklyn Parviz attends the circumcision party for the Mendelson twins and remembers a photo of himself similarly displayed on a pillow (311), an image of a group identity forged out of pain and loss: "each generation welcoming the next with an irreversible scar—a covenant with God, yes, but perhaps also a covenant with pain" (311). The parallels draw the three different "families"—Islamic, Hassidic, secular—together. Spatial and chronological synchronicity and intercultural syncretism bring together Iran and America, Muslim and Jew, modernity and tradition.

In some senses the parallels seem to work in favour of the Hassidic group rather than the secular groups. In Iran Isaac buries his father, the last of the family to be interred in the family tomb, and prepares for exile, while in Brooklyn the Mendelsons are celebrating new life, the birth of male twins. Iran is marked by death, America apparently by life. The collective has its points; individualism is a lonely affair. Even before he was imprisoned, Isaac was "a specialist in solitary confinement" (199), allowing distance to grow between himself and his family. The alternating sections of the novel reinforce the sense of a fractured nuclear family, a group of four individuals rather than a collective entity, as the Muslims and Hassids seem to be. The bridges between the family members are subliminal, unexpressed, tenuous. Parviz likes to walk on Brooklyn Bridge, because there he can exist "with no connection to any land—or any person—but with the reassurance that connection is possible" (111). Sofer's narrative method works in ironic terms to undermine certainties, but also to indicate the possibility of connection, as the reader draws the parallels across different locations and groups.

Significantly, when the Amins escape, they do embrace a group identity. Earlier in the novel Shirin had been horrified by the erasure of individual identity involved when her mother sets to work to tear up all the family photographs. She could hardly bring herself to start ripping apart her own image. Where should she begin, she wonders, should she tear through the eye or the hair? (119). She recalls her detestation of magic tricks and magicians' assistants. "What kind of person volunteers to be erased?" (115). Her father has already disappeared, and now his life also seems to be being torn up. But when the family set off for exile, they realise that their only unconfiscated passport is Shirin's, from which, by removing her photograph and erasing the details of her identity, Isaac is able to forge a family passport. The individual image is erased in favour of a strengthened group identity.

One final image draws a tentative moral. Just as the Mendelsons are celebrating, the Amins also come together in a fragile image of Jewish survival. A lamb is sacrificed to celebrate Isaac's release. Just as Parviz reflected on the pain of the circumcision, so Shirin wonders why people "thank God with blood" (266). There is a power-outage, "the lights go out, the city going black" (266), and the Amins light their table with candles, using the only ones they have left, usually reserved for commemorating the dead on holidays. At this point, Isaac enters the room, the white of his beard stark in the light of the candles. For a moment we are back in a black and white world. But for Shirin her father suddenly recalls Rembrandt's painting, *Old*

Jew Seated. A poster of the painting once hung over her father's desk, and Shirin had seen the figure's gaunt, aged hands and downcast eyes, as the epitome of sadness. Now she suddenly understands the painting and sees its beauty. In its sepia tones the painting is somewhere between the blackness of Islamified Tehran and the highly coloured nationalist past; it is almost all in shades of brown. Her father now looks old, like the painting, but he has survived. The scene ends with the candles guttering, supposedly a sign of the unquiet spirit of the person commemorated, with Shirin wondering if there are enough candles to account for all those who have not left the earth peacefully. This is a scene which indicates the numbers lost, and the continuity across the ages, linking the Amins with their Jewish heritage and ancestors, but also, importantly, with other groups. The meat from the sacrificed lamb has been shared with their Muslim neighbours; the painting evokes a past age of tolerance. As H.W. Janson notes,

> Rembrandt had a special sympathy for the Jews, as the heirs of the biblical past and as the patient victims of suffering.[39]

Rembrandt, proverbially known as the friend of Jews, lived in the Jewish quarter of Amsterdam where many of his neighbours were refugees from the Spanish Inquisition, given shelter in tolerant Amsterdam. The Old Jew, painted in 1654, wears a tattered robe and large flat beret, typical garb for an Ashkenazi Jew, at this date, probably a penniless refugee from Poland, paid to serve as a model.[40] So the picture is an image of the possibility of survival, continuity and tolerance.

Sofer puts all the pictures into a different book, her own ekphrastic photo-essay on the revolution, and by her words makes for a more subtle and nuanced understanding of the past. Reframing the pictures, she indicates that neither the highly coloured nationalist image, the Eurocentric view, or the monochrome photograph express the whole truth of Iran. As W.J.T. Mitchell argues, in his analysis of ekphrasis, the visual is always in some sense "other" to the verbal.[41] The alien visual object of verbal reproduction can emphasise separation and distance between reader and object, historical distance in the case of Keats' urn, or exotic distance, in the case of Orientalism. Sofer's novel however indicates the problems of distances—but also operates to build bridges across them.

7 Updike's Many Worlds
Local and Global in *Toward the End of Time*

Utopia + colonialism.

Where Sofer offered a dystopian account of the evils of Islamic religious fundamentalism, John Updike broadens the scope to examine the relationship between colonial empire and religion, including Christianity, exploiting scientific thought to challenge the demonologies of American political rhetoric. Bill Ashcroft has argued that Utopia is a deep repository of colonial thinking. In More's tale, King Utopus is a conqueror who renames his island (formerly Abraxa) and civilises its wild inhabitants, imposing the idea of a regulated commonwealth, with productive agriculture a defining characteristic.

> Here is the colonial process defined: the land was conquered; its name was changed, the indigenous inhabitants were "civilised", what was previously wasteland was cultivated; and the land was physically reconstructed.[1]

In Utopia land must be cultivated to be considered properly colonised; if any of Utopia's neighbours choose not to cultivate their land, they are invaded. If any writer has understood the argument that Utopia goes hand in hand with colonisation, it is John Updike. Ever since *The Coup* (1978), set in the imaginary African kingdom of Kush as its newly decolonised inhabitants encountered the forces of neo-colonialism, Updike has demonstrated a keen interest in empire, and its aftermath. Apparently disparate novels focus upon imperialism, whether in the shape of an American empire in decline (*Rabbit is Rich*, 1981), or under threat (*Terrorist*, 2006), in the postcolonial fantasia of *Brazil* (1994), or the satiric take on the new powers of transnational corporatism in the utopian religious community in *S.* (1988). In his first novel, *The Poorhouse Fair* (1959), written in 1957, Updike situated events some twenty years later in a socially engineered secular utopia, which swiftly becomes dystopic. Global peace has been assured by "The London Pacts with the Eurasian Soviet" but as a result America has no cause left to strive for. "Heart had gone out of these people" and "the conception 'America' had died in their skulls."[2] Their world is explicitly compared to the decadent Rome of Nero, as an empire in decline.[3] *Toward the End of Time* is also located in a post-imperial setting, in order to interrogate the relationships between empire and religion, exploiting debates in modern cosmology and drawing upon the work of Elaine Pagels and Lewis Mumford to promote the local over the global, and to undermine Manichean images of global conflict. As a result the novel provides a provocative investigation of human cultural development and evolution, locating hope for the future in the marginal and the ordinary, as opposed to a dystopian vision of centrally directed societies.

Leading his troops into the assault on the Iraqi city of Falluja, Lt. Colonel Gareth Brandt of the US Marines had no doubts about the identity of the force ranged against him. "The enemy has got a face. He's called Satan. And we're going to destroy him."[4] As John Gray has argued, as the twentieth century drew to a close, the pursuit of utopia entered the political mainstream, as Western governments committed themselves to establishing democracy worldwide, influenced by patterns of belief dependent upon religious formations.[5] Fundamentalist religion, a mixture of apocalyptic myth and utopian hope, emerged as a major force in world politics. After 9/11 utopian thinking came to shape foreign policy in America, but as a utopianism of the Right. Whereas older conservative movements have tended to accept human frailty, distrust notions of progress and assume only qualified victories for their causes, the new Right embraced the belief that evil could actually be defeated once and for all. Apocalyptic religion shaped the views of both George W. Bush and President Ahmadinejad of Iran. Americans who believe in the Rapture, the ascent of believers to heaven following the final battle between Christ and the forces of Anti-Christ on the plain of Armageddon in modern Israel, have their counterparts in radical Islamists for whom revolutionary violence is similarly purifying, and martyrdom a ticket to paradise. Christianity and Islam are both monotheistic, militant faiths with a mission to convert humankind, and the millennial and prophetic content of their political rhetoric has common roots. Falluja is thus a city "razed by rival fundamentalists."[6] Prophetic beliefs shaped America, from the moment of John Winthrop's famous invocation of New England as a "city on a hill" involving a new contract with God, and the nation remains marked by a high level of religiosity, a widespread belief in Satan, and the influence of powerful anti-Darwinist groups for whom the battle between science and religion is still taking place. A large segment of the population believe the events of 9/11 were predicted in the Bible, as did twenty-five per cent of Americans responding in July 2002 to a Time/Life poll.[7]

Lt. Colonel Brandt's confidence in Falluja drew upon that of his government. In 2003 some months after the US invasion of Iraq, George W. Bush told the Palestinian Prime Minister, Mahmoud Abbas that

> God told me to strike al-Qaeda and I struck them, and then he instructed me to strike at Saddam, which I did.[8]

For Bush the war was a struggle between good and evil. Invoking the First Great Awakening of Christian fervour in America in the mid-eighteenth century and the Second Great Awakening in the early nineteenth century he informed the world that

> A lot of people see this as a confrontation between good and evil, including me. . . . It seems to me that there's a Third Awakening.[9]

Similarly, national security was understood in terms of concepts derived from demonology. In 2004 the Homeland Security Planning Scenario Document described the terrorist threat facing the US as being perpetrated by the "Universal Adversary" for example.[10] Updike's novel focusses upon the dangers of harnessing empire in the service of religion (and vice versa), using scientific and technological analyses to challenge Manichean notions of cosmic conflict.

In the novel Updike exploits the branching paths of many worlds theory to transport his readers from America in 2020, balkanised by global conflict, to ancient Egypt, the Roman Empire, monastic Ireland and Poland in 1944. Conflict between rival forms of globalisation—anglobalisation and Sinicization—has led to war between America and China, and created a post-global, post-Imperial America with a return to local conditions, as emphasised by the closely focussed descriptions of local flora and fauna in Ben Turnbull's seasonal diary of a calendar year. Updike drops hints gradually in the novel so that the reader does not realise right away that it is set in the future, creating a disquieting sense that it is altogether later than we think. The reader learns successively that the last Siberian tigers "perished in the recent war";[11] that the American economy has collapsed and the local currency is now "welders" (8), named for Bill Weld, governor of Massachusetts; and finally that the year is 2020 (22). The disaster is the result of the Sino-American conflict, with Japan on the American side (148). Lest the reader consider that this scenario is recklessly provocative on Updike's part, it is worth noting that it closely resembles the vision of the future projected by Richard Bernstein and Ross H. Munro in *The Coming Conflict with China*, in which the authors argue that America should be much more willing to oppose Chinese policies, and suggest that some sort of face off might be needed. Referring to Samuel P. Huntington's proposition that the emerging world order will be dominated by the clash of civilizations, Bernstein and Munro depict China as an emerging superpower with whom conflict is very likely, and urge the United States to assist Japan as a counterweight to the growth of China.[12] In Updike's novel Japan is now too ruined to compete (148), millions of Chinese civilians have been killed (101), radiation has badly affected the Third World (286) and Hong Kong has been given back to the British (191). Relatively few Chinese missiles have hit Massachusetts, though Chinese-Americans have been interned on the Boston harbour islands (209) after pro-Chinese riots in Chinatown. But

Stone Age conditions prevail in California; there is no proper communication between the coasts and the Mid-West is so depopulated that there are plans for a new Homestead Act (77). It is not all bad. A vaccine has cured AIDS (146) and there are no taxes, since the ghost of federal government which lingers in Maryland and Virginia is unable to collect them (119). Because Mexico remained neutral, its economy is thriving and US citizens are sneaking across the border as illegal immigrants (184). The overall picture of the future, however, is decidedly dystopian.

A striking image underlines the novel's dominant concern with notions of colonisation and empire. Over Ben's head hangs a second moon, an abandoned space station, on which the last colonists have slowly died out, as the government could no longer maintain connection via shuttle ships. As Ben notes, "all of us who dwell on earth are in a position exactly the same, if on a larger scale" (36). If in one sense the novel gives us global domination reduced to the local, it also expands its focus from the globe of the earth to the scale of the universe, with earth as a dying planet and man's best hope the potential colonisation of other planets and the effective globalisation of the universe. When Ben is returning from Boston he is struck by two emblematically global images. First he watches a young woman blowing a bubble of gum, expanding it out toward him, and then wolfing it back, a small globe contracted back into the darkness of her oral cavity (30), its own black hole. Looking out of the train window he sees his own eye reflected back "like the visage of a spy from outer space" (30), as if there were life beyond the globe, looking in on Ben. Throughout the novel images of globes appear and disappear: the two moons, the wheel of Ben's thermostat and its bead of mercury (50), even his golf balls which are either soaring into the sky or disappearing into a black hole, so that there is a continual expansion and contraction from global immensity to local smallness, and from airy heights to fleshy earthiness.

In order to consider the scenario of a potential extension of empire beyond the globe itself, Updike engages with debates in cosmology, particularly the "many universes" theory (16): the idea that at every instant when a wave-function collapse seems to occur, the entire universe may be said to split into parallel worlds, each containing one of the possible outcomes of measurement of a quantum system. In an alternative theory the observer may split into many selves—as in the novel's epigraph:

> We cannot tell that we are constantly splitting into duplicate selves because our consciousness rides smoothly along one path in the endlessly forking chains.

Updike borrowed his epigraph from Martin Gardner's hostile review of the account given by John D. Barrow and Frank J. Tipler of the "anthropic principle", the idea that our planet was carefully designed to create human beings, implicitly supporting the design argument for God.[13] Gardner described the four types of anthropic principle under the convenient abbreviations of WAP, SAP, PAP, and FAP.[14] In the essay from which Updike drew his epigraph, Gardner comprehensively demolished Barrow and Tipler, cheerfully adding his own fifth principle (the Completely Ridiculous Anthropic Principle: CRAP). Updike was well-read in cosmology and has referred to such eminent cosmologists as Paul Davies on several occasions, notably when he discussed the anthropic principle in a review of interviews with twenty-seven cosmologists,[15] and later in an essay, in which he argued that only a cruel God could have adopted such a lengthy, wasteful and painful method as evolution, to breed an intelligent species, and that such a God would be "an unescapable tyrant".[16]

Discussing Paul Davies's account of the likely end of the universe, Updike reviewed the various compensatory theories on offer.[17] As that second moon suggests, modern cosmology implicitly supports an imperial or colonial mission, which would expand man's domination over the entire universe. Barrow and Tipler discuss the potential colonisation of the universe using artificial machines.[18] Paul Davies has also argued that colonisation of other planets is likely, probably proceeding by planet-hopping, rather as the Polynesians moved from island to island across the Pacific, and has suggested that such colonists need not be human in form, but adapted to the conditions of other planets.[19] Updike takes a less sanguine view of this scenario of an advanced civilisation conducting exploration and colonization via self-reproducing intelligent machines. In the novel he invents the "metal-lobioforms", inorganic but evolving, machine-like creatures, feeding either on waste oil or electricity, with heads like chainsaws, which they use in ruthlessly attacking living creatures. Tipler argued that man would colonise further planets until the entire cosmos teemed with life—possibly computer life—until all the universes would get together to create a super mind, essentially the Almighty.[20] Updike uses this idea of the evolving mind in the shape of the "torus" (151) an apparition in the sky which offers a moment of mystical transcendence, and seems to offer evidence that somewhere in the universe mind has triumphed over matter. The torus is only a fleeting presence, however, with no lasting effects.

Updike pays much more attention to the idea of many universes, though his usage of the theories on offer is syncretic and creative. Such universes have been variously envisaged as parallel worlds flourishing side by side in our familiar three-dimensional space, or in other spaces in some way invisible to us; or as alternative worlds following one another in some sort of Supertime, exploding into and out of life, expanding, contracting and vanishing. In the novel Ben appears to exist in different universes. His wife Gloria disappears at one point (the possibility lingers that Ben has shot her (41)) and is replaced as Ben's lover by a deer, or a girl called Deirdre, who loots his house and sells off his valuables. But suddenly Gloria is back, Deirdre is gone, and most of the looted objects have also returned. Deirdre, perhaps, still exists in some other universe. Or the story has branched from a universe in which Gloria is dead to another in which she remains alive. On the one hand, therefore, Updike offers a very dystopian image of the future, as globalisation produces conflict and devastation, and on the other hand, in the use of many universes theory, a highly utopian image of worlds without end in which there is effectively no death, whether for the individual or his world.

So is this a utopian or a dystopian novel? In fact, when Ben enters alternative worlds, his experiences do not support the utopian scenario. In the novel there are four moments when Ben shifts into parallel universes. Each excursion concerns the end of an Empire: ancient Egypt as the pyramids are looted, Rome as the Christians expand in all directions, Irish monasticism during the Holy Roman Empire as the Vikings appear upon the horizon, the Third Reich with defeat imminent. As David Malone has argued, these passages focus on historical transition, the dying of one power and the emergence of another.[21] The excursions suggest a continuing cycle of resurgent imperialism, as the death of one civilisation contains within it the seeds of the next. Each of these parallel universes casts Ben in an ironic light, undercutting an American imperial self and more broadly interrogating the complicity between religion and Empire. Ben is in most respects a thoroughly unpleasant anti-hero, described by Updike as having spent his working life "in a world as opaque and menacing to me as that of Neanderthal hunters, the world of financial investment."[22] A retired investment counsellor, Ben is also a sexual imperialist, for whom paid sex with Deirdre has all the attractions of an auction (47). His likeness to primitive man, as a caricature caveman, is emphasised in the opening pages as he tracks prints in the snow (4), while his fur clad wife demands he turn hunter to kill the deer who is eating her roses. Ben is fascinated by the extinction of the Neanderthals, which he ascribes to a primal clash of civilisations: murderous conflict with the Cro-Magnons (126). Updike said of Ben that, like other members of the upper classes, he had evaded the problems of global disaster, insulated by wealth. In each of the excursions, however, he takes on the role of a much more lowly, even endangered, figure in a declining empire, and has to engage with the consequences of the belief in global conflict, a tyrant God and technological triumphalism. The "alternative worlds" thus satirise the overconfidence and pretensions of an American capitalist, suggesting that America is just one in a series of empires, and offering a corrective to exceptionalist delusions of grandeur.

In the first excursion (61–66) Ben features as one of a pair of grave robbers, looting a pyramid, where "we robbed our victims not merely of life's passing illusion but of an eternity"(62–63). Ben had previously noted that grave robbing was a skilled craft practised by whole villages, successfully matching the "divinely inspired technological achievements of the tomb-builders" (62). The reader follows Ben through the intricate passageways of the tomb, promising either a world of riches if he chooses the right path, or a fatal trap if he enters a booby-trapped pathway. As he glimpses the rubble-strewn entrance to the central treasure chamber, he has an uneasy sense of the crushing weight of stone above him, and in a moment of claustrophobic horror his lamp is blown out, leaving him immured in darkness. A sudden draft from an intersecting passageway functions as the breath "of the outraged gods" (63). The continually branching passageways lead only to confinement and death, not to an alternative universe which triumphs over death. Updike's imagined world is informed here by Lewis Mumford's analysis of the Pyramid Age in *The Myth of the Machine*, which draws analogies between America's commitment to technology and empire and what is usually thought of as the rise of civilisation in the great river valleys (Jordan, Nile, Euphrates, Tigris) in the fourth millennium BC.[23] Mumford argues that the rise of civilisation was the product of a new type of socioreligious organisation, authoritarian, centrally directed and under the control of a dominant elite. Its major features were an increase in mechanical and mathematical order, (derived from the use of astronomical knowledge to plot the procession of the seasons and the revolutions of the planets) and a replacement of the gods of vegetation and fertility (fallible and local) by the implacable Sky gods—sun, moon and planets.

> The remarkable fact about this transformation technically is that it was the result, not of mechanical inventions, but of a radically new type of social organization: a product of myth, magic, religion, and the nascent system of astronomy.[24]

The inflexible, predictable order which was represented by the calendar was transferred to the regimentation of human components, in a disciplined and specialised labour force.

Ben's diary of a calendar year in Massachusetts therefore sets the stage for an exploration of Mumford's major ideas. In Mumford's argument our own technological age has its origins not in the invention of individual machines in the Industrial Revolution, but in the age of the Megamachine, a social machine composed of human parts. At the centre of this new type of society is the idea of divine kingship, as kings draw on the authority of the gods. Cosmic order was the basis of the new human order. Because the sun is the central point of reference in the motions of the planets, the sun-king occupies the centre of a society conceived in its regularity as a replica of cosmic order, with all phenomena measurable, controlled and repetitive. Society therefore became hierarchical, in the shape of a social pyramid, with many at the bottom supporting an elite class at the social apex. The resulting culture was also dedicated to expanding its collective power, by war and conquest. Mumford argued that as far as later kingships declined to more modest dimensions, it was through the stubborn resistance of village communities—essentially the relation between local and global has been played out since the beginnings of civilisation. Egypt was Mumford's prime example of the new form of power. Only a complex power machine could build the immense construction of a pyramid, which demands knowledge of mathematics and astronomy, and the use of manpower on a large scale. What, he wondered, was a pyramid, if not the equivalent of modern space technology, a device for securing passage to an afterlife for a favoured few. Mumford drew explicit parallels with the way the modern world had developed.

> The ideological fabric that supported the ancient megamachine had been reconstructed on a new and improved model. Power, speed, motion, standardization, mass production, quantification, regimentation, precision, uniformity, astronomical regularity, control, above all control—these became the passwords of modern society in the new Western style.[25]

Essentially Updike updates Mumford to the era of globalisation, presenting America as pyramid in the mordant symbolism of Ben's enormous mansion, referred to as The Hill. He and Deirdre (described as looking Egyptian, 43) explore its "seldom-visited chambers" (59), where rubble and fallen plaster lie underfoot, and the menacing noise of the steam pipes, like the breath of "a captive serpent" (59), creates the illusion that the portraits of Gloria's ancestors "so confident in their luxurious appropriations, hiss crushingly in our ears" (61). Treasures are stacked everywhere, from Meissen and Limoges china and Wedgwood chairs to a safe-room full of silver. Earlier Ben had noted scratches on his asphalt driveway.

> Ominously ancient, Egyptian, these man-induced grooves, as if slaves had dragged one huge stone across another in the construction of a pyramid so gigantic that death itself would be defeated. (37)

Just as the pyramid represents an attempt to defeat death, filled with grave goods for the afterlife, Ben's treasures offer a mirror image of an imperial civilisation. Ben has spent a lot of time plumbing the mysteries of Deirdre's dark passages, describing her vagina as "that sacred several-lipped gateway to the terrifying procreative darkness" (54). But Deirdre, a villager, represents the local, female opponent of male imperial power, and she loots his treasures just like a grave robber; the dark female gods reassert their power over the gods of light and mock the pretensions to immortality of an Imperial class. David Malone has drawn attention to the mythological elements of *Toward the End of Time*, and sees these references as essentially unsystematic, if richly productive of non-realistic ways of reading.[26] Arguably, however, they relate to Mumford's argument, in which the decline of local fertility religions was part of the new order. Cosmic conflict between rival gods of fertility underscores the plotting of the novel, with the male god (Ben) rampant at the beginning of the year with Deirdre, declining in power in the arms of a maiden (Doreen) and subsiding into impotence at year's end. At the close he is about to be replaced as king of the hill, as Gloria (the crone) brings in the deer-hunter with his bow and arrow.

Mumford discusses a change in social leadership between the ninth and sixth centuries BC, with a retreat from the great centres of power into smaller communities, and the emergence of men of humbler, more modest proportions, bringing life back towards the village scale, men like Socrates (a stone-cutter), Jesus (a carpenter) and Paul (a tent-maker).[27] In the second excursion (124–134) Ben features as Saint Mark in the first century AD, accompanying Saint Paul, preaching in Iconium in the Roman province of Galatia, where Paul preached in 47–48 AD. Again the emphasis is on empire and its colonists. Iconium was founded by Emperor Claudius as a colony of army veterans, and became an important Christian centre, though like most of the many places where Paul preached, it is so no longer.

> His travels seem wormholes in petrified wood, the already rotten eastern end of the Empire, dotted lines traced from one set of ruins to another, or to empty Turkish spaces where even the names Paul knew— Lystra, Derbe—have been wiped away by time's wind. (123)

In the excursion Paul is characterised as intent on expansion, and wants to take advantage of empire to spread the Christian message, to sail to Ephesus because he believes the word of Jesus will spread best from the "teeming ports" (126). He goes on to Rome. "Cities are unholy places, but their mobs were needed for the spread of the Word" (133). The new power, Christianity, depends upon the imperial infrastructure for its spread, the roads, ports and cities. As in Egypt, there are complicities between religion and empire, just as in America Ben's house recalls the American sense of divine mission, the city on a hill of American exceptionalism. Ben had previously reflected that the Roman Empire had made the spread of Christianity possible (121). Christianity needed roads or would never have got out of Jerusalem.

> And it needed to get out of Jerusalem. It would have been squelched by the Jewish establishment. The Jews hated it, though it *was* Jews at first. (121)

At an Easter service he had been struck by the contrast in the stained glass windows between the "wistful, genteel Aryan faces" and the gesticulating Jewish rabble-rousers (112). In the alternative world of the first century Mark quarrels with Paul over the question of relations between Jews and Christians, and the fact that Paul is taking Christ to the Gentiles. Paul argues that once Christ has come "there are Jews no more" (130); Christ is a new life for all nations. Mark takes a narrower point of view, arguing that Jesus is the fulfilment of the Law of the Old Testament, and that Jesus is not "conjuring away all difference, decreed from the days of Abraham, between Jew and Gentile" (134).

In this excursion, Updike draws upon another thinker concerned with the connection of global conflict to religion, Elaine Pagels. In *The Origin of Satan*

Pagels argues that Paul was inclusivist, but Mark's Gospel (written about 70 AD) sets the story of Jesus firmly in the context of conflict, both in relation to the struggle of the Jews against Rome and a cosmic conflict between good and evil in the universe.[28] Mark's gospel was written in the violent years of Jewish rebellion and Roman suppression, when offence to the Romans had to be avoided. The New Testament gospels are wartime literature, written during or in the aftermath of the Jewish revolt of 66 AD that culminated in the destruction of Jerusalem. Although Mark knew that Pilate had ordered the crucifixion of Jesus, the two trial scenes in his gospel indict the Jewish leaders for Jesus's death and semi-exonerate the Romans. Pilate, in reality a brutal colonial governor, becomes a well-meaning weakling intimidated by Jewish priests and the mob. Reviewing Pagels, Updike noted how the other three gospels took their cue from Mark to indict the Jewish high priests, "sowing the seeds for 2000 years of Christian anti-Semitism".[29] Mark also emphasises the cosmic dimensions of the struggle. If Jesus was the Messiah, his capture and death had to be construed not as a final defeat but as a preliminary skirmish in a vast cosmic conflict. Satan had not been a major figure in the Old Testament; his name in Greek merely characterises him as "the obstructor", one who throws something across one's pathway. (If the path is the wrong one the obstruction may have a positive effect.) Mark, however, emphasises the role of Satan from the start, constructs the gospel in terms of temptation scenes, and casts the Jews as the agents of darkness rather than light. As a result, Updike argued, the Manichean image of a universe at war still remains a narrative of great imaginative force, as exemplified in science fiction fantasies, and films such as *Star Wars*, or *Independence Day*.[30] Thus, in this excursion, Updike focusses again on the ways in which religion depends on or collaborates with empire, with consequences on a global scale, particularly in the demonisation and persecution of the Other.

The point is expanded upon in the excursion to the Third Reich (240). After a golf game Ben bumps into his doctor, Aaron Chafetz, in the shower room. Usually it is Ben who is naked and vulnerable, not his doctor, but here

> another universe, thinner than a razor blade, sliced into the sinister locker room. Chafetz was a naked Jew, and I a uniformed good German recruited to guard an extermination camp. (241)

Again, one empire, the Third Reich, is at the point of collapse. It is Poland in 1944, Allied planes are overhead and America is about to pick up the reins of power. This anti-Semitic universe is the consequence of St Mark's. The showers evoke a killing machine memorably interpreted as the product of order, mechanisation and calculation, a successor to the Pyramid Age. Ben had described the death camps as "orderly" and as ending forever the concept of "the Western world as proceeding under a benign special Providence" (20). The imagined scene emphasises technology: "the iron of guns and barbed-wire fences and of the rails upon which the steam engines dragged their crammed human cargo" (241). The branching passageways of the pyramid, the roads Paul travelled exhaustively, the railways of Europe, all alike appear to lead to images of conflict and death, rather than to new worlds.

So far, so dystopian. But Ben makes one other excursion, which casts the relationship between religion and empire in a different light. Shaving, he alters his usual method and

> It was as when a measurement is taken in the quantum realm of an electron's position or momentum, and the wave function collapses and another universe floridly sprouts on the spot. (215)

Suddenly he becomes a young monk in an Irish monastery in the ninth century, happily rejoicing that the white crests of the waves are "a divine sign of safety" (215), since the sea is too rough for the arrival of "the fair-faced demons from far Lothland" (215), the "Antichrists", who are "eternally condemned" (217): the Vikings. Clearly the idea of the power of the devil has gone on expanding since Mark's days; the monk repeatedly describes the Vikings as "fiends", and as the "evil from the sea" (216), operating with the consent of Providence, as a test for the faithful, so that the latter may become angels, replacing "the ranks depleted by Satan and his defiant and banished legions" (216). By now, Satan has been promoted from an obstruction on the path to the leader of a cosmic army. The monk, unfortunately, is over confident; the dreaded sails appear and he faces the Viking axe. The actual marauder, however, is not a "roaring demon" (219) but a frightened boy.

> The instant of time to which our lives have converged has two sides of terrible brightness. . . . Darkness and light are one" (220).

Updike deliberately undercuts the Manichean image, and demotes the demonic. But why select this particular clash of cultures? The Vikings are not normally seen as imperialists, and in the monk we see Christianity in humble guise, clinging to a rock off the Irish coast in a subsistence economy. What is this monk's relation to empire?

The answer lies in Thomas Cahill's book, *How the Irish Saved Civilization*. Cahill quotes the poem by John Scotus, an Irish monk, which underlies Updike's setting.

> Bitter is the wind this night
> Which tosses up the ocean's hair so white.
> Merciless men I need not fear
> Who cross from Lothland on an ocean clear.[31]

Cahill argues that before the Viking attacks in the ninth century, Ireland's position on the margins of empire made it a cultural leader, in preserving the legacy of Western civilisation. As the Roman Empire fell and the barbarians looted it, the Irish took on the task of copying all of Western literature. Their scribes served as the conduits through which Greco-Roman and Judaeo-Christian cultures were transmitted to the tribes of Europe. Without the Irish monks, the world that came after them would have been quite different, a world without books. As Kenneth Clarke comments,

> Looking back from the great civilizations of twelfth century France or seventeenth century Rome it is hard to believe that for quite a long time, almost a hundred years, Western Christianity survived by clinging to places like Skellig Michael, a pinnacle of rock eighteen miles from the Irish coast rising seven hundred feet out of the sea.[32]

The monk's location on his "island hill" (215) off the Munster mainland with its "beehive" (219) shaped stone huts, accessed by narrow crawl-way passages, is recognisably Skellig Michael, raided by the Vikings in 823. The monk's medicinal herb garden is described in some detail, as an example of the creation of a God who pervades all aspects of the creation with peace and love (218), a benevolent deity rather than a tyrannical power. At the same time the monastery is clearly envisaged as a bastion of culture. The monk mentions brother Guaire copying books in the scriptorium, and even though he is himself illiterate he is aware that the herbs which he tends were also known to the pagan Greeks, "the king of whose wisdom was named Aristotle" (218). Updike clearly evokes the notion that classical learning survived because of the Irish, who then reexported it, founding monasteries all over Europe.

The Irish therefore apparently represent here the salvatory qualities of the marginalized, a validation implicitly of Mumford's locals as pitted against the centralised Imperial machine. Mumford made much of the role of the monastery as offering civilised order on a human scale, and argued that the first labour-saving machines came not from the technically advanced centres of empire but from people on the fringes. Monks mechanised work (e.g. grinding) to have more time for prayer.[33] Ben is increasingly fascinated by the overlooked corners of time and space, especially the Dark Ages from the fall of Rome to 1000 AD, and becomes aware that these centuries included major breakthroughs for mankind; the stirrup, crank and horseshoe in the ninth century, watermills, the wheeled plough and crop rotation by 1000 AD, things which the tyrants of Rome never imagined.

> In humble, anonymous farmsteads and workshops, technological leaps never dared by the theorizing, slave-bound ancients were at last executed. (279)

Once again, the novel validates the progressive role of the marginal, as opposed to the centralised totalitarian machine, and in addition demonstrates the possibility of religion as disconnected from Imperial power.

The return to Ben's own world, however, depicts an aggressive America, still in the grip of fantasies of global conflict. Ben's excursion as a monk takes place on the day before Independence Day and the local hoodlums who are running a protection racket on Ben's land are aware that lots of outsiders will soon be trying to access the nearby seashore. Ben notes that the local fireworks always attract "Bare-chested Vikings, already drunk" (223), lugging coolers of beer towards the beach. The date also evokes cosmic conflict. The movie *Independence Day* was screened on the eve of the fourth of July in 1996, the year in which Updike took the naturalist notations which he uses for Ben's diary of the seasons.[34] In the film, alien beings invade the earth from outer space and trigger global conflict. Updike described "this summer's no-brainer megahit" as an example of the popularity of the Manichean image of a universe at war.[35] In response to the Viking threat, Ben suggests that the young hoodlums charge a fee for beach-access, of which he will take a cut. He also suggests ways in which they can improve their protection racket, to extort cash from his neighbours: killing pets, kidnapping children or burning down a beach house. Civilisation is indeed extremely precarious. Vikings and monks now appear to have changed sides. Ben's locals are more like pillaging, burning Vikings than the "Vikings" they are supposedly opposing. In the upshot, the deal Ben brokers condemns his young associates to violent death at the hands of more powerful outside forces—like the monk in the alternate universe. The Manichean opposition of good and evil may have been deconstructed but by the close of the novel Ben's dreams—his other excursions into other worlds—are filled with images of atrocity and he feels as if an "infernal machinery of some local or global conspiracy . . . was closing in on me" (287).

The novel closes, as it began, with an image of man-the-hunter, as Gloria hires an archer to kill the deer in her garden. Updike's selection of weaponry is well-chosen, taking advantage of the fact that in residential areas of Massachusetts it is illegal to discharge a rifle within 150 yards of a residence whereas the limit for bow hunters is fifty yards, making the "archaic" technology safer and more effective.[36] Mumford had described the bow and arrow as the first machine, invented by Palaeolithic man, and ascribed the development of the initiative, self-confidence and ruthlessness that kings need to get and hold power, to the development of hunting as an activity, and the subsequent emergence of the hunting chief.[37] Small farmers were then an easy target for hunters seeking tribute or "protection money" and social violence was the result.[38]

> The efficiency of kingship, all through history, rests precisely on this alliance between the hunter's predatory prowess and gift of command, on one hand, and priestly access to astronomical lore and divine guidance.[39]

At the start of the novel the deer escaped unscathed, but this time the fatal arrow, symbolically the arrow of time, which flies in only one direction, meets its target. Time is linear once more and Ben's alternative pathways have been closed off.

At the close, conflict is on the horizon again and the American empire is beginning to regroup. Mexico has repossessed Texas, New Mexico, Arizona and Lower California (290) and Gloria feels "It's about time somebody took charge, before the Mexicans invade" (290). And somebody does: FedEx, which arms its postal workers, reconnects the coasts, takes over the protection rackets and assumes most of the functions of government. The president is rumoured to have resigned (291) and America is about to be run by—and as—a transnational corporation. The smaller operators, like the local hoodlums, have been removed, and most of the roads and airways are under FedEx control—or soon will be. FedEx has plans to remote control the metallobioforms, which will then be "the biggest thing in warfare since the taming of the horse" (293). There is talk of moving the government to Memphis—not the Egyptian location, but FedEx HQ, emblematically the site of the next Pyramid Age.

Updike sensibly sidesteps a definitive conclusion on the future of the universe, or of man's place in it, though the long view of humanity does not tend towards excessive optimism. In the novel, however, technological triumphalism, centrally-directed societies and religious empires are repeatedly undercut by small, local inventions and the imaginative engagement with the marginalised. What the sallies into alternate universes demonstrate is not a celebration of some utopian project of colonisation, global expansion across the universe, or a divine mission for humanity, but rather the reverse. The local is at least partly validated, in the village world of the grave robbers, and the marginalized monks, and the religious underpinnings of the discourse of global conflict are undercut. While the primary thrust of the novel is satirical, offering a corrective to American exceptionalism, Updike repeatedly brings life back to a village scale, to celebrate the resistance of ordinary people across the centuries to totalitarian forces, and to urge the importance of local solutions. In his review of Pagels, Updike argued that while the concept of absolute evil may once have been useful in calling forth heroic virtues, now these need to be called forth

> on behalf of the more modest goals of standoff, accommodation, piecemeal amelioration, and forgiveness of one's obstructor.[40]

8   The Black Atlantic as Dystopia
Bernardine Evaristo's *Blonde Roots*

In a study of fictions of utopia it might well appear that there is little space for the consideration of race, still less in the context of slavery. Yet utopian thought lies at the heart of one of the most influential discussions of American racial history, Paul Gilroy's *The Black Atlantic*. In interview Paul Gilroy acknowledged the utopian nature of his thinking, not (as might be thought) as the utopianism of a tradition, Marxist or otherwise, but in relation to utopian thinkers in the philosophical sense.

> I have been very influenced by Ernst Bloch, his conceptions of utopia, and particularly his understanding of the relationship between music and utopia and also his sense of the place of the fragments—the shards of utopian thinking in everyday life.[1]

To recap, Ernst Bloch expanded the concept of utopia from the narrower image of a description of an alternative society designed to evoke or facilitate a better way of life, to such phenomena as daydreams, religious visions, myths of a golden age, circuses, fairy tales, glossy magazines and travel literature, with the capacity for hope envisaged as a prime source of human creativity, dynamism and progress, part of our capacity for imagination.[2] Similarly for Gilroy, utopias are thought experiments which restore to people the ability to imagine a better or a different world to the one that they inhabit. He poses the question:

> how do we cultivate the ability to do what Bloch called dreaming forward and what value does it have to be compelled to imagine a different world.[3]

Following Bloch, music is a key element of the analysis, as Gilroy emphasises utopias as involving the politics of transfiguration, the emergence of qualitatively new desires, social relations and modes of association, both within the racial community and between that group and white oppressors. The issue of how utopias are conceived is complex, not least because they strive continually to move beyond the grasp of the merely linguistic, textual and discursive.[4] Such utopias may embody an imaginary anti-modern past and a postmodern future.

Gilroy argued that the vernacular arts of the descendants of slaves suggest a role for art which is strikingly similar to that described by Adorno in relation to European artistic expression after the Holocaust.[5]

> Art's utopia, the counterfactual yet-to-come, is draped in black. It goes on being a recollection of the possible with a critical edge against the real; it is a kind of imaginary restitution of that catastrophe which is world history.[6]

A major problem in critical response to the Black Atlantic concept is the lack of awareness of its utopian nature, as a catalyst to thought and action, rather than as a hard-edged theoretical definition. The term has been rapidly canonised and institutionalised in the US academy and concretised as a formal space.[7] As Brent Hayes Edwards notes

> It is sometimes overlooked that Gilroy himself is careful to propose *black Atlantic* as a provisional or heuristic term of analysis, more in order to open up a certain theoretical space that would radically dislodge any inquiry grounded in singular frames—whether "race", "ethnicity", or "nation"—than in order to formalize that space.[8]

Although the term was never meant to be comprehensive, the areas missing from the analysis remain striking. As the editors of a recent volume of essays note, Gilroy's case studies focus on middle class male intellectuals in America (Alexander Crummell, Martin Delany, W.E.B Du Bois), make little of class and gender, largely ignore Latin America and appear somewhat oblivious to potential collusion between Black Nationalism and patriarchy. Crossing the sea tends to be the province of men, obscuring the importance of women, land and agency. In addition, the book's Americo-centrism appears paradoxical given the agenda of debunking the notion of African-American provincialism by taking the African-American experience as paradigmatic of the black diaspora.[9] More generally, the rapid adoption of the term as a shorthand for the cultural richness of the black diaspora tends to obscure the fact that these riches came at the cost of pain and suffering; slavery may be too high a price for the global dissemination of rap music.

How better to challenge Gilroy's thinking, therefore, than by a dystopian novel? In *Blonde Roots*, Bernardine Evaristo constructs a deeply felt and trenchant critique of the utopian qualities of Gilroy's model, in a revision which is also an act of homage and a creative extension to his work. Evaristo is not an American writer by nationality, but her novel engages with the legacy of slavery in North and South America and Europe, specifically critiquing the dominance of Anglo-American paradigms. In her African,

British and Afro-Brazilian family history Evaristo herself encapsulates the diasporic reach of the black Atlantic. Born in 1959 in South London, she is the daughter of a white mother and a black, Nigerian father, born in Cameroun in 1927, whose own father "returned" from Brazil to Lagos in 1888, when slavery was abolished. The epigraph to the novel evokes the long history of Portuguese chattel slavery:

> Remembering the 10 to 12 million Africans
> taken to Europe and the Americas as slaves
> . . . and their descendants
> 1444–1888 [10]

In 1444 Lançarote de Freitas landed 235 enslaved Africans in Lagos, Portugal, the first large group of slaves to be brought to Europe. In her semi-autobiographical verse-novel, *Lara*, Evaristo travels back 150 years, seven generations and three continents, telling the tale of Yorubas enslaved in Brazil, "emancipados" in colonial Nigeria and finally immigrants into Britain.[11] The novel includes multiple narratives describing other immigrant forebears, impoverished Irish Catholics and Germans (her mother's family), including one white ancestor who makes his way in London by boiling West Indian sugar night and day. It includes a rich Yoruba-Brazilian glossary, and a powerful evocation of the Brazilian Quarter in central Lagos. As the epigraph indicates, this is a family which has known transnational roots and routes, which has crossed several seas and is deeply imbricated in the flows and currents of the triangular trade. Lara is the short form of the Yoruba Omilara, meaning (as the novel's epigraph states): "the family is like water." Evaristo's verse novel *The Emperor's Babe*, set in multicultural Roman Londinium in 211 AD, also takes a very broad canvas to emphasise the antiquity of the black diaspora, and of the black presence in Britain, which was still largely absent from the history books in 2001 when the novel appeared. As its epigraph reads, quoting Oscar Wilde's maxim, "the only duty we have to history is to rewrite it."[12] The novel takes its cue from Peter Fryer's account of the presence of blacks in Britain long before the English came, and significantly it also introduces the topic of white slavery.[13] The heroine, Zuleika, a Sudanese Roman citizen who has an affair with the Libyan-born African Emperor Septimus Severus, is not a slave but an affluent cosmopolitan and a member of the ruling class. As Evaristo commented,

> Zuleika's husband Felix buys her two Scottish women as slaves and I was interested in the way Zuleika reacts to them. What struck me is how rarely we read about slavery as something that occurred outside of the black/white axis.[14]

The Emperor's Babe clearly anticipates Evaristo's 2008 novel. *Blonde Roots* is a classic reversal narrative, like *Lord of the Flies* (children as savage adults) or *Planet of the Apes* (animals rule men), essentially a "what if?" novel, in this case, "what if blacks had enslaved whites?" In interview Evaristo said that her intention was to make readers focus on what, if the tables had been turned historically and Africans had enslaved Europeans, that would mean for the way we view history.[15] In her account

> The slave trade is a subject that elicits strong responses including anger, defensiveness, resentment, self-righteousness, guilt, sadness. So I decided to ask the question What if? What if the history as we know it is turned on its head and Africans enslaved Europeans for four centuries? What if Africans assume the moral and intellectual high ground and notions of savagery and civilisation are inverted?[16]

This does not mean that the history of slavery is casually erased, however. Nor are its horrors scanted. As Evaristo argued, "It's a 'what if?' book but it's also a 'This is what was' book."[17]

The novel incorporates almost all the familiar elements of the slave narrative genre: capture, failed escape, Middle Passage (with slave insurrection, multiple deaths, rape, torture and mutilations), branding (18), slave auctions (33), family separation (23), renaming, whippings, the acquisition of literacy (20) and a final escape to freedom, to a long-established community of maroons. Along the way the heroine, Doris Scagglethorpe, kidnapped from the "Cabbage Coast" of Northern England (a replacement for the Gold Coast of Africa) is enslaved in "Londolo", a mixture of London and Mombasa, which has recognisable landmarks such as "Paddingto" and "Mayfah", but also a tropical climate and crocodiles in the "Temz." Doris works as a house slave, then a field slave, as a White Mammy to her master's son Nonso, in a sugar mill on a Caribbean plantation, and as a Topsy-like companion to Little Miracle, a thinly disguised caricature of Harriet Beecher Stowe's saintly Eva. (Though when Little Miracle threatens to send a disobedient Doris to the port brothel, Doris shoves her into the river, where her tight dress and heavy neck-rings ensure instant drowning.) Spirituals are sung, notably "Gahd save we grashus chief" (176) and "Should ole akwaintaunce be forgot" (215) and there are minstrels in "whyteface", their black faces smeared with chalk as they attempt the hop, skip and jump of Morris dancing, in clogs and bells. While the reversals certainly offer a counterfactual image of historical restitution, it is a risky strategy. On the plus side, as Stephanie Merritt argued in *The Observer*, the creation of a photographic negative in which black becomes white and vice versa, does maintain the shock of the atrocities of slavery.[18] But as Joan Smith observed in *The Times*, it also risks criminalising blacks by giving them some of the worst characteristics of eighteenth century Europeans.[19] Nor does the reader ever discover why blacks became dominant rather than whites, though they are described as having once sent their own people to the New World as slaves and bond servants (28), much as the British used transportation to stock the Carolinas with a labour force. Evaristo herself observed that it was important to remember that North Africans did enslave a million Europeans from the sixteenth to the nineteenth century, though that paled in comparison with the slave trade's twelve million, its creation of intergenerational slavery, and subsequent wholesale depletion of the resources of African countries.[20] Evaristo's imaginative reversals none the less maintain the reader's awareness of the main features of slavery, while compelling a continual translation between racialised spaces and cultures, which effectively transforms black into white and vice versa, propagating Gilroy's anti-essentialist agenda. The way in which renaming by masters destroys personal identity is vividly brought to life in the novel. It is often difficult for the reader to remember that Doris, renamed Omorenomwara, is white, that Ye Memé is a Dane, that Yomisi began life on a Bavarian wheat farm as Gertraude Shultz, or that Sitembile was taken hostage from a palace in Monaco in a war with the French.

The most startlingly original element in the novel however is the reorganisation of time and space. Evaristo makes the Middle Passage a metaphor for both temporal and geographical dislocation by setting events in an unspecified time (both futuristic and historical) and by rearranging the geography of the globe so that "Aphrika" and the "United Kingdom of Great Ambossa", though on the Equator, lie to the north of "Europa", whence "whyte" slaves are kidnapped by "blaks", to be exported across the Atlantic to work on the plantations of the "West Japanese Islands". By moving everything South, Evaristo effectively transfers the Black Atlantic from Northern to Southern hemispheres, correcting Gilroy's Anglophone bias, and relegating "Amarika" to the sidelines. Just as the concept of the Black Atlantic "dislocates the whole geographic and thematic focus of British cultural studies by shifting it to a space between national borders"[21] so Evaristo undercuts the centrality of African-American culture in the African diaspora, exposes the arbitrary nature of cultural values and questions the notion of a counterculture of modernity. As the title indicates the satire cuts in several directions. The fair-haired narrator longs for her roots, for cloudy skies and cabbages, much as one of Alex Haley's characters might yearn for yams. At the same time the reference to blonde roots showing through dyed-black hair evokes the satire on radical chic in the novel, in which free whites ape black appearance and fashions. In a sense Evaristo takes Gilroy at his word, and imagines a different world in which blacks are not enslaved, but the results are decidedly dystopian for both blacks and whites. The rich diasporan intermingling of cultures celebrated by Gilroy is little compensation for Doris, who suffers the full horrors of slavery. And in the example of Nonso, a drunken, dissolute planter, Evaristo charts the evil effects of slavery on the slave-holders.

Throughout the novel notions of modernity are questioned. In *The Black Atlantic* Gilroy alerted his readers to a non-Western experience of modernization induced by the suffering of the Middle Passage as a cataclysmic instance of dislocation and a sudden shift in the horizon of expectations. This African-American focus has been rightly critiqued as neglecting other African experiences of modernization. Walter Goebel and Saskia Schabio, for example, have challenged unified concepts of modernization from a postcolonial perspective.[22] Benita Parry, in particular, has invoked Marx's concept of the historical time of capitalism as involving a complex and differential temporality, so that modernity is not necessarily Western but rather coextensive with capitalism's worldwide consolidation.[23] As far as Gilroy's understanding of slavery as the entry into modernity is concerned, Evaristo's satirical world deliberately questions any such easy periodisation. Doris's escape on the Underground Railroad (the now-defunct London tube) apparently takes place in some unspecified future, yet the scene is also set with crinolines and bonnets, knee breeches, eighteenth century coffee houses, witch-burnings, and a quasi-Caribbean plantocracy. Contemporary colloquialisms ("glamazon"189) coexist with consciously archaic terms ("Baked chewetts" 53, "oftentimes" 114); tanning studios, hip hop and skateboarders share textual space with feudal landlords. The anachronism is even more obvious in the short story which was the germ of the novel, "Otakemehomelord.com", published in *The Guardian* in 2005, which transplanted slavery to the digital age.[24] In the short story Doris has a secret email account, Please!@ohtakemehomelord.com, on a free server set up by the not-for-profit Abolitionist's Co-op and protected by AntiMasterGuard (AMG). She worries that proslavery viruses operating in cyberspace may hunt out abolitionists, corrupt their hardware and hack into their conversations, but she also uses the internet for revenge by siphoning off funds from her master's account at the Tate Bank (her master has made a fortune from sugar) before escaping on the tube which has been abandoned in favour of futuristic air trains on radar-controlled pathways. In the novel times are similarly scrambled, though with less of a "sci-fi" emphasis. Coffee houses such as Coasta Coffee, Hut Tropicana, Café Shaka and Starbright (33) mimic contemporary London, though they also stage slave auctions, just like eighteenth century coffee houses in London and Liverpool.[25] Shuga is noted for its rumpaccino, and for the daily news relayed through talking drums, while bearing on its blackboard, the chalked advertisement, "Fresh slaves". The smells of tobacco, coffee, sugar and rum evoke the trades which were fed by slavery (34). The 1791 revolution in Haiti is mentioned (221) as a recent event, but slaves bear names which evoke black heroes and heroines from the fifteenth to the twentieth century: Shaka Zulu and his mentor Dingiswayo, Cleopatra, Cetewayo, Sonni Ali, Tutankhamun and Yaa Asantewa (178), the latter a Ghanaian ruler until 1921. On one level the technique challenges the legitimacy of all official histories, unsurprisingly given that the novel was completed in 2007, the bicentenary of the abolition of the slave trade, in the midst of bitter debates concerning reparations and the extent to which the profits of slavery still prop up Western economies. Anachronism prevents the easy separation of past and present. In *The Emperor's Babe*, the Armani and Versace Roman togas are a case in point.

Satirically the target is also, more generally, the British love affair with costume drama and the "heritage" industries, exemplified in "bonnet and bustle" movies and television, utopian shards in contemporary culture, which evoke a past which never was, with its horrors airbrushed out. Evaristo makes it clear that Doris was never really free, but a serf to Lord Percy, owner of the Montague estate, who is in cahoots with the slave traders. In other words, Britain was never a land of freedom, and there is nothing idyllic about its history, nor (if we translate the mirror imagery) African history, where aristocratic Africans also sold slaves. The family history of the aristocratic Montagues crosses *Jane Eyre* with *The Turn of the Screw* and several Dickensian novels: a wife who looked "suspiciously foreign" (53), went mad and was locked up in an attic, illegitimate children, a child who died in mysterious circumstances on a lake, and an adulterous governess. As Doris comments, the Montagues "gave our lives drama by association, glamour by proximity, status through acquaintance" (53). They offer a utopian image, not unlike Bloch's glossy magazines or fairy stories. In its scrambled, Medieval-Regency-Victorian quality, therefore, the novel calls attention to a delusive, mystified utopian history, rather like images of mythical African pasts, a history which prevents imaginative awareness of liberatory possibilities. As a result it also powerfully underlines the importance of economic class. For the poor, history may be much the same whether medieval or Victorian. The upper classes are robbers and criminals whatever the date. Indeed, given her Brazilian background, there may be a certain glee to Evaristo's description of the capture and enslavement of the King and Queen of Portugal and their entire family (63). This is restitutive history with a vengeance. Just as Parry argued that modernity is coextensive with capitalism's worldwide consolidation, so Evaristo sees the profit motive as the one constant in history. Doris notes that many of the slave traders in the "Business" (27) are Arabs, who came to "Slavery HQ" with impressive CVs detailing their exemplary horsemanship and skill at raiding villages for slaves, only to find their skills redundant in Ambossa "where the task of slavery was somewhat more managerial" (27). She is perfectly certain that the Ambossans will never give up "their cash cow" (5). The spoof advertisements in the novel target institutions which have been associated with profiting from slavery (by insuring slave ships for example) and which still flourish: Lloyds of Londolo, The General Council of Holy Men (aka the Synod of the Church of England) and Barings Bank (25). Throughout the novel, radically different moments of history are conjoined so that modernity is comprehensively scrambled in a Benita Parry model of differential temporality, cohering only as a result of the glue of capitalism. Gilroy will never read quite the same again. As a result Evaristo is able to construct the Black Atlantic less as a social imaginary than as a set of material conditions.

None the less cultural matters are not neglected. Following on from the treatment of time and space, the novel engages forcefully with three more of Gilroy's major preoccupations. The novel is divided into three books, firstly Doris's capture, enslavement and her first escape attempt; interrupted in the second book by the voice of a "blak" intellectual writing a pamphlet on the nature of the slave trade, in a parody of scientific racism; and finally a third book following her recapture and export to the sugar plantations on the other side of the Atlantic. The first focusses particularly on cultural values, the second on the collusion of Western rationalism with terror, and the third on the world that the slaves made, especially strong women slaves. In Book One, set in Londolo, "blak" is no longer a counterculture but dominant. The Ambossans consider the Whytes' belief in privacy and monogamy ample evidence of their inferiority, and "blak" cultural norms are the ones which hold sway. Evaristo turns a satiric eye on the cultural transmission of " blak" styles, the fashionable adaptations by "free whytes" of " blak" cultural icons, including music, "Aphro" hairstyles and dyes, skin-darkeners and nose-flattening jobs. An "Aphrikan" aesthetic dominates standards of beauty. For all its comic verve, the novel makes a serious comment on the construction and irreversible effects of racism, exemplified in Doris's self-hatred as a white. A slender strawberry blonde, she has "image issues" (31), is tormented by the nickname "Barbee", and keeps trying to forget that she is a size four figure with long blonde hair, a concave stomach, and slim nostrils—all marks of ugliness by the standards of the "glamorously fat" (3) Ambossan women. In parody of the mantra "black is beautiful" Doris stands before her mirror reciting

> I may be *fair* and *flaxen*. I may have *slim* nostrils and *slender* lips. I may have *oil-rich* hair and a *non-rotund* bottom. I may blush easily, go *rubicund* in the sun and have *covert yet mentally alert* blue eyes. Yes, I may be whyte. But I am whyte and I am beautiful. (32)

As a house servant she is told that she has to look "respectable" when she opens the door to guests, and therefore must appear topless, with her hair in plaited hoops. The poster advertising a reward for her capture describes her as a "scrawny blonde slave woman" (45). Fortunately for the Ambossans all scrawny blondes look alike, which facilitates her escape.

In Londolo the counterculture flourishes—but it is "whyte". Most of the free whites live in the crowded ghettoes of the "Vanilla Suburbs" as opposed to the spacious townhouses and compounds of the central "Chocolate Cities" (29), a reverse image of the American phenomenon of white flight to leafy suburbs from blighted black inner cities. Evaristo thus engages in witty dialogue with contemporary ways of "performing blackness" in urban-popular cultures and media, and with the discourse of whiteness as a trope of "minority culture". In the Burbs it is possible to buy exotic clothing (sporrans, knickerbockers, boleros and bustles) and "lovely plain food"

(30) without peppers or spices (Brussels sprouts, tapioca pudding, and of course cabbage). The Burbs also attract the cultural tourism of "blaks" from "Aphrika", effectively on township tours, gawking in anthropological fascination at the free whites from the safety of carriages escorted by Masai or Zulu warriors. Class remains an important factor complicating a racial reading of slavery. There are "poor blaks" living in shantytowns, many of them hostile to the slaves, at whom they shout, "Wigger, go home! You're taking our jobs!" (28). The reader has to translate black into white and vice versa to yield the historical referents (in this case South African township tours in the twentieth century, and American antebellum poor whites). In the Burbs there are also underground venues for "whyte" music, featuring madrigal boy bands and recorder recitals—not quite what Gilroy imagined as the musical diaspora. For Gilroy diasporic music is the supreme signifier of black countercultural modernity and (as Laura Chrisman has argued) he has a tendency to idealise music as categorically emancipatory for black expression.[26] But music can also be an obstacle to black self-realisation rather than a utopian anticipation of it. It has a highly visible commercial value. Later in the novel Ye Memé laments the way in which each of the boys of the community is dressed ("cotton pants worn so that the waist hung . . . beneath his bum" 204) and their fashion of calling themselves names like Bad Bwoy, Totallee Kross or Machete Monsta. For Ye Memé they are bent on self-destruction by adopting the poor role models of "dose wotless gang boys" (249). Rap carries no utopian charge here. When Dingiswayo describes himself, rapper-style, as irresistible to "de hos and bitches" (207) his adoptive mother whacks him on the head with a hefty iron pan, reducing him to childish tears.

One problem with the satiric method is that it tends to emphasise physicality rather than inner lives or emotions and therefore cuts in many different directions. While there are vigorous sideswipes at the slave holders, Ezinwene, the liberal-left abolitionist who facilitates Doris's escape, and embodies the condescension of the middle class do-gooder, is also physically caricatured, in her expensive tastes. For Ezinwene Doris is just one more fashion accessory, like her Ylang Ylang perfume, the cocoa butter with which she adorns her cinnamon skin, or her gold-capped teeth, each fashionably sharpened to a point. Evaristo clearly indicates here the way in which abolitionism could function as a liberatory fantasy in which freedom is represented as being handed over by whites to grateful blacks, crushing the agency of the latter and buttressing the moral superiority of the former. The corrective balance comes in the second book, where Evaristo gives the reader full access to the thought and emotions of a "blak" racist intellectual. The text is that of "The Flame", reflections on the nature of the slave trade, by Doris's master, Chief Kaga Konata Katamba (whose initials KKK are branded into her skin), also known as Bwana. The pamphlet, a supposed defence of slavery against abolitionists, advances a creed of pseudo-scientific racism and shares its name with a newspaper of the British far-right party, the National Front, indicating the long reach of racist ideology. It claims the rational high ground from the first page, beginning "I am a reasonable man and a man with reasons" (110) and is written "in defence of my rights" (110), describing its author as having gained access to objective truths through "Serious Contemplation, Erudite Debate, as well as Rigorous Scholarly research and the analysis of Vital Statistics" (112).

In interview Evaristo argued that anti-black racism, portraying Africans as less than human, or as savages, developed as a justification for and in tandem with the growth of the transatlantic slave trade.[27] Evaristo has acknowledged the influence of Peter Fryer's arguments that racism developed in the eighteenth century to provide a defensive ideology for the planter class, the slave-merchants and planters of the Caribbean, not merely to the rest of society but to justify themselves in their own eyes.[28] Edward Long's *History of Jamaica* (1774) is probably the first sustained example justifying slavery on the grounds that Africans were inherently inferior, in a text with overt pretensions to scientific rigour and authority. In Fryer's view, racism is not a causal factor in slavery, but develops in its defence. Whereas race prejudice tends to be scrappy, oral and confused, racism is transmitted by the written word and attempts to look "rational". Its functions are political and economic, as opposed to race prejudice's psychological and cultural functions. The pamphlet promotes the "civilising mission" justification of slavery (notoriously pilloried in Conrad's *Heart of Darkness*) in which whites supposedly rescue blacks from their own barbarity. Conrad also creates an image of Britons as slaves. The narrator, Marlow, imagines what the Romans must have thought when they arrived in Britain to be confronted with "cold, fog, tempests, disease, exile, and death" and envisages the depopulating effect on the area between Deal and Gravesend of Romans enslaving the locals.[29] In *Europa*, on his first slaving voyage, the Chief reacts similarly to the climate of the "grey Continent" (123), with its stormy and influenza-ridden coasts, parodies of the Western images of disease-ridden African jungles. He is horrified by the practice of criminals being hung, drawn and quartered (132), witch-burnings (135), beheadings (135) and the display of heads on poles (132), a direct reference to Conrad.[30] European history has little to boast of here. In the fields of the "dark heart of Europa" (13) Bwana notes sinister pagan idols with hair made of straw (scarecrows). The irrational "Europanes" are characterised as deeply superstitious, whereas Bwana's task is a "Mission of Liberation-the Saving of Souls" (121). Paradoxically he studs his defence of reason and science with thanksgivings to the gods (particularly Yemonja) who have providentially delivered him from shipwreck and death. The developed nation (here "blak") denies the coevalness of the other (here "Europa), stigmatising it as backward. Bwana is forthright:

> Dear Reader, the natives of those lands are just now emerging from the abominable depths of savagery which we civilised nations left behind in prehistoric times. (118)

A short essay on cranial anthropometry follows, "proving" that the hierarchy of races runs from Negroid, to Mongoloid and (lowest) Caucasoinid, in which the skull is too narrow, with a small brain and a weak orthognathous jaw, effectively a Neo-Primate, unable to feel pain as the Chief does. Even worse he describes the natives as "hirsute beyond decency", their visible flesh covered "in hideous hair like that of a monkey or gorilla" (126). It was common in the eighteenth and nineteenth century for skull-shapes to be analysed as an index of human development.[31] The father of craniology, Johann Friedrich Blumenbach coined the term "Caucasian" to describe white skulls, preferring these to those he called "Mongolian" and "Ethiopian". Pieter Camper then introduced the notion of the "facial angle" (the extent to which the jaw juts out) thought to indicate a higher forehead, bigger brain and greater degree of intelligence and beauty. The resultant popular image was of a hierarchy as the angle grew wider, in which Europeans were top, followed by Indians, Africans and lastly apes. In Conrad's novella, famously, a doctor measures the head of Marlow, the narrator, with callipers.[32] Chief Bwana's comment on the hairiness of the "Europanes" reveals the irrationality of racial classification. As Winthrop D. Jordan has pointed out, if the amount of bodily hair had been chosen as the criterion of ranking, Africans would have come out top, followed by Indians, Europeans and apes.[33] When Europeans set out to rank the varieties of man, their decision that the white was at the top and the black at the bottom was not dictated by the facts of biology. While tracing his path towards "Property, Prosperity, and Enlightenment" (112) Bwana engages in strenuous moral gymnastics to rationalise his inhumanity and portray himself in a rosy light, skipping over the details of the close-packed slave voyage with its heavy casualties, to proclaim that

> Dear Reader—suffice it to say that running a slaver meant having to be responsible for the welfare of the cargo—rather as a parent for its children. (146)

In some respects this section of the novel runs closest to Gilroy, who argued that

> The overcoming of scientific racism (one of modernity's more durable intellectual products) and its post-war transmutation into newer cultural forms that stress complex difference rather than simple biological hierarchy may provide a telling, concrete example of what scepticism towards the grand narratives of scientific reason adds up to.[34]

But whereas Gilroy can only deride rationalism in a rational manner, the novelist has a distinct advantage. The pamphlet is most striking for its positioning. Gilroy argues that racial terror is not just compatible with Western rationality but cheerfully complicit with it. Evaristo deliberately positions

the pamphlet between the scene at the close of Book One where Doris, terror-stricken, thinks she is about to be recaptured by Bwana, and the moment
when the chief does recapture her, and she suffers a brutal whipping. The
reader leaves Doris trembling with terror at the close of Book One and
moves to the pseudo-rational pamphlet, remaining on a cliff-hanger before
the story takes up again, recounting her desperate flight, brutal recapture
and the administration of the sentence of 201 lashes. Anxiety concerning
her fate permeates the reader's experience of the pamphlet. Bwana resur-
faces briefly at the whipping, still claiming the moral high ground: "The
humane thing would have been to finish her off. But I was not and will
never be a murderer (170).

In the final book of the novel, Evaristo leaves the "rational" male behind,
to present a world in which women characters dominate. Where Gilroy's
model tends to focus on the male, obscuring the role of women, land and
local agency, Evaristo brings women firmly back on board. Transported
across the Atlantic to the sugar plantation, Doris finds herself in a tight-knit
community of fellow slaves. The slaves' quarter is described as "like another
world on a Sunday; busy, lively, normal" (185) with children playing games,
and adults gossiping and singing, weaving and gardening. The emphasis is
on the resilience and resistance of the slave community, and their attempts
to assure the survival of their original culture. Under the pretence of a Voo-
doo mass (the official Ambossan creed) they celebrate a Christian service,
preserving their own customs and beliefs. In the slave quarter, as Doris says,
"we ran *tings*, more or less" (191). After two years Doris has become accli-
matised to an alarming degree, in the world the slaves have made (211). She
evokes a feeling of mutual solidarity and even a degree of agency. "It was
almost as if our lives were normal. As if we were free" (211).

Throughout there is an emphasis on strong women and on families surviving and clinging together despite the odds, culminating in a sentimental
series of reunions reminiscent of the end of *Uncle Tom's Cabin*. Doris is
reunited with her sister, her nephews and her lost husband (now a maroon
leader.) But sentimentality is evoked only to be scotched. It is tempting
to see in the characterisation here a feminist corrective to Gilroy's male
model, particularly in the portrayal of the proud slave matriarch Ye Memé
and her friend Ma Majani, raising fatherless families with strict religious
and moral discipline and struggling against the odds to prevent their sons
becoming the irresponsible rappers of Gilroy's musical utopia. In the final
analysis, however, class solidarity is prioritised over gender. The women's
apparent sisterly feeling for Doris is immediately threatened when they discover her former identity as an urban, literate house slave. Ye Memé and
her friends are "blue-collar" (182) slaves, doing heavy mechanical work in
the "factory quarter" (176) of sugar mill, boiling house, water mill and dis-
tillery. When Doris's past is revealed, she fears for a moment that Ye Memé
will knock her out as a "lyar an deceeva" (247). Doris does gain a sister,
but in the shape of Sharon, now the plantation owner's concubine, part of

"the slave aristocracy" (214), depicted resplendent in frothy cream taffeta and heavy gold jewellery. Her sons are slave drivers and overseers. Doris escapes to freedom, but it is Ye Memé who pays the price. When the escape is discovered she is whipped, tortured and gets her tongue cut out.

Above all the plantation episode turns towards a fresh emphasis on slavery as a business, with a sustained evocation of the hard labour attending the industrial processes of sugar refining (180). House slaves and field slaves are part of one connected economic system. Even worse Doris is warned to be careful what she says; some slaves are treacherous and will betray for money (194). The utopian image of a community with a degree of agency, forging its own new social practices, while clinging to cultural survivals, is just that, utopian. In the end, it is capitalist practices which offer the only means of real resistance. To outwit her owners Doris has to play them at their own game. In Londolo Doris had been trained as a skilled bookkeeper and when Nonso realises that his father is planning to audit the plantation accounts, he brings her back from the mill to the comfort of the Big House so that she can save his bacon by cooking the books. This gives Doris the chance to erase from the records the names of the slaves whom Nonso planned to sell, and thus to help them escape. Finally, therefore she wields power not because of any cultural solidarity or utopian inspiration, but by turning the weapons of capital back upon itself. Modern profit making capitalism is the distinctive element in slavery—and it continues into the present. At the end of the novel we are told that the Chief's descendants still own the sugar estate and are among the grandest and wealthiest families in Great Ambossa, where they reside. Implicitly, Evaristo acknowledges here the risk that a reconceptualisation of culture as transnational, going beyond national borders, may be just what corporate capitalism ordered, replacing nation states with a borderless space allowing for a free flow of capital. Arguably, therefore, satire and dystopian imaginings are politically more strategic than utopianism, because they allow the writer to register the strength of capitalist and materialist domination.

9 Disaster Utopias
Chitra Divakaruni, *One Amazing Thing*

As Dubus and Faludi emphasise in their different ways, in the immediate aftermath of 9/11 the US media made the event more like the movies than the reality, telling an old story reminiscent of those disaster action movies in which what mattered was accomplished by masculine heroes, largely professionals and men of action.

> Lost in this epic version was the fact that most people effectively evacuated themselves from the towers and from the area without much uniformed assistance, and those who rescued others included unathletic gay men, older women executives, school principals, Hasidic Jews in distinctly unheroic outfits, a gang of accountants carrying a paralyzed coworker down sixty-nine flights of stairs, young men who stepped up while police were overwhelmed, homeless people, nurses, and chauffeurs. Everyone, in other words, as usual in disaster.[1]

For Rebecca Solnit, civil society had triumphed in the hours and days after the attacks, but failed in the face of more familiar stories told by the government, and retold again and again by the media. The spirit of brave resolve and the sense of solidarity were overwhelmed by the Bush administration's encouragement to people to stay home, go shopping, buy big cars, support wars, spy on their neighbours and live in fear of further attacks.[2] While 9/11 was certainly a moment of intense anxiety and fear, Solnit emphasises the group solidarity involved when 25,000 people helped each other in an orderly evacuation of the towers; people on the long descent of the stairs gave way to injured people being brought down; an armada of little boats spontaneously formed to evacuate the south tip of Manhattan; citizens in the streets rallied to help the wounded and stranded; and commissaries, supply chains and collection sites sprang up to support workers at Ground Zero. Volunteers came from all over North America, donations from around the world, as people sought a sense of connection in helping others, a sense of being valued, needed and part of something larger than themselves. Most people experience altruism not as self-sacrifice but as both giving and receiving.

The streets of New York were flooded with people desperate to find something to give, to do, someone to help, some way to matter. In a sense they were taking care of themselves, but a society in which this was how people ordinarily did so would be a paradise indeed.[3]

In short, as Solnit's title proclaims, disaster may be utopian, *A Paradise Built in Hell*.

The dominant wisdom would argue otherwise. In *The Shock Doctrine: The Rise of Disaster Capitalism* Naomi Klein argues for a decidedly dystopian view of disaster which she sees as an opportunity for the implementation of brutal free-market programs when the public have been disorientated by wars, coups or natural disasters. Klein cites as an example Milton Friedman's comment in the wake of Hurricane Katrina, on the ruin of the New Orleans school system. "This is a tragedy. It is also an opportunity to radically reform the education system."[4] In her argument neo-liberal economics dominates societies not through a peaceful battle of ideas but through a string of shocks, beginning with a collective trauma which leaves people unable to resist an economic program (privatization, deregulation, cuts in social services, pro-corporate policies) often backed by torture and terror. Klein's examples include the other 9/11 (the 1973 coup in Chile), US Intervention in Kosovo, the Tiananmen Square uprising, the Iraqi war, and the tsunami of 2004 among others. In terms of the Iraqi war, her views were persuasive, demonstrating how deeply enmeshed the private sector has been with the war, from surveillance cameras to biometric technologies, and privately built detention centres.[5] The auctioning of land to foreign corporations in the wake of the tsunami also appeared to be a paradigmatic case of disaster restructuring.[6] Free market economics thus appear to rely on social upheaval and an aftermath to disaster in which people are dazed, helpless and dependent on outside sources of relief. Charles E. Fritz (who carried out methodical investigations of dozens of disasters) noted that the conventional belief is that disaster leads to mass panic, wild stampedes, looting, selfish behaviour, social conflict and widespread immorality. Klein herself describes New Yorkers after 9/11 as in a state of "profound disorientation, extreme fear and anxiety, and collective regression."[7] As Solnit comments, "it's a surprisingly disempowering portrait for the Left".[8]

In fact Klein's case is based on unexamined and false assumptions about post-disaster reactions. Disaster sociologist Kathleen Tierney argues that it is not the public who panic but the ruling classes. "Elite panic" is the problem. "It is the few who behave badly and the many who rise to the occasion".[9] Those who are afraid of the poor, minorities or migrants exacerbate the disaster, memorably in the case of Hurricane Katrina, where elite panic, fed by racism, reached enormous levels, with the victims of the hurricane portrayed as menaces and monsters. As Charles E. Fritz established, however, altruism is much more typical in the wake of disaster.[10] Movement towards the disaster scene is more significant than panicked flight, and "tend and befriend" more common than "fight and flight". Disaster involves sharing loss, danger and deprivation and produces intimate group solidarity among survivors, and a source of emotional and physical support. In Fritz's view people are often already surviving a very different disaster that consists of the social order enforced upon them from above and out-side. "Everyday life is already a disaster of sorts, one from which actual disaster liberates us."[11] The result may be the evolution of a set of values to which all subscribe, merging individual and social needs. In disaster it is relatively easy to know who to be and what to do; it is everyday life that is hard with its complications and ambiguities and problems that resist easy solutions. Michael Barkin coined the term "disaster utopia" in 1974, argu-ing that disaster produces the questioning required for social change.[12] In his argument the survivors of disaster often experience moments of intense warmth, community and comradeship, an alternative to the alienations and isolation of ordinary life. Solnit notes that "Utopia is in trouble these days" with many people no longer believing that a better world is possible.[13] But while she acknowledges that a certain type of utopian idealism has died, the belief that we can erase everything and start over, she contends that utopia has evolved into more viable, modest versions. Her book examines ubiquitous, if fleeting, utopias that are neither coerced nor countercultural: disaster utopias.

In short, Solnit's argument is that disasters provide glimpses of utopia, rediscoveries of altruism, civic life, engagement, grassroots community and meaningful work. From the San Francisco earthquake of 1906 through the 1917 Halifax explosion, the 1985 Mexican earthquake, 9/11 and Hurricane Katrina (among others) she argues that disaster shows us that human nature is not necessarily as bad as we imagine, and that life can be good when the state breaks down. Disaster can promote social change. In Nicaragua, for example, the earthquake only allowed Somoza to strengthen his power tem-porarily before he was brought down. In Mexico the disaster utopia lasted; citizens discovered their own power and reshaped their nation.

> Horrible in itself, disaster is sometimes a door back into paradise, the paradise at least in which we are who we hope to be, do the work we desire, and are each our sister's and brother's keeper.[14]

In this respect story has a crucial role. The image of the selfish, panicking and regressively savage survivor has little truth to it. The worst behaviour is on the part of those who believe others will behave savagely and who take pre-emptive defensive measures. Their beliefs betray them to violence. Changing the story, diminishing the gap between common beliefs and actual disaster behaviour could change a great deal more. Solnit's account is studded with hundreds of stories of ordinary people who rose to the challenge of disaster, and she argues that stories have a powerful role in changing beliefs and in connecting those to whom they are narrated. She cites a friend's account of being trapped in a terrible fog in California, with all traffic halted on the highway. For two days her friend was stranded in a small diner with many others. Although food and water began to run out, the experience was positive.

> The people gathered there had little in common, but they all opened up, began to tell each other the stories of their lives.[15]

By the time the road reopened they were reluctant to leave; it was the first time her friend's husband, a Native American, had felt a sense of belonging in society at large. Disaster created an intensely absorbing experience, a feeling of immersion in the present and solidarity with others.

Chitra Divakaruni's 2009 novel, *One Amazing Thing*, sets out to investigate the role of story in relation to disaster. In the novel nine characters are trapped in the basement of an Indian consulate's visa department following an earthquake in San Francisco. The location, a state building which has collapsed, is emblematic. The Indian official, Mr Mangalam, and his secretary Malathi cede control of the group to Cameron Grant, an African-American war veteran; state structures of leadership have collapsed from the very beginning. The others in the group have little in common: Jiang, a Chinese-American grandmother and her granddaughter, Lily, a teenage Goth; Tariq, an American Muslim, newly politicised by 9/11; Mr and Mrs Pritchett, moneyed white Americans; and Uma, an Indian-American student of literature, who comments that it is like "a mini UN summit."[16] All are stuck in the queue for a visa, anxiously watching that nobody takes their place and frustrated by Kafkaesque bureaucratic slowness. Divakaruni was drawn to the topic by her own experience. She was closely involved with the survivors of Hurricane Katrina, and was herself evacuated during Hurricane Rita, during which she was stuck in a mass of people on the interstate for ten hours with the hurricane heading straight for them. She saw how it brought out the worst in some people. Some were getting into fist fights, toting guns and calling each other names.

> And other people it just brought out the best in them. They were sharing water, they were trying to comfort families with children, they were just being wonderful. And I said, there's something here that I have to explore in a novel.[17]

At first glance Divakaruni's novel might appear to have more in common with Klein than Solnit. In the wake of the earthquake, suspicion and distrust are general; violence erupts almost immediately. Cameron, aware that the door may be holding up the ceiling and that it is important not to open it precipitately, has to knock out Tariq, who has disputed his authority and lunged for the door. Malathi fears Cameron purely because he is black, while Uma assumes that Tariq is violent because he is Muslim. Though they pool their supplies of food and drink, Uma suspects that some of them have hidden supplies (and is subsequently proved correct). Malathi initially refuses to provide her sari to bandage broken and injured limbs then shoots Uma a look of hate while handing it over; and initially nobody admits to possessing any form of pain relief, though Mrs Pritchard is well-provided with Xanax. On regaining consciousness Tariq announces that he will kill Cameron; Uma resolves to share nothing more with him. Mangalam lies that there are no additional water supplies in order to conceal the existence of his private bathroom (and whisky supply); Malathi (infuriated by his attempt to kiss her) promptly denounces him. Mr Pritchett is intent on smoking even though there may be a gas leak. He and his wife (who has previously overdosed) fight when he tries to take away her pills; Malathi makes him return them. Mangalam reproaches her and when she lambasts him in Tamil, slaps her; Lily launches herself at him, raking his cheek; and Tariq comes to her defence. Cameron's attempt to intervene peacefully ends up with Tariq punching him in what swiftly becomes a general melee. As disaster survivors they appear to conform to the popular stereotype of regressive, selfish behaviour, violence and panic. For Uma they have all turned into savages; "it was like their very own *Lord of the Flies*" (67).

What alters the situation, restoring a degree of order and eventually building a community is story. Story bridges the gap between the individuals which has bred violence. Uma, who has been studying *The Canterbury Tales*, suggests that to focus their minds and avoid taking out their stress on each other, each of them should narrate an important story from their own lives, the experience of one amazing thing (69). The nine stories follow, each with a pause in which the characters comment or react in the frame tale. It is no accident that Cameron is the master of ceremonies who decides the order in which the tales are told. The model for the story cycle with frame tale, while not unlike *The Canterbury Tales,* is more closely connected to Boccaccio's *Decameron*. Chaucer's pilgrims tell tales to amuse themselves on their way to Canterbury. Boccaccio's *Decameron* is a disaster utopia.

The *Decameron*, written in the mid-1350s, is not the first example of the story cycle with frame tale; the format can be traced back through Spanish, Arabic, and Persian works to the Indian *Panchatantra*. Cycles of this nature often confront the figure of death, as in *The Thousand and One Nights* where Scheherazade tells a tale each night to delay dawn execution, and the *Decameron*, written in response to the Black Death. As Richard F. Kuhns comments, the model in which stories interrupt the everyday frame has the result of expanding the sense of time. To tell a story is "to stand outside time in the sense of lifetime time, moving towards death."[18] In the *Decameron* the Black Death has produced a social earthquake; plague is in Florence, and normal restraints on conduct have given way to selfish and indulgent actions and a loss of sexual inhibitions. Seven women and three men flee the city for a villa near Fiesole where over ten days the ten narrate 100 stories (plus one more narrated by the author himself, whose

presence is felt at the beginning and end of each day.) Although the stories are sometimes bawdy, emphasising physical and emotional vitality as
opposed to death, the "brigata", the little company of friends, maintain
their own restraint and moral decorum. The storytellers are located in a
garden in spring, occupying themselves with games, songs and dances, in
a little utopia of order and pleasure. Storytelling is just one of the games
played in the garden. In this way the group create a fiction of perfect order
with each day dedicated to a particular theme, in a context which is hierarchical but not authoritative, pleasurable but not promiscuous, free but not
anarchic, a modest utopia. [19]

Divakaruni's story cycle is on a smaller scale, covering only a couple of
days, but also has ten narrators (Malathi insists that Mr Mangalam translate
her story as she tells it in Tamil), and stories which are full of sexual desire
and vitality as well as darker topics. Like *The Canterbury Tales* and the
Decameron it involves a company of travellers (here, would be travellers to
India) who meet by chance and tell stories linked by connecting passages in
the present, with one of the tellers acting as the director. Unlike the authors
of other story cycles, Divakaruni, however, does not allow her characters
to tell their stories in their own voices, even when competence in English
is not a factor. The third person narrator assumes control, filling in some
missing details, supplying memories for several characters, and producing a
sense of many voices merging into one. The narrator is not, however omniscient, but only partially knowing. In response to Jiang's account of her
pregnancy, for example, the narrator wonders for a paragraph how she felt
about the event, whether she was joyful, worried, resentful or resigned (82).
It is almost as if the narrator became a reader, pondering the story while
it is still in mid-narration. The overall effect is to create a narrative style
which produces a community of tale-tellers and receivers, without authoritative exegesis. The reader never knows, for example, whether the group
are rescued, or die. As a result the stories largely sidestep any clear moral.
Indeed, Uma recalls her mother's distaste for Aesop's fable of the ant and
the cricket, with its apparent anti-altruistic moral, her voice indignant as the
ant sent the cricket off into the winter to die (24). Just as in the *Decameron*
these stories offer "a kind of education against an absolutism of truth and
morality"[20] with some stories explicitly revising earlier false impressions or
hasty judgements. Mangalam's story corrects Malathi's image of him, for
example; Mr Pritchett's explains to his wife why he became materialistic;
Jiang's revises her granddaughter's image of her. Uma, Tariq and Cameron are singleton-storytellers, and their stories remain incomplete. The
stories do not merely expand time, in the sense of everyday time leading
to death (though because they concern life experiences several cover a considerable space of historical time), but also space. Although the horizon is
completely blocked and it is dangerous even to open a door, the stories open
out into a whole succession of other worlds: Chinese Calcutta, underclass
America, Coimbatore, American Muslims, Delhi, the African-American

community, the world of art and, at the end, the constellations and cosmos. Story explodes the confining frame and offers escape from their situation. Most of the stories portray hostile relations between different ethnic, gendered or social communities: African-Americans against the white world, Muslims persecuted after 9/11, caste hostilities and Chinese versus Hindus in India, women subjected to patriarchal regimes, with a repeated motif of characters ineffectually resisting a social order enforced upon them from above. The pauses between the stories, and the opportunity presented for commentary and reflection, suggest a model of narrative in which story is envisaged as a way of thinking through and resolving human conflicts and contradictions, revising and reconsidering along the way.

One structural element, however, is crucially different to Boccaccio, or, indeed, Chaucer. Boccaccio hardly varies the frame/tale relation over the ten days. It is a vision of order which produces utopia. Divakaruni proceeds otherwise, progressively eroding the distinction between frame tale and inset story, in parallel with the further collapses of the shelter occupied by the group. The survivors bond into a community in proportion as the disaster escalates in the collapse of material structures, and the narrative structures also merge into each other, creating community and a fleeting utopia out of disaster and collapse, rather than from order and structure. (Significantly, Uma is reading "The Wife of Bath's Tale" but turns from it to the events in the passport office. The Wife of Bath's tale is unusual in Chaucer's work in that it is a point where frame and inset story almost reverse; the Wife's prologue, describing her own life experience with five husbands, is much longer and more interesting a story than the short tale she subsequently tells.) In this connection the spatial organisation of the basement in which they are trapped is unobtrusively symbolic. There are four doorways (entrance, bathroom, and two doors to Mangalam's office). Each offers a frame of refuge during aftershocks; doorframes are the safest places to be in an earthquake. In the opening sequence, keeping the entrance door closed in its frame is paramount. The door may be supporting their part of the room. If it were to be opened suddenly, something else might collapse. But for a door to be a refuge it has to be opened. When the time comes to open the door, it sticks and all the able bodied have to cooperate to pull together, collapsing in a mass when it finally flies open. Tariq rushes recklessly out and is buried by fallen rubble. Again the group pull together and combine to rescue him. Lily risks her life to climb over the pile of rubble, using story as a refuge in her mind. "'*I'm Gulliver*' she tells herself. '*This is a mountain in Lilliput*.' Making it into a fantasy helped a little" (52). Later, ominous creakings and aftershocks become more common and the group have to shelter in the three other doorways. When Tariq's story is interrupted by an aftershock in the frame tale, the survivors rush into the doorframes, almost as if they were moving spatially from inset back to frame tale. Eventually frame and inset merge as Cameron is narrating. Cameron describes how he was in the consulate to apply for a visa to visit

[handwritten marginal note: Stories as refuge.]

an orphan he is sponsoring and continues "Then the earthquake struck and–." (200). The chapter ends on the dash, and the ensuing one continues in the frame tale:

> It was as though the giant in the earth had heard Cameron speak his name. (201)

A huge aftershock sends everyone to their doorways, ending his story. As the structure of the building undergoes successive collapses, so the stories become repeatedly interrupted or unfinished, but at the same time the bonds between the survivors strengthen, the barriers of race, class or gender break down, and the walls between individuals crumble. Altruism increases; the store of food is mysteriously replenished as individuals stop hoarding their own supplies (154); dry clothes are shared with those caught in the rising waters (161); they become physically closer. Lily offers Tariq a place to stay; Uma hugs Cameron; the group splits up into different threesomes to occupy the doorways, cooperating without any need for instruction. They have become a closely bonded, cooperative group, looking out for each other. Divakaruni has commented that

Story creates community

> I believe strongly in the power of story in creating a community. It is when we learn about the core of the lives of strangers that they become family to us.[21]

Disaster liberates.

But what of the inset stories themselves? How do the stories accomplish this bonding process? Although Divakaruni had not read Solnit when she wrote the novel she commented in a later interview that Solnit's premise that everyday life is "already a disaster of sorts from which actual disaster liberates us" corroborated her own understanding of her novel's action.[21] Despite the emphasis on bonding into community the novel is a far cry from any form of heart-warming, Oprahfied uplift. The stories are of lost loves (Jiang, Mangalam, Malathi); war and persecution (Jiang, Tariq, Cameron); wretched childhoods which are not overcome (Cameron, Mr Pritchett); and quests for economic or self-improvement which backfire spectacularly (Cameron, Lily, Malathi). The stories also darken as the novel advances, becoming progressively death-saturated. The final three feature a near-death experience with attendant ghost (Mrs Pritchett); a haunting by an aborted child plus multiple deaths in Vietnam (Cameron) and Uma's last words to her dying friend Jeri. While the stories stand alone, their meaning is linked to reception and context. Listeners' reactions alter each story as the action unfolds, changing its meaning. Interpreting a story depends not only on its internal economy, symbol and content, but also on the reactions of the listeners and the ways in which any single story relates to those that follow. And the stories alter the ways the characters understand their world.

Jiang's story, the first, takes the reader across the threshold from frame to inset tale, introducing her listeners to a secret house in Calcutta's Chinatown. An inconspicuous low door, just like its neighbours, opens onto a brick wall, the spirit wall built on Feng Shui principles for the purpose of deflecting the outsider's gaze. Beyond lies a beautiful courtyard with mango trees and roses, and a central fountain, around which on full moon nights there are parties, games and poetry reading—a world not unlike that of the *Decameron*. As prosperous leather workers, the Calcutta Chinese wall themselves off from their neighbours, in a secret world. But Jiang falls in love with Mohit Das, a Hindu Bengali, to the consternation of their families, each of whom prays to their respective gods to end the relationship. Three days later the outbreak of the Sino-Indian war of 1962 and the attendant persecution and internment of the Chinese minority accomplishes their wishes. Mohit gives up and Jiang is married off in the blink of an eye to a total stranger in order to secure a safe exit ticket to America. She says little of her subsequent emotions, deflecting the curiosity of the others with a well-crafted tale. Jiang's story also operates on Feng Shui principles; her internal walls remain firmly in place. In America Jiang and her husband are almost as confined as in India. Jiang need never leave Chinatown, which provides schools, friends, markets and movie theatres, and she gives up English, communicating with her grandchildren only in Mandarin. Hers is a story in which the walls between and within people appear to be unshakable. In a sense she tells her story to avoid communicating her intimate emotions. It is only now, as a widow, that she is experiencing a desire to return to Calcutta, but at the end of the story she closes off further analysis.

> "Why am I going?" Jiang said. She shrugged and spread her hands. "Not sure. End of story." (84)

But it is not the end of the story. In the silence as she stops talking, "each member of the company—for listening had made them into that" (85) is busy with his or her own thoughts. Jiang's defensive story has brought the listeners together, and each now connects it to parts of their own life stories. Tariq, newly politicised after 9/11, considers the perfidiousness of governments which turn on their minority groups. Malathi regrets her own family, left behind in India; Mangalam wonders if, like his own, marriage between Mohit and Jiang would have killed passion stone dead; Lily is astounded to discover her grandmother's fluent English; Mrs Pritchett (who gave up her dream of running a bakery to marry Mr Pritchett) reacts with longing to the description of the cakes enjoyed by Jiang and Mohit at Flury's bakery. Cameron is non-committal (later we learn that he too had abandoned the woman he loved). Uma thinks that if people were houses, Cameron would be as secretive as Jiang's former home. "Who lived within his shuttered inner rooms?" (87). But suddenly Jiang pulls up the shutters and continues her story. Stuck in an arranged marriage with small children, hard work and constant fatigue there was, she says, no time for romance, but after four years when her husband was taken sick she astonished herself by crying out, "Don't die. I love you" (89). In the everyday disaster of her life she did find happiness, and it is happiness described as the result of barriers breaking down and internal walls collapsing. Looking back she could not pinpoint any special time when it had happened.

> That's what is amazing. We can change completely and not recognise it.We think terrible events have made us into stone. But love slips in like a chisel—and suddenly it is an axe, breaking us into pieces from the inside. (90)

Many of the stories are about a similar "inner tectonic shift" (17) as Malathi describes love, though not all are as optimistic as Jiang's, as the companion tale demonstrates. Mr Pritchett makes no response to Jiang's tale but instead immediately volunteers his own, a wretched story of childhood poverty, the death of a beloved kitten, a mother both loved and loathed, and a lifelong retreat from emotion. Mr Pritchett, an accountant, owes his unlikely name, Lancelot, to his mother's fascination with *King Arthur and His Knights of the Round Table*, "its complicated cat's cradle of stories" (96). The subtitle of the *Decameron*, *Prencipe Galeotti*, refers to Lancelot's best friend and mentor, Galehaut, in whose grave he was buried. Once a lover of stories, Lancelot Pritchett has closed them off and found solace instead in the world of mathematics, and in the cold reliability of numbers. Though his math problems are posed like stories, involving Aunt Anna driving from Boston to Philadelphia at a certain speed, or a bathtub where the stopper doesn't quite fit, and the time it takes to fill it, the words transform themselves into numbers "that can be trusted to perform the way they're supposed to" (105). Mr Pritchett has concealed his past and his emotions for years but Jiang's story—narrated by an equally secretive individual—opens the way for him to admit to them, and to communicate to his wife why worldly success meant so much to him, and why he argued that the future was all that mattered. Mrs Pritchett goes over to join him, but to his disappointment offers no comment, no validation of his boyhood suffering, and the others remain silent, uncomfortably aware of a wound that has not healed.

At this point the stage is set for some decidedly necessary comic relief. Malathi's rueful, self-mocking account of her beautification in Miss Lola's Lovely Ladies Salon, and her subsequent employment as a beautician, is voiced by Mr Mangalam, forced to translate from Tamil. As a result the dapper Lothario finds himself announcing that he would "require more work than my sisters" (109), and that a sari had to be pinned on him "to manufacture curves where none had existed before" (111), not to mention offering a detailed account of depilation, skin-bleaching, exfoliation and the application of slatherings of hair oil and face creams so that in the

Bridal Special Silver Level with Hair Oil photograph he can pass as one of Lola's lovely ladies (111). It is a whole ritual of vengeful humiliation on the part of Malathi, incensed by his adulterous flirtation. The narrative is doubled, mocking both Mangalam himself and "the complex and painful process of improving upon nature" (110) in the salon, satirising the ways in which women are forced to conform to oppressive standards of beauty in order to land a rich husband.

The quest for perfection has its more serious consequences, however. The story sets up a clear dichotomy between idealistic and pessimistic images of human nature. Mrs Vani Balan, a regular visitor to the salon, is horrified when her idealistic son Ravi starts a school to improve the lives of illiterate girls, and even more so when he extends the project to the family servants. The latter are largely impervious to the lure of literacy. Only the maid, Nirmala, proves a ready pupil and promptly falls in love with Ravi. Malathi has already poured scorn on Ravi's father, an adulterous chaser of secretaries (a pointed dig at Mangalam) and she portrays Ravi as his idealistic opposite, with no plans to compromise Nirmala. Challenged by his mother, Ravi declares that rigid class boundaries are the bane of Indian society and should be broken down, and praises her virtue and intelligence, "her belief in the goodness of the world, and her willingness to improve herself." (118) Mrs Balan appears initially to subscribe to Ravi's vision, and instructs Malathi to work on Nirmala to make her as beautiful as possible (119), but then takes her on a visit to her playboy brother, Gopalan, who promptly seduces Nirmala, who confounds Ravi's view of her innate goodness by allowing Gopalan to install her overnight as his mistress. Physical and educational improvement apparently leads to moral downfall, a decidedly anti-utopian image of human nature. Worse, by "improving" Nirmala, Malathi feels that she had contributed to her fate. When Mrs Balan returns to the salon for a permanent wave, ready for Ravi's engagement party to the bride she has selected for him, Malathi wreaks a terrible revenge, applying the wrong strength of lotion to her hair to ensure that it all falls out. Lola detects the plot by the smell of the lotion, but collaborates by offering Mrs Balan a pedicure to make sure that the chemicals have enough time to produce their full results. The story is thus a double revenge, on a man (Mangalam) in the frame and a woman, in the tale itself. The humiliation of Mrs Balan is contemporaneous with that of Mr Mangalam. Male and female boundaries are crossed so that the reader hears the tale as if from a man and a woman at the same time, with its targets also both male and female. Paradoxically, the result of Malathi's revenge is a distinct improvement in her own situation; to ensure her safety the kindly Lola finances a move to Hyderabad, English lessons and employment in America.

When the story ends, Uma does not want to return to the present, lost in a dream of Lola's pink salon, with its herbal shampoos, sandalwood paste and "the calm ministering hands of Lola's girls" (127). Story has provided an escape from their plight. But with the exception perhaps of Lola,

Malathi's story appears to confirm a low estimation of human character, in which improvement is neither possible nor desirable. When the others discuss the story Mrs Pritchett, Jiang and Lily focus on the women characters, and in particular Mrs Balan's cruelty. For Jiang the reason is class; Nirmala was a servant and therefore a lesser being. But Tariq raises the question on everyone's mind. "Why would Nirmala do something so stupid, give up Ravi for a creep like Gopalan?" (128). The women understand her better. Wealthy Mrs Pritchett ascribes it to the love of luxury; Jiang, who has also experienced family opposition, to the realisation that their match would never be permitted; Uma wonders if Gopalan had raped Nirmala (as the Knight rapes the maiden in "The Wife of Bath's Tale"). Lily wonders if Ravi was merely infatuated; Malathi whether he gave Nirmala up because his ego was dented. Only Mr Mangalam argues that Ravi's heart was broken.

When Mangalam tells his story in his own voice the point springs into significance; his heart was broken when he was forced to separate from his beloved Latika by the machinations of his powerful wife and her family. Unknowingly Malathi told a story which forced Mangalam to revisit his own past history. In his story (the sixth to be narrated) his persona is oddly congruent with that foisted upon him by Malathi. He reveals that he came from a poor background but was inspired by an astrologer's prediction that his face would be his fortune (161). Though he works hard to gain a degree, he swiftly realises that without wealthy connections he will never find a good job. The parallel with Nirmala is striking. By dint of improving the way he appears, posing as wealthy and cultured, he manages to attract a rich bride, Naina, whose father finds him a job. After the wedding however his wife undergoes a Jekyllean transformation, calling all the shots because of her wealth and making him thoroughly miserable. When he falls in love with Latika and demands a divorce she and her father refuse point blank, frame Latika as a thief and separate the lovers forever. Without Latika he admits to feeling that the part of him which was tender and moral has been crushed, and he wreaks revenge on his wife by serially seducing as many of her friends as possible until the humiliation forces her at least to allow him to leave the country. In America however he finds that the adulterous persona has become the reality; he cannot break the flirtatious habit. He got away geographically but not legally or psychologically. The adopted role had become his character. Now, however, Mangalam ends his story by turning to Malathi and apologising for his previous behaviour; she in her turn thanks him for translating her story "which I chose partly to jab at you, the kind of man I thought you were" (173). Mangalam's image has been thoroughly revised, and the adulterer set in stone shattered, by the telling of the tale. His story also revises the conclusions of Malathi's, demonstrating that improvement is possible, in his own revised behaviour.

Two stories deal directly with politics and with art. Tariq recounts how in the wake of 9/11 his father was abducted and returned after four days, visibly shaken, suffering a stroke shortly afterwards. As a result his parents have decided to leave America behind and return to India. In response Tariq has become a much more observant Muslim and has moved in with a group of activists, persuaded by his friend Ali that "Bad things were happening here to our people, and we needed to fight them" (140). He is clearly becoming radicalised, and leaving behind his Westernised suburban background. What attracted him to the activists was how close they were to one another. "Like brothers. Watching one another's backs" (143). Importantly however Tariq's description of the activists is interrupted for some pages by severe aftershocks which cut off the water supply, and bring down the ceiling in a fall of debris which includes a dead body. When he resumes his tale, sunlight falls onto some of the survivors' faces. Tariq is now less certain of his plans for the future. Comparing his story with the others' has led to a sea change. Now he sees that everyone suffers in different ways and no longer feels so alone. Lily offers him a place to stay, putting her arm through his. Although his story is about social polarisation and a community coming apart after 9/11, rejecting broader social formations in favour of more isolated micro-identities, the result of the group narration is to replace a defensive political grouping with a different kind of fellowship. His story came apart, was interrupted, as people fled the collapsing ceiling to the frames, but as a result there is a breaking down of barriers which offers stray rays of hope.

After previously asking several times to tell her own, it was Lily who requested Tariq's story, having finally learned to wait for her turn on stage, as her story demonstrates. Lily's tale engages directly with the dangers of perfectionism. Lily's parents believe that her brother Mark is a perfect child, polite, obedient, gifted and idealistic, with plans to study medicine and cure cancer. In response, unable to compete for their parents' attention Lily decides to be bad, to cultivate small rebellions, skip homework, sleep late and miss classes, and adopts a Goth makeup with body-piercings. Mark (very much his sister's keeper) saves the day by secretly teaching her the flute, for which she has real aptitude. But the result is that Lily goes to the other extreme, becoming obsessively focussed on perfection, and practising continually to win competitions. For both there is a moment of burn out. At university Mark's grades slip and he develops a drinking problem; Lily freezes onstage and gives up. Salvation comes for Lily when she begins to play only for her own pleasure. Mark had taught her in the local park, and she abandons the competition stage to return there, composing her own melodies, her only audience a group of small boys. She begins playing a melancholy tune, but as she makes her way through it, finds that it is not sad all the way through. "It had leaps and trills and a ribbon of joy that kept looping back" (153). Perhaps a little obviously, Lily's story, which occupies central position in the novel, acts as an analogy to the novel itself. The tale attests to the importance of interactive, non-competitive art, the importance of audience rather than individual solo performance and demonstrates how art can cross barriers. The boys are sufferers from Down's syndrome. Art is not in this model something reserved for the highest levels of competence and technique, but flourishes in improvisation, even in imperfection. Lily finds the little ribbon of joy, the paradise in hell, by creating her own music. The story is perhaps too fabular, offering a clearer moral than the others—not to push for perfection, but also not to decide that anything less than perfection means embracing a negative vision of human behaviour. Rather there are moments of joy in even a melancholy, or an apparently "imperfect" life. There are no comments at the end of Lily's story. It is a moment of stillness and poise in the novel, with the music speaking for itself to the listeners. At the end of the chapter Lily plays a serene melody, and the light falls through the ruins above and shines on her for a few seconds before it dies away. Lily is in the spotlight, but she is no longer courting individual success.

Death is always the hardest of counter-utopias. The three remaining stories from Mrs Pritchett, Cameron and Uma, are darker in tone than those preceding them, and permeated by ghosts and spiritual mentors. Cameron had concealed the existence of the dead body floating near them but now it makes death a touchable horror which has to be confronted. In Mrs Pritchett's story her life is changed not by wars, seductions, persecution or death, but by watching an old man help his wife with her coat, and recognising the lack of tenderness in her own marriage. Mr Pritchett had never explained his past. Now she understands his chilliness and his need for material security, but it is too late. She has been contaminated by his own mindset. With unintentional irony, she uses the language of maths to describe their emotional bankruptcy. Her activities, friendships, gardening and home making, "were all so many zeroes" (179). Narrowly surviving an overdose, she now has medication which at times places her in a kind of limbo, not quite connected to the others. The story which Mrs Pritchett tells is a ghost story. In hospital she finds an Indian night nurse, unmoving at the foot of her bed, who tells her that this is her last night at the hospital and Mrs Pritchett her last patient. The nurse tells her to remain where she is, forgive her husband, and work on her heart. "Once you're dead it's much more difficult" (184). She invokes the notion of karma, warning that death may not necessarily mean that she will end up in a better place (181), and advises concentrating on inner change, so that outer change will follow. Just as the notion of karma involves alternating cycles of good and bad, so the nurse emphasises the impossibility of a new beginning, but the possibility of improvement. But should Mrs Pritchett believe her? The nurse's hands are chilly (184), her face invisible; in the dark her uniform appears grey, wraith-like; and her whispery statements are oracular. When a second nurse appears later and Mrs Pritchett mentions the preceding one she is marked as delusional on her chart. "Had she actually been a nurse? Was she even a real person?" (185). After her suicide attempt, Mrs Pritchett finds it too difficult to improve, and when she sees a picture in a magazine of an Indian palace decides to go to

India with her husband and leave him there, to begin a new life. After her story, Mr Pritchett sits in silence, horribly humiliated, his head bowed. "Hell is other people" thinks Uma on his behalf (187). It seems clear to Uma that the whole group now believe that they are going to die. Only Lily remains optimistic—because unlike Mrs Pritchett she and her grandmother believe in ghosts. Jiang describes them as the spirits of those who have died in the same place, returning to warn others. Lily takes comfort in the belief that the ghosts of all the others who have died in the quake might yet come to save them.

Death and belief also run like a ribbon through Cameron's tale, which opposes social mobility to group loyalty in a companion story to Tariq's. Tariq was ready to give up on integration into the larger community and retreat into a Muslim world, whereas African-American Cameron tries to rise in society and leave his people behind him. He allows a counsellor to parlay his apparent handicaps—orphanhood, poverty, race—into a university scholarship. Fearing the ghetto closing in on him, Cameron abandons his pregnant girlfriend who aborts their child and curses him. In her view he can see only the negative aspects of his community, not the positives:

> you already decided you going to leave, so you can't see nothing good even if it up and smack you in the face. (190)

Cameron chooses individual success over community and he pays the price. His success turns to ashes. Out of place in a college for rich white kids, he falls behind and leaves university, ending up in Vietnam. Now haunted by the ghosts of those he killed, particularly the unborn child, he has encountered a holy man of sorts, Jeff, a lay Buddhist priest who volunteers with him at a hospice for the dying. Despite his beliefs, Jeff, another "nurse" figure and mentor, can find no way to comfort Louie, dying of Aids. Cameron is similarly ineffectual; he finds that watching the interminable process of dying makes him nervous, and he has to be transferred to gardening duties. Unlike Lily, neither Jeff nor Cameron is able to take comfort from their beliefs. Story seems to be losing the battle with death. Even worse, between Cameron's unfinished tale and Uma's there is an interruption, noises above, tapping and banging, the sound of engines revving and a door slammed shut (203). Elation at the prospect of rescue propels everyone to the hole in the ceiling, frantically trying to signal, and shouting for help—everyone except Cameron. But only silence is heard. Hope is snatched away and the group are devastated.

It is against this background that Uma tells the final story. Uma recounts how she had set off for college only to learn shortly after her arrival that her father planned to leave her mother. Everything seems pointless.

> Could all the things of the world crumble so suddenly? What was the point, then, of putting our hearts into any achievement? (209)

Instead she decides to abandon college, and drive to New York with her friend Jeri and a randomly picked-up hitchhiker. Later that night, stopping in a field, she looks up to see a vision of colours, swathes of red and green and yellow, curtains of light with bursts of brightness, the aurora borealis. The vision is enough to transform her view of the world, she returns to college, and commits herself to life again. Later she discovers that the aurora was actually the product of a disaster, a massive fire in a chemical factory.

> This explanation of my aurora was disappointing, but no matter what its source, the dance of lights over the night field had given me something facts couldn't take away. (216)

Uma has seen an amazing thing, an image of "the oldest histories of all: earth and sky" (216) and gained a broader perspective. When her father decides not to leave, she keeps his secret, but seeing just how fragile her mother's security is makes Uma withhold the deep core of her being in her relationships. It is only now that she realises how that defensive withholding was a betrayal of her own self. Fresh noises interrupt her, but now nobody moves. "They were aware of the possibilities and ready to accept them" (218), whether rescue or death. The group have re-formed while Uma was talking; Jiang and Lily have their heads on Tariq's shoulders; Mangalam has his arm around Malathi, even Mrs Pritchett has wrapped her husband in a shawl; and Cameron is pressed close to Uma. As she finishes her story he pats her knee approvingly; somehow, in revealing the core of her own self, she has brought them back together.

The novel continues: "But what they didn't know was that the story wasn't over yet" (219). For the reader it is not immediately clear if this is a comment on the frame tale or the inset story—or both. Uma thinks that she only has a few minutes to finish her tale, to find the right words and begins to rehearse it in her head. It turns out that long after their road trip, Jeri, who was dying, had phoned Uma to ask if it had really been the aurora which they had seen. She demands the truth in the face of death. "People lie to me all the time. I want the truth about this one thing before I die" (220). Where Mrs Pritchett and Cameron failed in their encounters with death, Uma lies in its teeth. She tells Jeri twice that it was an aurora. Jeri is comforted; "At least I saw one amazing thing" (220). It was this phrase of Jeri's, vaguely remembered, which had prompted Uma's storytelling project at the outset. But did Uma do the right thing? Should she have told the truth? Or has she actually told the truth? Had the lights in some way become an aurora?

> their magic transforming Uma, giving her the courage to turn her life around—because she had believed so completely that they were (220).

As in the two previous stories, belief is at the core of the tale. Uma has chosen fiction not fact for Jeri, based upon her idea that a strong enough belief can change the story and the world. But this ending to her story reaches the reader only through the third person narrator. Will it ever get told to the group? The novel ends with renewed clankings.

> The giant was on his way down. Were those voices, calling to them? As they waited to see what would happen next, Uma began the end of her story. (220)

As readers we have been given a story which has not reached the group of survivors. Their story ended as Uma was regretting her self-betrayal. The aurora, the product of a disaster, illuminated her life and gave her courage to change because of her belief in it. She tells the group the truth (a chemical fire) but tells Jeri a lie. The novel ends poised between truth and lies, rescue and death, frame and inset, and only belief will decide what story to tell, how to determine what happens next. The belief in the aurora was enough to make Uma change her life. Stories may have power to change us, where facts do not. If we believe that things can be better, then perhaps they will become so, by the power of our convictions. And if we know other stories, particularly utopian stories, they may lead us in optimistic directions. In the *Decameron* the "brigata" appear to survive. Near the end the author remarks in the introduction to the ninth day that "Either these people will not be vanquished by death, or they will welcome it with joy."[23] If the reader knows Boccaccio's story, he or she may also believe in the possibility of survival for the modern group, by the process of intertextual prolepsis. Just as in the *Decameron*, storytelling is a better defence against the powers of death than any other, for it doubles reader, author and character, by sympathetic identification—a form of love.[24] The result is to produce a multiplication of roles as audience, narrators and characters exchange positions. The third person narrator functions in places as a reader, pondering meaning; narrators are doubled (Malathi and Mangalam for example) or paired; every narrator is also a character in an inset tale; and every character is also an interpreter, reading the meaning of the stories. As a result the narrative has a reparative function, expanding the individual into a plenitude of different roles in the community of storytellers. As Paul Coates puts it:

> Works of fiction exist in a space between the Double and the Other. To enter into a work of fiction is in a sense to transform the Other into a Double : to discover in the apparent foreignness of another person the lineaments of one's own aspirations and hopes.[25]

Conclusion

Utopias are impossible, unbelievable, unrealistic, in short imaginary, and their proponents tend to be dismissed as naïve idealists. Bill Ashcroft, a vigorous defender of utopia, argues however that

> although not everything we imagine may be achievable, what is never imagined cannot be achieved.[1]

Art is almost inevitably utopian, in its capacity to imagine new or better worlds, even in the most dystopian conditions, though as Kim Edwards demonstrated the human propensity to push its ideas to the limit may give us reservations about imagination. In Margaret Atwood's 2003 novel, *Oryx and Crake*, genetic engineers have dreamed up and then created such creatures as the snat (combining the worst traits of rat and snake), the pigoon (pig and racoon) and the viciously aggressive wolvog (wolf and dog), creatures which once at liberty prove a nightmare for the human race (and indeed for the susceptible reader). Set circa 2017 on the Eastern coast of America, in a world of decadent consumerism and corporate greed, the events of the novel involve a world in which biological experimentation has unleashed mega-plagues, destroying most of humanity. One of the few survivors, Jimmy, is left tending the "Crakers" a group of genetically engineered humanoids. Interspecies gene-splicing and part-gene-splicing has been developed and applied to ordinary human embryos, with the resulting beautiful creatures apparently an improvement upon human beings. Aggression is foreign to them. Racism has been eliminated (they do not recognise skin colour) as has territoriality, property and sexual jealousy. (The Crakers come into heat at regular intervals, cheerfully mating in groups, and sexual activity ceases upon conception.) They are docile, have no strong emotions, and live in perfect harmony with their environment, munching on plant foods. Suffering is at an end: they have superior immune systems, built in insect-repellents and sunscreen, and because they are programmed to drop dead at thirty without any illness, have no fear of death. Crake claims to have produced them purely as floor-models, walking advertisements for the designer-baby technologies (about to hit the market) which he has evolved in the "Paradice" dome of his firm, RejoovenEsence. Actually, however, Crake is a utopianist, who has evolved a killer haemorrhagic virus with which he intends to wipe out humanity, replacing it with a better model, in a re-invention of Eden without temptation or evil. Human nature has been altered, apparently forever. The novel draws upon the Frankenstein story to condemn Crake for assuming god-like powers of creation, in creating new life-forms; yet narrative creativity is eventually validated as the only route back to humanity. Crake's own society has exploited the human imagination to terrible ends, and importantly it appears that art has been complicit in the process. The novel is partly constructed around a series of computer games, for example. Crake is particularly skilled at playing EXTINCTA-THON, in which human beings, soon to be extinct if he has his way, adopt the code names of extinct species. "Blood and Roses" is a trading game in which one side play with human atrocities, the other with works of art or human achievements. One Mona Lisa equals Bergen Belsen; one Armenian genocide equals the Ninth Symphony plus three Great Pyramids, with the winner the person who retains the largest number of human achievements. As Jimmy notes, the Blood player usually wins, but it is a Pyrrhic victory since he inherits only a wasteland. The arts appear to be always on the losing side.

But what Crake is unable to eliminate from the gene pool is the desire for storytelling. When Jimmy leads the Crakers out of Paradice and into their new world, he keeps having to invent simple narratives to explain their surroundings, each narrative leading inevitably to further questions and fresh inventions, however uncomplicated he tries to keep the story. At first this process appears to be merely a form of brainwashing, as Jimmy imposes his own master-narrative.

> These people were like blank pages, he could write whatever he wanted on them.[2]

Telling stories becomes his means of survival; the Crakers catch fish for him in return for them. "A story is what they want, in exchange for a slaughtered fish" (117–8). As time goes on, however, story acquires more than a utilitarian or exchange value. Jimmy's tales rapidly turn into myths and legends, including exalting his dead mistress, Oryx, to the status of a benevolent deity, a companion god to Crake. In "Writing Utopia" Atwood argued that utopias are a product of monotheistic cultures, or cultures in which there is a single idea of the Good, whereas polytheistic cultures do not seem to produce them.[3] Jimmy's doubling of the deity undermines the possibility of one truth, one perfect state, or belief. And story is equally slippery, as it multiplies and spreads. When Jimmy tells the Crakers that Crake (now dead) cannot be seen by them because he has turned into a plant, he astounds himself. "Now where had that come from?" (421). His own imagination has supplied an image that immediately escapes from his control. When he briskly redefines Crake as a tree, not an edible plant, the follow up question asks how Crake can talk, and the tree has to acquire an invented mouth. Jimmy realises that

> He has made a narrative mistake. He has the sensation that he's lost his balance at the top of a flight of stairs. (421)

When he returns to the group after an excursion in search of food he is astonished to discover them seated in a semi-circle around an effigy, a reasonable facsimile of himself, chanting and banging percussion instruments. The Crakers have built upon the stories which he told them and created a myth for themselves, with Jimmy as godhead. He recalls Crake's warning:

> Watch out for art. As soon as they start doing art, we're in trouble. Symbolic thinking of any kind would signal downfall. . . . Next thing they'd be inventing idols, and funerals, and grave goods, and the afterlife, and sin, and Linear B, and kings, and then slavery and war. (419–20).

Now that they have art, they will in time become human beings, just like Jimmy. The imagination, in short, even amongst the Crakers, is irrepressible. Storytelling simply will not go away, even in the most extreme social conditions, and the bioterrorist is going to lose the game.

Notes

NOTES TO CHAPTER 1

1. Amy Waldman, "Freedom," *Boston Review* July/August 2009: 39. Subsequent page references follow citations in parentheses.
2. For the distinction between "product" and "process" utopias see Eugene W. Holland, "Utopian Thought in Deleuze and Guattari," in Andrew Milner, Matthew Ryan and Robert Savage, ed., *Imagining the Future: Utopia and Dystopia* (North Carlton, Australia: Arena Publications, 2006), 217–42.
3. Jess Whyte, "Critiquing the Violence of Guantánamo: Resisting the Monopolization of the Future," in Andrew Milner, Matthew Ryan and Robert Savage, ed., 123–35.
4. Robin Wright, "Chinese Detainees Are Men Without A Country," *Washington Post*, August 24, 2005, accessed June 29 2012, http://www.washingtonpost.com/wpdyn/content/article/2005/08/23/AR2005082301362. Overtures were made to Palau in the Western Pacific, and, notoriously, four Uighurs were resettled in Bermuda, a British overseas territory, without the prior consent of the British government. See also Amy Waldman *et al.*, "Guantánamo and Jailers. Mixed Review by Detainees," *New York Times*, March 17, 2004, accessed June 29, 2012, http://www.nytimes.com/2004/03/17/world/guantanamo-and-jailers/mixed-review-by-detainees.
5. "UK told US won't shut Guantanamo," *BBC News*, May 11, 2006, accessed June 29, 2012, http://news.bbc.co.uk/1/hi/uk_politics/4760365.stm.
6. John Gray, *Black Mass: Apocalyptic Religion and the Death of Utopia* (London: Allen Lane, 2007), 167.
7. Harry Lee Poe, *Edgar Allan Poe: An Illustrated Companion to His Tell-Tale Stories* (New York: Metro Books, 2008), 39. Poe published his poem "Al Araaf" in 1829.
8. Oscar Wilde, *The Soul of Man Under Socialism and Selected Critical Prose.* Edited Linda Dowling (Harmondsworth: Penguin, 2001), 141.
9. Bill Ashcroft, "Critical Utopias," *Textual Practice* 21, 3 (2007): 420.
10. Ernst Bloch, *The Utopian Function of Art and Literature: Selected Essays*, trans. Jack Zipes and Frank Mecklenburg (Minneapolis : University of Minnesota Press, 1989).
11. Ashcroft, "Critical Utopias," 418.
12 Dunja Mohr, "Transgressive Utopian Dystopias: The Postmodern Reappearance of Utopia in the Disguise of Dystopia," *Zeitschrift für Anglistik und Amerikanistik* 55 (2007): 5–24.
13. E.H. Carr, *The Twenty Years' Crisis, 1919–1939* (London: Macmillan 1951).

14. Karl R. Popper, *The Open Society and its Enemies*. Volume 2. (London: Routledge and Kegan Paul, 1945).

15. Russell Jacoby, *The End of Utopia: Politics and Culture in an Age of Apathy* (New York: Basic Books, 1999), x.

16. Richard Rorty, *Philosophy and Social Hope* (London: Penguin, 1999), xiii.

17. Ernst Bloch, *The Principle of Hope* (Cambridge, Massachusetts: MIT Press, 1986); Ruth Levitas, *The Concept of Utopia* (Syracuse: Syracuse University Press, 1990); Tom Moylan, *Scraps of the Untainted Sky: Science Fiction, Utopia, Dystopia* (Boulder, Colorado: Westview Press. 2000); Lyman Tower Sargent, "The Three Faces of Utopianism Revisited," *Utopian Studies* 5, 1 (1994): 1–37.

18. Immanuel Wallerstein, *Utopistics: Or Historical Changes of the Twenty-First Century* (New York: New Press, 1998); Russell Jacoby, *Picture Imperfect: Utopian Thought for an Anti-Utopian Age* (New York, Columbia University Press, 2005); John Rawls, *The Law of Peoples* (Cambridge: Harvard University Press, 1999); Pierre Bourdieu, "A Reasoned Utopia and Economic Fatalism," *New Left Review* 227 (Jan.–Feb. 1998): 125–30.

19. Lyman Tower Sargent, "Ideology and Utopia: Karl Mannheim and Paul Ricoeur," *Journal of Political Ideologies* 13, 3 (2008): 263–73.

20. Patrick Hayden and Chamsy El-Ojeili, ed., *Globalization and Utopia: Critical Essays* (London: Palgrave, 2009).

21. Hayden and Ojeili, *Globalization and Utopia*, 51.

22. See Judie Newman, *Fictions of America: Narratives of Global Empire* (Routledge, 2007), Chapter 1, for a full discussion of different approaches to globalization.

23. Thomas L. Friedman, *The Lexus and the Olive Tree: Understanding Globalization* (New York: Farrar, Strauss, Giroux, 1999); Francis Fukuyama, *The End of History and the Last Man* (London: Penguin, 1992).

24. Ulrich Beck, *The Cosmopolitan Vision* (Cambridge, Polity, 2006).

25. John Gray, *Black Mass*.

26. Lucy Sargisson, "Religious Fundamentalism and Utopianism in the 21st century," *Journal of Political Ideologies* 12, 3 (October 2007): 269–87.

27. David Bell, "Fail Again. Fail Better. Nomadic Utopianism and Deleuze and Guattari and Yevgeny Zamyatin," *Political Perspectives* 4, 1 (2010), accessed July 21, 2012, http://politicalperspectives.org.uk.

28. Derek Attridge, "Once More With Feeling: Art, Affect and Performance," *Textual Practice* 25, 2 (2011): 329–43. Attridge argues that there is no critical agreement on a definition of affect as opposed to feelings or emotion and surveys the various definitions on offer.

29. Nigel Thrift, "Intensities of Feeling: Towards a Spatial Politics of Affect," *Geografiska Annaler. Series B. Human Geography* 86, 1 (2004): 58.

30. Richard Gray, *After the Fall: American Literature Since 9/11* (Chichester: Wiley-Blackwell, 2011).

31. Fredric Jameson, *Postmodernism, or the Cultural Logic of Late Capitalism* (Durham, North Carolina, Duke University Press, 1995), xvii.

32. Liz Bondi, "Making Connections and Thinking Through Emotions: Between Geography and Psychiatry," *Transactions of the Institute of British Geographers. New Series.* 30, 4 (2005): 433–48.

33. Arlie Russell Hochschild, *The Managed Heart. Commercialization of Human Feeling* (Berkeley, University of California Press, 1983).

34. Nigel Thrift, "But Malice Aforethought: Cities and the Natural History of Hatred", *Transactions of the Institute of British Geographers. New Series.* 30, 2 (2005): 133–50.

35. Karen Cerulo, *Never Saw it Coming: Cultural Challenges to Envisioning the Worst* (Chicago: University of Chicago Press, 2006).

36. Barbara Ehrenreich, *Smile or Die: How Positive Thinking Fooled America and the World* (London: Granta, 2009),13.
37. Jess Walter, *The Zero: A Novel* (New York: Harper, 2007), 169. Subsequent page references follow citations in parentheses.
38. C.B. James, "*The Zero* by Jess Walter," accessed July 6, 2012, http://ready-whenyouarecb.blogspot.co.uk/2012/06zero-by-jess-walter.html.
39. Elizabeth Kübler-Ross, *On Death and Dying* (London: Tavistock, 1970).
40. Clark Blaise and Bharati Mukherjee, *The Sorrow and the Terror: The Haunting Legacy of the Air India Tragedy* (New York: Viking 1987), ix. For accounts which bring the story up to date see Kim Bolan, *Loss of Faith: How the Air-India Bombers Got Away with Murder* (Toronto: McClelland and Stewart, 2005); Fred Ribkoff, "Bharati Mukherjee's 'The Management of Grief' and the Politics of Mourning in the Aftermath of the Air India Bombing," in Bill Ashcroft, Ranjini Mendis, Julie McGonegal and Arun Mukherjee, ed. *Literature For Our Times. Postcolonial Studies in the Twenty-First Century* (Amsterdam: Rodopi, 2012): 507–22.
41. Bharati Mukherjee, "The Management of Grief," in *The Middleman and Other Stories* (Virago, 1990), 177–97. First published New York: Grove Press, 1988. Quoting page 183. Subsequent page references follow citations in parentheses. The spatial nature of the story has also been explored, without reference to Marin or utopia, by Deborah Bowen, "Spaces of Translation. Bharati Mukherjee's 'The Management of Grief'," *Ariel* 28, 3 (July 1997): 47–60.
42. Louis Marin, *Utopics: Spatial Play*, trans. Robert A. Vollroth (Atlantic Highlands, New Jersey: Humanities, 1984). First published as *Utopiques: jeux d'espaces* (Paris: Minuit, 1973).
43. Eugene D. Hill, "The Place of the Future: Louis Marin and his *Utopiques*," *Science Fiction Studies* 9 (1982): 167–79.
44. Ruth Levitas, *The Concept of Utopia*.
45. Judie Newman, "Slave Narratives and Neo-Slave Narratives," in Sharon Monteith, ed., *The Cambridge Companion to the Literature of the American South* (Cambridge: Cambridge University Press, 2013), forthcoming.
46. Kathryn Hume, *Aggressive Fictions: Reading the Contemporary American Novel* (Ithaca: Cornell University Press, 2012), ix. Hume's analysis of the potential rewards of the fiction in question is consistently percipient and the book marks a major intervention in the field. The present reader admits to enormous glee as she recognised her most detested works of American fiction on Hume's list.

NOTES TO CHAPTER 2

1. Kim Edwards, *The Memory Keeper's Daughter* (London: Penguin, 2006), 15.
2. Edwards, *The Memory Keeper's Daughter*, 17–18.
3. Kim Edwards, "Paradise," *Ploughshares* (Fall 1990): 88.
4. Edwards, "Paradise," 88.
5. Janet Whitaker, Chela Kaplan and Amy O'Brien, "A Conversation with Kim Edwards," accessed September 9, 2009, http://www.ket.org/bookclub/books/1999_feb/interview.htm.
6. Kim Edwards, *The Secrets of A Fire King* (London: Penguin, 2007), 104. Subsequent citations follow quotations in parentheses. The collection was first published in 1997 by W.W. Norton, without the following stories: "Aristotle's Lantern," *Zoetrope* 6, 1 (Spring 2002); "In the Garden," *Ploughshares* (Fall 2003): 21–42; "Thirst," *Mid-American Review* XXIV, 1 (Fall 2003).

7. Karl R. Popper, *The Open Society and its Enemies*. Volume 2. (London: Routledge and Kegan Paul, 1945), 6.

8. Jeanna Bryner, "Surprise! Your cousin's a sea urchin," *LiveScience*, November 9, 2006, accessed March 10, 2009, http://www.livescience.com.

9. Ian Hill, "The Human Barnyard and Kenneth Burke's Philosophy of Technology," *KB Journal* 5, 2 (Spring 2009), accessed September 14, 2009, http://www.kbjournal.org.

10. Eric Shouse, "Suicide: or the Future of Medicine. (A 'Satire by Entelechy' of Biotechnology)," *KB Journal* 4, 1 (Fall 2007), accessed September 14, 2009, http://www.kbjournal.org.

11. Kenneth Burke, *Language as Symbolic Action. Essays on Life, Literature and Method* (Berkeley: University of California Press, 1966), 16.

12. Burke, *Language as Symbolic Action*, 40.

13. William Rueckert, "Some of the Many Kenneth Burkes," in Hayden White and Margaret Brose, ed., *Representing Kenneth Burke. Selected Papers from the English Institute* (Baltimore and London: Johns Hopkins University Press, 1982), 15–16.

14. Stan A. Lindsay, *Implicit Rhetoric: Kenneth Burke's Extension of Aristotle's Concept of Entelechy* (Lanham: University Press of America, 1998).

15. See also Kenneth Burke, *On Human Nature: A Gathering While Everything Flows. 1967–1984*, ed. William H. Rueckert and Angelo Bonadonna (Berkeley: University of California Press, 2003); Stephen Bygrave, *Kenneth Burke's Rhetoric and Ideology* (London: Routledge, 1993); Merle E. Brown, *Kenneth Burke*. Minnesota Pamphlets on American Writers 75 (Minneapolis: University of Minnesota Press, 1969).

16. Tzvetan Todorov, *Hope and Memory* (London: Atlantic Books, 2003), 19.

17. Bill Ashcroft, "Critical Utopias," *Textual Practice* 21, 3 (2007): 412.

18. Ashcroft, "Critical Utopias," 412.

19. Ashcroft, "Critical Utopias," 413.

20. Marie Curie, *Pierre Curie* (New York : Macmillan 1923), 104.

21. Eve Curie, *Madame Curie*, trans. Vincent Sheean (London: William Heinemann, 1938), 173.

22. Janet Whitaker, Chela Kaplan and Amy O'Brien, "A Conversation with Kim Edwards," 28.

23. Robert Reid, *Marie Curie* (London: Collins, 1974), 314.

24. Susan Quinn, *Marie Curie: A Life* (London: Mandarin, 1996), 180.

25. Eve Curie, *Madame Curie*, 384.

26. Eve Curie, *Madame Curie*, 282.

27. For details see David I. Harvie, *Deadly Sunshine: The History and Fatal Legacy of Radiation* (Stroud: Tempus, 2005).

28. Ruth Levitas, "The future of thinking about the future," in John Bird *et.al.*, ed., *Mapping the Futures: Local Cultures, Global Change* (London : Routledge, 1993), 257–69.

29. Ernst Bloch, *The Principle of Hope* (Cambridge, Mass: MIT Press, 1986), 364.

NOTES TO CHAPTER 3

1. Susan Choi, *A Person of Interest* (New York: Viking Penguin, 2008), 5. Subsequent citations follow quotations in parentheses.

2. Theodore Kaczynski, *Industrial Society and Its Future*. Paragraph 25, accessed February 28, 2009, http://en.wikisource.org.wiki/Industrial_Society_and_Its_Future.

3. Allston Chase, *Harvard and the Unabomber: The Education of an American Terrorist* (New York: W.W. Norton, 2003), 41.
4. Vince Passaro, "Dangerous Don DeLillo," *New York Times Magazine*, 19 May 1991, p. 36–38.
5. Ryan Simmons, "What is a terrorist? Contemporary Authorship, the Unabomber and *Mao II*," *Modern Fiction Studies* 45, 3 (1999) 675–695. *Mao II* was published in 1991, four years before the Unabomber's manifesto, and five before his arrest.
6. Silvia Caporale Bizzini, "Can the Intellectual Still Speak? The example of Don DeLillo's *Mao II*," *Critical Quarterly* 37 (1995): 111.
7. Margaret Scanlan, *Plotting Terror: Novelists and Terrorists in Contemporary Fiction* (Charlottesville and London: University Press of Virginia, 2001), 155–63. As she notes, Conrad's irony prevents any reading of the novel as supportive of terrorism; his portrayal of the anarchists intent on blowing up Greenwich observatory offers a ferocious satire on the revolutionary mindset.
8. Kaczynski, *Industrial Society and Its Future*, Paragraph 96.
9. John Douglas and Mark Olshaker, *Unabomber: On the Trail of America's Most-Wanted Serial Killer* (New York: Pocket Books, 1996), 120.
10. Chase, *Harvard and the Unabomber*, 41.
11. Wen Ho Lee (with Helen Zia), *My Country Versus Me* (New York: Hyperion, 2001), 71.
12. Jessica Murphy, "The Moment of Origin," *Profile*, Jan.–Feb. 2008, p. 40.
13. Kaczynski, *Industrial Society and Its Future*, Paragraph 192.
14. David T. Lykken, *A Tremor in the Blood: Uses and Abuses of the Lie Detector* (New York and London: Plenum, 1998); Andrew Stephen, "The Truth About the Lie Detector," *New Statesman*, October 16, 2006, accessed April 1, 2009. http://www.newstatesman.com/200610160033.
15. Wen Ho Lee, *My Country Versus Me*, 74.
16. Wen Ho Lee, *My Country Versus Me*, 329.
17. Wen Ho Lee, *My Country Versus Me*, 328.
18. Wen Ho Lee, *My Country Versus Me*, ix.
19. Susan Choi, *The Foreign Student* (New York: HarperCollins, 1998), 186.
20. Chase, *Harvard and the Unabomber*, 370.
21. Liz Brown, "Margins of Terror," *Time Out* 644, Jan. 30–Feb 5, 2008, accessed February 2, 2009, http://www.timeout.com/newyork/articles/books/25963/margins-of-terror.
22. Chase, *Harvard and the Unabomber*, 89.
23. Timothy W. Luke, *Capitalism, Democracy and Ecology* (Urbana: University of Illinois Press, 1999), 171–95.
24. Ron Arnold, *Ecoterror. The Violent Agenda to Save Nature: The World of the Unabomber* (Washington: Free Enterprise Press, 1997), 6.
25. Luke, *Capitalism, Democracy and Ecology*, 177.
26. Kaczynski, *Industrial Society and Its Future*, Paragraph 183.
27. Cynthia Ozick, *Quarrel and Quandary: Essays by Cynthia Ozick* (New York: Alfred A. Knopf, 2000), 4.
28. Paul Harris, "Fictions of Globalization: Narrative in the Age of Electronic Media," *PhiN* 7 (1999): 27.
29. Franco Moretti, *Graphs, Maps, Trees: Abstract Models for Literary History* (London and New York: Verso, 2000), 81.
30. Moretti, *Graphs, Maps, Trees*, 82.
31. Mieke Bal, *Narratology: Introduction to the Theory of Narrative* (London and Toronto: University of Toronto Press, 1985), 47.

32. The term became controversial when used in 2001 by the Attorney General in relation to whether Dr Steven J. Hatfill was a suspect in the 2001 anthrax attacks case.

33. Dorrit Cohn, *Transparent Minds: Narrative Modes for Presenting Consciousness in Fiction* (Princeton: Princeton University Press, 1978), 99–143.

34. Julie Newberger, "Susan Choi. Interview," *failbetter.com*. September 23, 2008, accessed February 26, 2009, http://www.failbetter.com/28/ChoiInterviw.php.

35. Newberger, "Susan Choi. Interview."

36. "A Conversation with Susan Choi," in *Penguin Readers' Guide. A Person of Interest*, p. 3, accessed September 8, 2011, http://us.penguingroup.com/static/rguides/us/person_of_interest.html.

NOTES TO CHAPTER 4

1. Samuel Moyn, *The Last Utopia: Human Rights in History* (Cambridge, Massachusetts: Harvard University Press, 2010). For a critique of Moyn's account of human rights as lacking historical antecedents before the 1970s see Gary J. Bass, "The Old New Thing," *New Republic*, November 11, 2010, p. 35–39.

2. Jean Bricmont, *Humanitarian Imperialism* (New York: Monthly Review Press, 2006).

3. Sally Kitch, "Gendered National 'Identity Politics': The U.S. and Afghanistan." Paper presented at the annual meeting of the American Studies Association, 2008, accessed abstract April 21 2008, http://www.allacademic.com/meta/p113693_index.html.

4. Gayatri Chakravorty Spivak, "Can the Subaltern Speak?" in Cary Nelson and Lawrence Grossberg, ed, *Marxism and the Interpretation of Culture* (London: Macmillan, 1988), 299.

5. Seymour Hersh, "The Iran Plans," *New Yorker*, April 17, 2006, accessed April 20, 2008, http://www.newyorker.com/archive/206/04/17/060417fa_fact.

6. Gary Sick, *All Fall Down: America's Tragic Encounter with Iran* (New York: Random House, 1985).

7. Hamid Dabashi, "Native Informers and the making of the American Empire," *Al-Ahram Weekly Online*, accessed July 10, 2007, http://weekly.ahram.org.eg/2006/797/special.htm.

8. Niall Ferguson, *Colossus: The Rise and Fall of the American Empire* (London : Allen Lane, 2004).

9. Michael Hardt and Antonio Negri, *Empire* (Cambridge, Massachusetts: Harvard University Press, 2000).

10. Chalmers Johnson, *Nemesis : The Last Days of the American Republic* (New York : Henry Holt, 2006), 6. See also Chalmers Johnson, *Blowback: The Costs and Consequences of American Empire* (New York: Henry Holt, 2000) and *The Sorrows of Empire* (London: Verso, 2004).

11. Johnson, *Blowback*, 65.

12. Johnson, *Blowback*, 8.

13. Johnson, *Blowback*, 17.

14. Hamid Dabashi, *Iran: A People Interrupted* (New York and London: The New Press, 2007).

15. Azar Nafisi, *Reading Lolita in Tehran: A Memoir in Books* (London: I.B. Tauris, 2003) is the most notorious. See Jennifer Worth, "Unveiling *Persepolis* as Embodied Performance," *Theatre Research International* 32, 2 (2007): 143–60, who also lists *Lipstick Jihad* by Azadeh Moaveni (2005),

Even After All this Time: A Story of Love, Revolution, and Leaving Iran by Afschineh Latifi (2005), *Journey from the Land of No: A Girlhood Caught in Revolutionary Iran* by Roya Hakakian (2004), *Funny in Farsi: A Memoir of Growing up Iranian in America* by Firoozeh Dumas (2004), *Saffron Sky: A Life between Iran and America* by Gelareh Asayesh (2000), *To See and See Again: A Life in Iran and America* by Tara Bahrampour (2000) and *Foreigner* by Nahid Rachlin (1999).

16. Gillian Whitlock, *Soft Weapons: Autobiography in Transit* (Chicago and London: University of Chicago Press, 2007), 13.
17. Whitlock, *Soft Weapons*, 22.
18. Seyed Mohammed Marandi, "Reading Azar Nafisi in Tehran," *Comparative American Studies* 6, 2 (June 2008): 179–89.
19. Dabashi, "Native Informers."
20. Fatemeh Keshavarz, *Jasmine and Stars: Reading More than Lolita in Tehran* (Chapel Hill: University of North Carolina Press, 2007); John Carlos Rowe, "Reading *Reading Lolita in Tehran* in Idaho," *American Quarterly* 59, 2 (June 2007): 253–75.
21. Donna Seaman, "Review of *House of Sand and Fog*," *Booklist* 95, 11 (February 1999): 961.
22. André Dubus III, *House of Sand and Fog* (New York: Vintage 1999), 73. Page references follow subsequent quotations in parentheses.
23. Stephen Kinzer, *All the Shah's Men: An American Coup and the Roots of Middle East Terror* (Hoboken, New Jersey: John Wiley, 2003). "Almost no one in the United States knew what the CIA did there in 1953." p. x.
24. Michael Donovan, "National Intelligence and the Iranian Revolution," in R. Jeffreys-Jones and Christopher Andrew, ed., *Eternal Vigilance? Fifty years of the CIA*(London: Frank Cass, 1997). I am grateful to Rhodri Jeffreys-Jones for his suggestions for readings in the history of Iran.
25. See Robert Graham, *Iran: The Illusion of Power* (London: Croom Helm, 1978) for a account of US aid.
26. Robert Graham, *Iran: The Illusion of Power* provides a good account of SAVAK.
27. Robert Graham, *Iran: The Illusion of Power*, 181.
28. Stephen Kinzer, *Overthrow: America's Century of Regime Change from Hawaii to Iraq* (New York: Henry Holt, 2006). Kinzer notes the consistent pattern in which American regime change tends to install repressive regimes which it then cannot control, weakening American security and producing generations of militants.
29. The action covers three weeks in August 1993, with a day by day chronology carefully indicated, followed by a final section covering a few weeks after the deaths, and ending with Kathy's mother's visit on Labor Day (the first Monday in September).
30. Judith Butler, *Giving an Account of Oneself* (New York: Fordham University Press, 2005), 7.
31. Gerald Turkel, "Property, Law and Violence. A Thematic Analysis of *House of Sand and Fog*," *Humanity and Society* 30, 4 (November 2006): 384.
32. Marc Galanter, Susan Egelko and Helen Edwards, "Rational Recovery: Alternative to AA for Addiction?" *American Journal of Drug and Alcohol Abuse* 19, 4 (1993): 499–510.
33. Googoosh, the most popular Iranian singer in the 1970s, did not record or perform from 1979 to 2000, as a result of the ban on female solo singers, envisaged as temptresses. She was briefly jailed and then lived under virtual house arrest.
34. Cyril Jones-Kellett, "The Home Builder: A Try for the American Dream," *San Diego Union-Tribune*, February 14, 1999, p. BOOKS 3.

35. *House of Sand and Fog*; produced by Michael London and Vadim Perelman. Directed by Vadim Perelman. Written by Vadim Perelman and Shawn Lawrence Otto. DVD DreamWorks, 2003.

NOTES TO CHAPTER 5

1. Janet Maslin, "A Terrorist in a Fleshpot Before Bidding Farewell to the Flesh," *New York Times*, June 9, 2008, accessed June 5,2009, http://www.nytimes.com/2008/06/09/books/09masl.html.
2. Anthony Giardina, "Why do they hate us?" *Washington Post*, June 22, 2008, p. BW07.
3. Sonia Baelo-Allué, "The Depiction of 9/11 in Literature: The Role of Images and Intermedial References," *Radical History Review* 111 (Fall 2011): 184–93.
4. Martin Amis, "The Voice of the Lonely Crowd," *The Guardian*, June 12, 2002, p. 4.
5. André Dubus III, *The Garden of Last Days* (New York: W.W. Norton, 2008), 23. Page references follow subsequent quotations in parentheses.
6. Malise Ruthven, *A Fury for God: The Islamist Attack on America* (London and New York: Granta Books, 2002) provides a succinct account of the Florida group.
7. Susan Faludi, *The Terror Dream: Fear and Fantasy in Post-9/11 America* (New York: Henry Holt, 2007), 23.
8. Faludi, 22.
9. Faludi, 5.
10. Faludi 7.
11. Faludi, 13.
12. Faludi, 251.
13. André Dubus III, *Townie* (New York: W.W. Norton, 2011), 44.
14. Dubus, *Townie*, 38.
15. Dubus, *Townie*, 51.
16. Dubus, *Townie*, 78.
17. Dubus, *Townie*, 215.
18. Dubus, *Townie*, 234.
19. Dubus, *Townie*, 332.
20. Dubus, *Townie*, 336.
21. Bree Nordenson, "Cowboys and Damsels," *Columbia Journalism Review* 46, 4 (November–December 2007): 59–62.
22. Lucy Sargisson, "Religious Fundamentalism and Utopianism in the 21st century," *Journal of Political Ideologies* 12, 3 (October 2007): 269–87.
23. For a compendium of such reports see "Context of Before September 11, 2001. Hijackers Drink Alcohol and Watch Strip Shows," *History Commons*, accessed June 5,2009, http://www.historycommons.org/.
24. Jody Benjamin, "Suspects' actions don't add up," *South Florida Sun Sentinel* September 16, 2001, accessed June 5, 2009, http://web.archive.org/web/20010916150533/http://www.sun-sentinel.com/news/local.
25. Jeff Baker, "Book Review of "The Garden of Last Days," *Bookmarks*, June 20, 2008, http://blog.oregonlive.com/books/2008/06/book_review_the_garden_of_last.html.
26. Michael Uebel, "Striptopia?," *Social Semiotics* 14, 4 (2004): 4.
27. Uebel, "Striptopia?," 7–8.
28. Danielle Egan, *Dancing for Dollars and Paying For Love: The Relationships Between Exotic Dancers and Their Regulars* (London: Palgrave Macmillan, 2006), 19.

29. Elizabeth Bernstein, *Temporarily Yours: Intimacy, Authenticity, and the Commerce of Sex* (Chicago: University of Chicago Press, 2007), 6.
30. Katherine Frank, *G-Strings and Sympathy: Strip Club Regulars and Male Desire* (Durham: Duke University Press, 2002).
31. Frank, *G-Strings and Sympathy*, 192.
32. Frank, *G-Strings and Sympathy*, 86.
33. Frank, *G-Strings and Sympathy*, 210.
34. For a ground-breaking discussion of emotional labour see Arlie Russell Hochschild, *The Managed Heart: Commercialization of Human Feeling* (Berkeley: University of California, 1983).
35. Uebel, "Striptopia?," 9.
36. Dubus, *Townie*, 213.
37. Dubus, *Townie*, 304.

NOTES TO CHAPTER 6

1. Dalia Sofer, *The Septembers of Shiraz* (London: Picador, 2008), 2. First published New York: HarperCollins, 2007). Subsequent page references follow quotations in parentheses.
2. Krishan Kumar, *Utopia and Anti-Utopia in Modern Times* (Oxford: Blackwell, 1987), 19.
3. Jaqueline Dutton, "'Non-Western' Utopian Traditions," in Gregory Claeys ed., *The Cambridge Companion to Utopian Literature* (Cambridge: Cambridge University Press, 2010), 223–58. I am greatly indebted to Dutton's account of Islamic utopianism.
4. Maryam El-Shall, "Salafi Utopia: The Making of the Islamic State," accessed July 18, 2012, http://clogic.eserver.org/2006/el-shall.html.
5. Fredric Jameson, *Archaeologies of the Future: The Desire Called Utopia and Other Science Fictions* (London: Verso, 2005), 27.
6. Sohrab Bedad, "Islamic Utopia in Pre-revolutionary Iran: Navvab Safavi and the Fada'ian-e Eslam," *Middle Eastern Studies* 33, 1 (January 1997): 57.
7. Bedad, "Islamic Utopia," 52.
8. "Judeo-Persian Communities VI. The Pahlavi Era (1925–1929)," *Encyclopaedia Iranica*, accessed September 8, 2010, http://www.iranica.com/articles/judeo-persian-vi-the-pahlavi-era-1925–12979.
9. Marla Harris, "Consuming Words: Memoirs by Iranian Jewish Women," *Nashim: A Journal of Jewish Women's Studies and Gender Issues* 15 (Spring 5769/2008): 149.
10. Deborah Solomon, "Tales from Tehran," *New York Times*, August 26, 2007, accessed August 18, 2010, http://www.nytimes.com/2007/08/26magazine.
11. Harris, "Consuming Words," 148.
12. Gina Nahai, *Cry of the Peacock* (New York: Simon and Schuster, 1991); *Moonlight on the Avenue of Faith* (New York: Harcourt, Brace, 1999); *Caspian Rain* (San Francisco: McAdam/Cage, 2007).
13. Until the recent translated and abridged version. See Habib Levy, *Comprehensive History of the Jews of Iran: The Outset of the Diaspora*. Edited and Abridged by Hooshang Ebrami. Translated by George W. Maschke. (Costa Mesa, California: Mazda, 1998)
14. Houman Sarshar, ed., *Esther's Children: A Portrait of Iranian Jews* (Los Angeles: Center for Iranian Jewish Oral history/The Jewish Publication Society, 2002).
15. Anna Free, "Moonlit Revelations: The Discourse of the End in Gina B. Nahai's *Moonlight on the Avenue of Faith*," *Papers: Explorations into Children's Literature* 16, 2 (2006): 35–39.

16. Roya Hakakian , *Journey from the Land of No: A Girlhood Caught in Revolutionary Iran* (New York: Three Rivers Press, 2004); Farideh Dayanim Goldin, *Wedding Song: Memories of an Iranian Jewish Woman* (Lebanon, New Hampshire: Brandeis University Press, 2003).

17. See Gina Nahai, "So What's With All the Iranian Memoirs," *Publishers Weekly* 26 November 2007, p. 58.

18. Soli Shahvar, "The Islamic Regime in Iran and its Attitude towards the Jews: The Religious and Political Dimensions," *Immigrants and Minorities* 27, 1 (March 2009): 82–117.

19. Dalia Sofer, "Of These, Solitude," in Danya Ruttenberg, ed., *Yentl's Revenge: The Next Wave of Jewish Feminism* (New York: Seal Press, 2001), 206–11. "In my experience, religion has not been a unifying force, but rather a source of rift" (211).

20. Sara Ivry, "Stolen Gems," *Tablet Magazine* August 20, 2007. (Audio interview), accessed August 18, 2010. www.tabletmag.com/podcasts/3202/stolen-gems/.

21. Stuart Cary Welch, *A King's Book of Kings; The Shah-nameh of Shah Tamasp* (New York and London: Thames and Hudson in association with the Metropolitan Museum, 1972), 112–13.

22. Souren Melikian, "Destroying a Treasure : The Sad Story of a Manuscript," *International Herald Tribune*, April 27, 1996, accessed September 8, 2010, http://.caissoas/CAIS/Art/manuscript.htm.171.

23. Stuart Cary Welch and Martin Bernard Dickson, *The Houghton Shahnameh* (Cambridge, Massachusetts: Harvard University Press, 1981), 7. See Volume I, no 23 for a full account of the image.

24. I am enormously grateful for an explanation of the miniature from Robert Hillenbrand, personal email, 8 September 2010. Note that Farnaz misreads the image in one respect. An angel, Sorush, intervened and prevented Faridun from killing Zahhak, whom he bound to Mount Demavend in the distant Elburz mountains.

25. Welch, *A King's Book of Kings*, 13.

26. Melikian, op.cit.

27. Elli Lester Roushanzamir, "Chimera Veil of 'Iranian Woman' and Processes of U.S. Textual Commodification. How U.S. Print Media Represent Iran," *Journal of Communication Inquiry* 28, 1 (January 2004): 9–28.

28. Abbas, *Iran Diary, 1971–2002* (Paris: Editions Autrement, 2002), 18. My translation, as in following quotations.

29. Paul Grainge, *Monochrome Memories: Nostalgia and Style in Retro America* (Westport, Connecticut: Praeger, 2002), 3.

30. Babak Ebrahimian, "Pictures from a Revolution: The 1979 Iranian Uprising," *PAJ :A Journal of Performance and Art* 25, 2 (May 2003): 27.

31. Abbas, *Iran Diary*, 135. He describes his photos as "fixés pour toujours—images suspendues dans le temps". In contrast words are seen as fluid, "le verbe n'est jamais figé."

32. Abbas, *Iran Diary*, 140.

33. Shiva Balaghi, "Abbas's Photographs of Iran," *Middle East Report* 233 (Winter 2004): 28–33.

34. Abbas, *Iran Diary*, 58.

35. Abbas, *Iran Diary*, 78. The dead include Abbas Ali Khalatbari, former Minister of Foreign Affairs, and General Hassan Pakhravan, former Deputy Prime Minister and former head of SAVAK. See www.a-w-i-p.com, accessed September 30, 2010.

36. Abbas, *Iran Diary*, 55.

37. Alfred Douglas, *The Tarot: The Origins, Meanings and Uses of the Cards* (London: Penguin, 1973.)

38. William Lobdell, "A Booming Sect Sends Jewish Emissaries Abroad," *Los Angeles Times*, September 11, 2006, accessed September 8, 2010, http://www.rickross.com/reference/lubavitch/lubavitch41.html.

39. H.W. Janson, *History of Art* (Englewood Cliffs, New Jersey: Prentice-Hall, 1974), 416 See also Steven Nadler, *Rembrandt's Jews* (Chicago and London: University of Chicago Press, 2003) for a critique of Janson.

40. Michael Zell, *Reframing Rembrandt: Jews and the Christian Image in Seventeenth Century Amsterdam* (Berkeley: Ahmanson, 2002).

41. W.J.T. Mitchell, *Picture Theory* (Chicago and London : University of Chicago Press, 1994.

NOTES TO CHAPTER 7

1. Bill Ashcroft, "Critical Utopias," *Textual Practice* 21, 3 (2007): 411–31.

2. John Updike, *The Poorhouse Fair* (London: Gollancz, 1959), 137.

3. Updike, *Poorhouse Fair*, 139.

4. Paul Wood, "Hunting 'Satan' in Falluja Hell," *BBC News*, November 23, 2004, accessed July 12, 2012, http://news.bbc.co.uk/go/pr/fr/-/1/hi/world/middle_east/4037009.stm.

5. John Gray, *Black Mass: Apocalyptic Religion and the Death of Utopia* (London: Allen Lane, 2007).

6. Gray, *Black Mass*, 184.

7. Gray, *Black Mass*, 119.

8. President George Bush, *Ha'aretz*, June 26, 2003. Quoted in Gray, *Black Mass*, 115.

9. Peter Baker, "Bush Tells Group He Sees a 'Third Awakening,'" *Washington Post* September 13, 2006, accessed July 12, 2012, http://www.washingtonpost.com/wp-dyn/contnet/article/2006/09/12/AR2006091201594.html?nav+rssnation.

10. Gray, *Black Mass*, 117. The web address given by Gray is no longer accessible.

11. John Updike, *Toward the End of Time* (New York: Knopf, 1997), 5. Subsequent page references follow quotations in parentheses.

12. Richard Bernstein, and Ross H. Munro, *The Coming Conflict with China* (New York: Knopf, 1997), 184; Samuel P. Huntington, *The Clash of Civilizations and the Remaking of World Order* (New York: Simon and Schuster, 1996). For a quite different view of the relation between American and China see Andrew Nathan and Robert S. Ross, *The Great Wall and the Empty Fortress* (New York: Norton, 1997).

13. Martin Gardner, "WAP, SAP, PAP and FAP," in *The Night is Large: Collected Essays 1938–1995* (London: Penguin, 1997), 44.

14. The four principles can be summarised as follows. The Weak Anthropic Principle (WAP) consists in the idea that because we exist the universe must be constructed to allow us to have evolved (the design argument.) The Strong Anthropic Principle (SAP) argues that life would be impossible unless the laws of nature are exactly what they are. If gravity were any stronger the cosmos would have stopped expanding ages ago and collapsed into a black hole; if any weaker it would have expanded too rapidly for the stars to form. The Participatory Anthropic Principle (PAP) holds that no universe can exist without a conscious observer, and the Final Anthropic Principle (FAP) maintains that life may exist only on earth but it is impossible to destroy, or the universe would lose all its observers.

15. John Updike, "At the Hairy Edge of the Possible," in *More Matters: Essays and Criticism* (London: Hamish Hamilton, 1999), 585.

16. John Updike, "Confessions of a Churchgoer," *The Guardian*, January 8, 2000, p. 3.
17. Updike, "Confessions of a Churchgoer," 3.
18. John D. Barrow and Frank J. Tipler, *The Anthropic Cosmological Principle* (Oxford University Press, 1986), 659.
19. Paul Davies, *The Last Three Minutes: Conjectures about the Ultimate Fate of the Universe* (London: Weidenfeld and Nicolson, 1994), 404–7.
20. Frank J. Tipler, "The FAP Flop," *New York Review of Books* 33, 19 (December 4, 1986), accessed March 2, 2010, http:/www.nybooks.com/articles/4946.
21. David Malone, "Updike 2020: Fantasy, Mythology and Faith in *Toward the End of Time*," in James Yerkes, ed., *John Updike and Religion: the Sense of the Sacred and the Motions of Grace* (Grand Rapids: Eerdmans, 1999): 88.
22. John Updike, "A 'Special Message' for the Franklin Library's Signed First Edition Society Printing of *Toward the End of Time*," in *More Matters: Essays and Criticism* (London: Hamish Hamilton, 1999), 833.
23. Updike also shows Mumford's influence in *The Witches of Eastwick*. See Judie Newman, *John Updike* (London: Methuen, 1988), 127–45.
24. Lewis Mumford, *The Myth of the Machine: Technics and Human Development* (London: Secker and Warburg, 1967), 11.
25. Mumford, 294.
26. Malone, "Updike 2020: Fantasy, Mythology and Faith in *Toward the End of Time*," 80–98.
27. Mumford, *The Myth of the Machine*, 258.
28. Elaine Pagels, *The Origin of Satan* (London: Random House, 1995).
29. John Updike, "Elusive Evil," in *More Matters: Essays and Criticism* (London: Hamish Hamilton, 1999), 480.
30. Updike, " Elusive Evil," 480.
31. Thomas Cahill, *How the Irish Saved Civilisation: The Untold Story of Ireland's Heroic Role from the Fall of Rome to the Rise of Medieval Europe* (London: Hodder and Stoughton, 1995), 216.
32. Kenneth Clarke, *Civilisation: A Personal View* (London: BBC and John Murray, 1969), 4.
33. Mumford, *The Myth of the Machine*, 269.
34. Updike, "Special Message," 833.
35. Updike, "Elusive Evil," 480.
36. I am grateful to Jack Ruttle for explaining the hunting laws, in email message to author, November 17, 2011.
37. Mumford, *The Myth of the Machine*, 114.
38. Mumford, *The Myth of the Machine*, 217.
39. Mumford, *The Myth of the Machine*, 171.
40. Updike, "Elusive Evil," 480.

NOTES TO CHAPTER 8

1. Tommie Shelby, "Cosmopolitanism, Blackness and Utopia: A Conversation with Paul Gilroy," *Transition* 98 (2008): 133.
2. Ernst Bloch, *The Principle of Hope* (Cambridge, Massachusetts: MIT Press. 1986).
3. Shelby, Cosmopolitanism, Blackness and Utopia", 133.
4. Paul Gilroy, *The Black Atlantic: Modernity and Double Consciousness* (London and New York: Verso, 1993), 37.
5. Gilroy, *Black Atlantic*, 38.

6. Theodor W. Adorno, *Aesthetic Theory* (London: Routledge, 1984), 196.
7. See Lucy Evans, "*The Black Atlantic*: Exploring Gilroy's Legacy," *Atlantic Studies* 6, 2 (2009): 255–268; Judie Newman, "Glocalizing Gilroy," *Journal of Commonwealth and Postcolonial Studies* 17, 1 (Spring 2011): 93–102.
8. Brent Hayes Edwards, "The Uses of Diaspora," *Social Text* 19, 1 (2001): 61.
9. Annalisa Oboe and Anna Scacchi, ed., *Recharting the Black Atlantic: Modern Cultures, Local Communities, Global Connections* (London and New York: Routledge, 2008).
10. Bernardine Evaristo, *Blonde Roots* (London: Hamish Hamilton, 2008). Page references follow citations in parentheses. Evaristo is not the first to reverse the races in a novel about slavery. In Steven Barnes, *Lion's Blood: A Novel of Slavery and Freedom in an Alternate America* (New York: Warner Brothers 2002) Carthage has destroyed Rome, Europe remains tribal and the New World is colonised by Islam. The American South in 1863 features as Bilalistan, a rich land of mosques, kraals and Moorish castles, where white slaves toil for both North African and Sub-Saharan masters.
11. Bernardine Evaristo, *Lara* (Tarset: Bloodaxe, 2009), 176.
12. Bernardine Evaristo, *The Emperor's Babe* (London: Penguin, 2001).
13. Peter Fryer, *Staying Power: The History of Black People in Britain* (London: Pluto, 1984).
14. Karen McCarthy, "Q & A with Bernardine Evaristo," *Valparaiso Poetry Review* 4.2 (2003), accessed July 9, 2011, http://www.valpo.edu/vpr/evaristointerview.html.
15. Laura Ashfeldt, "Bernardine Evaristo on Blonde Roots," *Pulpnet,* accessed September 1, 2009, http://www.pulp.net/57/interview-bernardine-evaristo.html.
16. "Orange Prize for Fiction: Interview with Bernardine Evaristo," accessed July 10, 2011, http://www.orangeprize.co.uk/show/feature/orange-2009-BE-q-and-a.
17. Michael Collins, "My preoccupations are in my DNA. An interview with Bernardine Evaristo," *Callaloo* 31, 4 (2008): 1201.
18. Stephanie Merritt, "When slavery isn't such a black-and-white issue," *The Observer*, August 24, 2008, p. 23.
19. Joan Smith, "Blonde Roots," *The Times*, July 25, 2008, accessed July 10, 2011, http://entertainment.timesonline.co.uk/tol/arts_and_entertainment/books/book_reviews/article4396396.ece.
20. Collins, "My preoccupations are in my DNA," 1202.
21. Paul Jay, *Global Matters: The Transnational Turn in Literary Studies* (Ithaca: Cornell University Press, 2010).
22. Walter Goebel and Saskia Schabio, ed., *Beyond the Black Atlantic: Relocating Modernization and Technology* (London and New York: Routledge, 2006).
23. Benita Parry, "The presence of the past in peripheral modernities," in Goebel and Schabio, ed., *Beyond the Black Atlantic*, 13–28.
24. Bernardine Evaristo, "ohtakemehomelord.com," *The Guardian*, June 25, 2005, p. 56.
25. Fryer, *Staying Power*, 59.
26. Laura Chrisman, "Black Modernity, Nationalism and Transnationalism: The Challenge of Black South African Poetry," in Goebel and Schabio, ed., *Beyond the Black Atlantic*, 29–46.
27. Collins, "My preoccupations are in my DNA," 1202.
28. Alastair Niven, "Alastair Niven in Conversation with Bernardine Evaristo," *Wasafiri* 16, 34 (2001): 25.

29. Joseph Conrad, *Three Short Novels* (New York: Bantam, 1968) 5, 21–22.
30. Conrad, *Three Short Novels*, 62.
31. Fryer, *Staying Power*, Chapter 7.
32. Conrad, *Three Short Novels*, 11.
33. Winthrop D. Jordan, *White Over Black: American Attitudes Towards the Negro 1550–1812*. (Chapel Hill: University of North Carolina Press, 1968), 226.
34. Gilroy, *Black Atlantic*, 44.

NOTES TO CHAPTER 9

1. Rebecca Solnit, *A Paradise Built in Hell: The Extraordinary Communities that Arise in Disaster* (New York: Viking, 2009), 212.
2. Solnit, *Paradise Built in Hell*, 227.
3. Solnit, *Paradise Built in Hell*, 197.
4. Naomi Klein, *The Shock Doctrine: The Rise of Disaster Capitalism* (London: Allen Lane, 2007), 5.
5. Michael Gould-Wartofsky, "Disaster Capitalism: An Offer You Can't Refuse—Or Can You?" *Monthly Review* 60, 1 (May 2008): 61.
6. Karenjit Clare, "Corporations, Catastrophes and Confusion," *The Geographical Journal* 174, 3 (2008): 284–7.
7. Klein, *Shock Doctrine*, 42.
8. Solnit, *Paradise Built in Hell*, 107. For a critique of Klein based upon the notion of capitalism as an everyday disaster, see Eric Cadzyn and Imre Szeman, *After Globalization* (Chichester: Wiley-Blackwell, 2011), 146.
9. Solnit, *Paradise Built in Hell*, 127.
10. Solnit, *Paradise Built in Hell*, 195.
11. Solnit, *Paradise Built in Hell*, 107. Solnit draws upon Charles E. Fritz, *Disasters and Mental Health: Therapeutic Principles Drawn From Disaster Studies* (Newark: University of Delaware Research Center, 1996).
12. Michael Barkin, *Disaster and the Millennium* (New Haven: Yale University Press, 1974).
13. Solnit, *Paradise Built in Hell*, 18.
14. Solnit, *Paradise Built in Hell*, 3.
15. Solnit, *Paradise Built in Hell*, 4.
16. Chitra Divakaruni, *One Amazing Thing* (New York: Hyperion, 2009), 5. Subsequent page references follow citations in parentheses.
17. Rob Neufeld, "Interview with Chitra Divakaruni about *One Amazing Thing*," accessed April 12, 2012, http://the readonwnc.ning.com/special/interview-with-chitra.
18. Richard Francis Kuhns, *Decameron and the Philosophy of Storytelling* (New York: Columbia University Press, 2005), 13.
19. In addition to the work of Kuhns, I have benefitted from the analysis of fourteenth-century storytelling in John M. Ganim, *Chaucerian Theatricality* (Princeton: Princeton University Press, 1990) and Leonard Michael Koff and Brenda Deen Schildgen, ed., *The Decameron and The Canterbury Tales* (London: Associated University Presses. 2000).
20. Ganim, *Chaucerian Theatricality*, 74.
21. "Chitra Divakaruni and *One Amazing Thing*," *Asia Society* February 2, 2010, accessed April 12, 2012, http://asiasociety.org/arts/literature/chitra-divakaruni-and-one-amazing- thing.
22. "A Conversation with Chitra Divakaruni," in Chitra Divakaruni, *One Amazing Thing* (New York: Hyperion, 2009), 223.

23. As translated in Kuhns, *Decameron*, 25.
24. As also in *The Thousand and One Nights*. See Peter Caracciolo, ed., *The Arabian Nights in English Literature* (London: Macmillan, 1988).
25. Paul Coates, *The Double and the Other: Identity as Ideology in Post-Romantic Fiction* (London: Macmillan, 1988), 1.

NOTES TO THE CONCLUSION

1. Bill Ashcroft, "Critical Utopias," *Textual Practice* 21, 3 (2007): 411.
2. Margaret Atwood, *Oryx and Crake* (London: Bloomsbury, 2003), 407. Subsequent page references follow citations in parentheses.
3. Margaret Atwood, "Writing Utopia," in *Moving Targets. Writing with Intent: 1982–2004* (Toronto: Anansi, 2004), 102–14.

Bibliography

Abbas, *Iran Diary, 1971–2002*. Paris: Editions Autrement, 2002.

Adorno, Theodor W. *Aesthetic Theory*. London: Routledge, 1984.

Amis, Martin. "The Voice of the Lonely Crowd." *Guardian*, June 12, 2002, p. 4.

Arnold, Ron. *Ecoterror. The Violent Agenda to Save Nature: The World of the Unabomber*. Washington: Free Enterprise Press, 1997.

Ashcroft, Bill. "Critical Utopias." *Textual Practice* 21, 3 (2007): 411–31.

Ashfeldt, Laura. "Bernardine Evaristo on *Blonde Roots*." *Pulpnet*. Accessed September 1, 2009. http://www.pulp.net/57/interview-bernardine-evaristo.html.

Attridge, Derek. "Once More With Feeling: Art, Affect and Performance." *Textual Practice* 25, 2 (2011): 329–43.

Atwood, Margaret. *Oryx and Crake*. London: Bloomsbury, 2003.

Atwood, Margaret. "Writing Utopia." In *Moving Targets: Writing with Intent: 1982–2004*, 102–114. Toronto: Anansi, 2004.

Baelo-Allué, Sonia. "The Depiction of 9/11 in Literature: The Role of Images and Intermedial References." *Radical History Review* 111 (Fall 2011): 184–93.

Baker, Jeff. "Book Review of *The Garden of Last Days*." *Bookmarks*, 20 June 2008. Accessed August 17, 2012, http://blog.oregonlive.com/books/2008/06/book_review_the_garden_of_last.html.

Baker, Peter. "Bush Tells Group He Sees a 'Third Awakening'." *Washington Post*, September 13, 2006. Accessed July 12, 2012. http://www/washingtonpost.com/wp-dyn/contnet/article/2006/09/12/AR2006091201594.html?nav+rssnation.

Bal, Mieke. *Narratology: Introduction to the Theory of Narrative*. London and Toronto: University of Toronto Press, 1985.

Balaghi, Shiva. "Abbas's Photographs of Iran." *Middle East Report* 233 (Winter 2004): 28–33.

Barkin, Michael. *Disaster and the Millennium*. New Haven: Yale University Press, 1974.

Barrow, John D. and Frank J. Tipler. *The Anthropic Cosmological Principle*. Oxford University Press, 1986.

Bass, Gary J. "The Old New Thing." *New Republic*, November 11, 2010: 35–39.

Beck, Ulrich. *The Cosmopolitan Vision*. Cambridge, Polity, 2006.

Bedad, Sohrab. "Islamic Utopia in Pre-revolutionary Iran: Navvab Safavi and the Fada'ian-e Eslam." *Middle Eastern Studies* 33, 1 (January 1997): 40–65.

Bell, David. "Fail Again. Fail Better: Nomadic Utopianism and Deleuze and Guattari and Yevgeny Zamyatin." *Political Perspectives* 4, 1 (2010). Accessed July 21, 2012. http://politicalperspectives.org.uk.

Benjamin, Jody. "Suspects' actions don't add up." *South Florida Sun Sentinel*, September 16, 2001. Accessed June 5, 2009. http://web.archive.org/web/20010916150533/http://www.sun-sentinel.com/news/local.

Bernstein, Elizabeth. *Temporarily Yours: Intimacy, Authenticity, and the Commerce of Sex*. Chicago: University of Chicago Press, 2007.

Bernstein, Richard and Ross H. Munro. *The Coming Conflict with China*. New York: Knopf, 1997.

Bizzini, Silvia Caporale. "Can the Intellectual Still Speak? The Example of Don DeLillo's *Mao II*." *Critical Quarterly* 37 (1995): 104–17.

Blaise, Clark and Bharati Mukherjee. *The Sorrow and the Terror: The Haunting Legacy of the Air India Tragedy*. New York: Viking 1987.

Bloch, Ernst. *The Principle of Hope*. Cambridge, Massachusetts: MIT Press, 1986.

Bloch, Ernst. *The Utopian Function of Art and Literature: Selected Essays*. Trans. Jack Zipes and Frank Mecklenburg. Minneapolis: University of Minnesota Press, 1989.

Bolan, Kim. *Loss of Faith: How the Air-India Bombers Got Away with Murder*. Toronto: McClelland and Stewart, 2005.

Bondi, Liz. "Making Connections and Thinking Through Emotions: Between Geography and Psychiatry." *Transactions of the Institute of British Geographers*. New Series. 30, 4 (2005): 433–48.

Bourdieu, Pierre. "A Reasoned Utopia and Economic Fatalism." *New Left Review* 227 (Jan.–Feb. 1998): 125–30.

Bowen, Deborah. "Spaces of Translation: Bharati Mukherjee's 'The Management of Grief'." *Ariel* 28, 3 (July 1997): 47–60.

Bricmont, Jean. *Humanitarian Imperialism*. New York: Monthly Review Press, 2006.

Brown, Liz. "Margins of Terror." *Time Out* 644, 30 (Jan.–Feb. 5, 2008. Accessed February 26, 2009. http://www.timeout.com/newyork/articles/books/25963/margins-of-terror.

Brown, Merle E. *Kenneth Burke*. Minnesota Pamphlets on American writers 75. Minneapolis: University of Minnesota Press, 1969.

Bryner, Jeanna. "Surprise! Your cousin's a sea urchin," *LiveScience* 9, November 2006. Accessed March 10, 2009. http://www.livescience.com.

Burke, Kenneth. *Language as Symbolic Action: Essays on Life, Literature and Method* Berkeley: University of California Press, 1966.

Burke, Kenneth. *On Human Nature: A Gathering While Everything Flows*. 1967–1984. Ed. William H. Rueckert and Angelo Bonadonna. Berkeley: University of California Press, 2003.

Butler, Judith. *Giving an Account of Oneself*. New York: Fordham University Press, 2005.

Bygrave, Stephen. *Kenneth Burke's Rhetoric and Ideology*. London: Routledge, 1993.

Cadzyn, Eric and Imre Szeman. *After Globalization*. Chichester: Wiley-Blackwell, 2011.

Cahill, Thomas. *How the Irish Saved Civilisation: The Untold Story of Ireland's Heroic Role from the Fall of Rome to the Rise of Medieval Europe*. London: Hodder and Stoughton, 1995.

Caracciolo, Peter, ed. *The Arabian Nights in English Literature*. London: Macmillan, 1988.

Carr, E.H. *The Twenty Years' Crisis, 1919–1939*. London: Macmillan 1951.

Cerulo, Karen. *Never Saw it Coming: Cultural Challenges to Envisioning the Worst*. Chicago: University of Chicago Press, 2006.

Chase, Allston. *Harvard and the Unabomber: The Education of an American Terrorist*. New York: W.W. Norton, 2003.

Choi, Susan, *The Foreign Student*. New York: HarperCollins, 1998.

Choi, Susan. *A Person of Interest*. New York: Viking Penguin, 2008.

Chrisman, Laura. "Black Modernity, Nationalism and Transationalism: The Challenge of Black South African Poetry." In *Beyond the Black Atlantic: Relocating Modernization and Technology*, edited by Walter Goebel and Saskia Schabio, 29–46. London and New York: Routledge, 2006.

Clare, Karenjit. "Corporations, Catastrophes and Confusion." *The Geographical Journal* 174, 3 (2008): 284–7.

Clarke, Kenneth. *Civilisation: A Personal View.* London: BBC and John Murray, 1969.

Coates, Paul. *The Double and the Other: Identity as Ideology in Post-Romantic Fiction.* London: Macmillan, 1988.

Cohn, Dorrit. *Transparent Minds: Narrative Modes for Presenting Consciousness in Fiction.* Princeton: Princeton University Press, 1978.

Collins, Michael. "My preoccupations are in my DNA. An interview with Bernardine Evaristo." *Callaloo* 31, 4 (2008): 1199–203.

Conrad, Joseph. *Three Short Novels.* New York: Bantam, 1968.

Curie, Eve. *Madame Curie.* Trans. Vincent Sheean. London: William Heinemann, 1938.

Curie, Marie. *Pierre Curie.* New York: Macmillan 1923.

Dabashi, Hamid. "Native Informers and the making of the American Empire." *Al-Ahram Weekly Online.* Accessed July 10, 2007. http://weekly.ahram.org.eg/2006/797/special.htm.

Dabashi, Hamid. *Iran: A People Interrupted.* New York and London: The New Press, 2007.

Davies, Paul. *The Last Three Minutes: Conjectures about the Ultimate Fate of the Universe.* London: Weidenfeld and Nicolson, 1994.

Divakaruni, Chitra. *One Amazing Thing.* New York: Hyperion, 2009.

Donovan, Michael. "National Intelligence and the Iranian Revolution." In *Eternal Vigilance? Fifty Years of the CIA*, edited by R. Jeffreys-Jones and Christopher Andrew. London: Frank Cass, 1997.

Douglas, Alfred. *The Tarot: The Origins, Meanings and Uses of the Cards.* London: Penguin, 1973.

Douglas, John and Mark Olshaker. *Unabomber: On the Trail of America's Most-Wanted Serial Killer.* New York: Pocket Books, 1996.

Dubus III, André. *House of Sand and Fog.* New York: Vintage 1999.

Dubus III, André. *The Garden of Last Days.* New York: W.W. Norton, 2008.

Dubus III, André. *Townie.* New York: W.W. Norton, 2011.

Dutton, Jaqueline. "'Non-Western' utopian traditions." In *The Cambridge Companion to Utopian Literature*, edited by Gregory Claeys, 223–58. Cambridge: Cambridge University Press, 2010.

Ebrahimian, Babak. "Pictures from a Revolution: The 1979 Iranian Uprising." *PAJ: A Journal of Performance and Art* 25, 2 (May 2003): 19–31.

Edwards, Brent Hayes. "The Uses of Diaspora." *Social Text* 19, 1 (2001): 45–73.

Edwards, Kim. "Paradise," *Ploughshares* (Fall 1990): 88–96.

Edwards, Kim. *The Memory Keeper's Daughter.* London: Penguin, 2006.

Edwards, Kim. *The Secrets of A Fire King.* London: Penguin, 2007.

Egan, Danielle. *Dancing for Dollars and Paying For Love: The Relationships Between Exotic Dancers and Their Regulars.* London: Palgrave Macmillan, 2006.

Ehrenreich, Barbara. *Smile or Die: How Positive Thinking Fooled America and the World.* London: Granta, 2009.

El-Shall, Maryam. "Salafi Utopia: The Making of the Islamic State." Accessed July 18, 2012. http://clogic.eserver.org/2006/el-shall.html.

Encyclopaedia Iranica. http://www.iranicaonline.org/

Evans, Lucy. "*The Black Atlantic*: Exploring Gilroy's Legacy." *Atlantic Studies* 6, 2 (2009): 255–68.

Evaristo, Bernardine. *The Emperor's Babe*. London: Penguin, 2001.

Evaristo, Bernardine. "ohtakemehomelord.com," *The Guardian,* June 25, 2005, p. 56.

Evaristo, Bernardine. *Blonde Roots*. London: Hamish Hamilton, 2008.

Evaristo, Bernardine. *Lara*. Tarset: Bloodaxe, 2009.

Faludi, Susan. *The Terror Dream: Fear and Fantasy in Post-9/11 America*. New York: Henry Holt, 2007.

Ferguson, Niall. *Colossus: The Rise and Fall of the American Empire*. London: Allen Lane, 2004.

Frank, Katherine. *G-Strings and Sympathy: Strip Club Regulars and Male Desire*. Durham: Duke University Press, 2002.

Free, Anna. "Moonlit Revelations: The Discourse of the End in Gina B. Nahai's *Moonlight on the Avenue of Faith*." *Papers: Explorations into Children's Literature* 16, 2 (2006): 35–39.

Friedman, Thomas L. *The Lexus and the Olive Tree: Understanding Globalization*. New York: Farrar, Strauss, Giroux, 1999.

Fritz, Charles E. *Disasters and Mental Health: Therapeutic Principles Drawn From Disaster Studies*. Newark: University of Delaware Research Center, 1996.

Fryer, Peter. *Staying Power: The History of Black People in Britain*. London: Pluto, 1984.

Fukuyama, Francis. *The End of History and the Last Man*. London: Penguin, 1992.

Galanter, Marc, Susan Egelko and Helen Edwards. "Rational Recovery: Alternative to AA for Addiction?" *American Journal of Drug and Alcohol Abuse* 19, 4 (1993): 499–510.

Ganim, John M. *Chaucerian Theatricality*. Princeton: Princeton University Press, 1990.

Gardner, Martin. "WAP, SAP, PAP and FAP." In *The Night is Large: Collected Essays 1938–1995*, 40–50. London: Penguin, 1997.

Giardina, Anthony. "Why do they hate us?" *Washington Post*, June 22, 2008, p. BW07.

Gilroy, Paul. *The Black Atlantic: Modernity and Double Consciousness*. London and New York: Verso, 1993.

Goebel, Walter and Saskia Schabio, eds. *Beyond the Black Atlantic: Relocating Modernization and Technology*. London and New York: Routledge, 2006.

Goldin, Farideh Dayanim. *Wedding Song: Memories of an Iranian Jewish Woman*. Lebanon, New Hampshire: Brandeis University Press, 2003.

Gould-Wartofsky, Michael. "Disaster Capitalism: An Offer You Can't Refuse—Or Can You?" *Monthly Review* 60, 1 (May 2008): 61.

Graham, Robert. *Iran: The Illusion of Power*. London: Croom Helm, 1978.

Grainge, Paul. *Monochrome Memories: Nostalgia and Style in Retro America*. Westport, Connecticut: Praeger, 2002.

Gray, John. *Black Mass: Apocalyptic Religion and the Death of Utopia*. London: Allen Lane, 2007.

Gray, Richard. *After the Fall: American Literature Since 9/11*. Chichester: Wiley-Blackwell, 2011.

Hakakian, Roya. *Journey from the Land of No: A Girlhood Caught in Revolutionary Iran*. New York: Three Rivers Press, 2004.

Hardt, Michael and Antonio Negri. *Empire*. Cambridge, Massachusetts: Harvard University Press, 2000.

Harris, Marla. "Consuming Words: Memoirs by Iranian Jewish Women." *Nashim: A Journal of Jewish Women's Studies and Gender Issues* 15 (Spring 5769/2008): 138–64.

Harris, Paul. "Fictions of Globalization: Narrative in the Age of Electronic Media." *PhiN* 7 (1999): 26–39.

Harvie, David I. *Deadly Sunshine: The History and Fatal Legacy of Radiation.* Stroud: Tempus, 2005.

Hayden, Patrick and Chamsy El-Ojeili, eds. *Globalization and Utopia: Critical Essays.* London: Palgrave, 2009.

Hersh, Seymour. "The Iran Plans." *New Yorker,* April 17, 2006. Accessed April 20, 2008. http://www.newyorker.com/archive/206/04/17/060417fa_fact.

Hill, Eugene D. "The Place of the Future: Louis Marin and his *Utopiques.*" *Science Fiction Studies* 9 (1982): 167–79.

Hill, Ian. "The Human Barnyard and Kenneth Burke's Philosophy of Technology." *KB Journal* 5, 2 (Spring 2009). Accessed September 14, 2009. http://www.kbjournal.org.

History Commons. "Context of Before September 11, 2001. Hijackers Drink Alcohol and Watch Strip Shows." Accessed June 5, 2009. http://www.historycommons.org/.

Hochschild, Arlie Russell. *The Managed Heart: Commercialization of Human Feeling.* Berkeley, University of California Press, 1983.

Holland, Eugene W. "Utopian Thought in Deleuze and Guattari." In *Imagining the Future: Utopia and Dystopia,* edited by Andrew Milner, Matthew Ryan and Robert Savage, 217–42. North Carlton, Australia: Arena Publications. 2006.

Hume, Kathryn. *Aggressive Fictions: Reading the Contemporary American Novel.* Ithaca: Cornell University Press, 2012.

Huntington, Samuel P. *The Clash of Civilizations and the Remaking of World Order,* New York: Simon and Schuster, 1996.

Ivry, Sara. "Stolen Gems." *Tablet Magazine,* August 20, 2007. (Audio interview). Accessed August 18, 2010. www.tabletmag.com/podcasts/3202/stolen-gems/.

Jacoby, Russell. *The End of Utopia: Politics and Culture in an Age of Apathy.* New York: Basic Books, 1999.

Jacoby, Russell. *Picture Imperfect: Utopian Thought for an Anti-Utopian Age.* New York: Columbia University Press, 2005.

James, C.B. "*The Zero* by Jess Walter," accessed July 6, 2012, http://readywhenyouarecb.blogspot.co.uk/2012/06zero-by-jess-walter.html.

Jameson, Fredric. *Postmodernism, or the Cultural Logic of Late Capitalism.* Durham, North Carolina: Duke University Press, 1995.

Jameson, Fredric. *Archaeologies of the Future: The Desire Called Utopia and Other Science Fictions.* London: Verso, 2005.

Janson, H.W. *History of Art.* Englewood Cliffs, New Jersey: Prentice-Hall, 1974.

Jay, Paul. *Global Matters: The Transnational Turn in Literary Studies.* Ithaca: Cornell University Press, 2010.

Johnson, Chalmers. *Blowback: The Costs and Consequences of American Empire.* New York: Henry Holt, 2000.

Johnson, Chalmers. *The Sorrows of Empire.* London: Verso, 2004.

Johnson, Chalmers. *Nemesis: The Last Days of the American Republic.* New York: Henry Holt, 2006.

Jones-Kellett, Cyril. "The Home Builder: A Try for the American Dream." *San Diego Union-Tribune,* February 14, 1999, p. BOOKS 3.

Jordan, Winthrop D. *White Over Black: American Attitudes Towards the Negro 1550–1812.* Chapel Hill: University of North Carolina Press, 1968.

Kaczynski, Theodore. *Industrial Society and Its Future.* Accessed February 28, 2009. http://en.wikisource.org.wiki/Industrial_Society_and_Its_Future.

Keshavarz, Fatemeh. *Jasmine and Stars: Reading More than Lolita in Tehran.* Chapel Hill: University of North Carolina Press, 2007.

Kinzer, Stephen. *All the Shah's Men: An American Coup and the Roots of Middle East Terror.* Hoboken, New Jersey: John Wiley, 2003.

Kinzer, Stephen. *Overthrow: America's Century of Regime Change from Hawaii to Iraq.* New York: Henry Holt, 2006.

Kitch, Sally. "Gendered National 'Identity Politics': The U.S. and Afghanistan." Paper presented at the annual meeting of the American Studies Association, 2008, accessed abstract April 21 2008, http://www.allacademic.com/meta/p113693_index.html.

Klein, Naomi. *The Shock Doctrine: The Rise of Disaster Capitalism.* London: Allen Lane, 2007.

Koff, Leonard Michael and Brenda Deen Schildgen, eds. *The Decameron and The Canterbury Tales.* London: Associated University Presses, 2000.

Kübler-Ross, Elizabeth. *On Death and Dying.* London: Tavistock, 1970.

Kuhns, Richard Francis. *Decameron and the Philosophy of Storytelling.* New York: Columbia University Press, 2005.

Kumar, Krishan. *Utopia and Anti-Utopia in Modern Times.* Oxford: Blackwell, 1987.

Lee, Wen Ho (with Helen Zia). *My Country Versus Me.* New York: Hyperion, 2001.

Levitas, Ruth. *The Concept of Utopia.* Syracuse: Syracuse University Press, 1990.

Levitas, Ruth. "The future of thinking about the future." In *Mapping the Futures: Local Cultures, Global Change,* edited by John Bird *et.al,*, 257–69. London: Routledge, 1993.

Levy, Habib. *Comprehensive History of the Jews of Iran: The Outset of the Diaspora.* Edited and Abridged by Hooshang Ebrami. Translated by George W. Maschke. Costa Mesa, California: Mazda, 1998.

Lindsay, Stan A. *Implicit Rhetoric. Kenneth Burke's Extension of Aristotle's Concept of Entelechy.* Lanham: University Press of America, 1998.

Lobdell, William. "A Booming Sect Sends Jewish Emissaries Abroad." *Los Angeles Times,* September 11, 2006. Accessed September 8, 2010. http://www.rickross.com/reference/lubavitch/lubavitch41.html.

Luke, Timothy W. *Capitalism, Democracy and Ecology.* Urbana: University of Illinois Press, 1999.

Lykken, David T. *A Tremor in the Blood: Uses and Abuses of the Lie Detector.* New York and London: Plenum, 1998.

Malone, David. "Updike 2020: Fantasy, Mythology and Faith in *Toward the End of Time.*" In *John Updike and Religion: The Sense of the Sacred and the Motions of Grace,* edited by James Yerkes, 80–98. Grand Rapids: Eerdmans, 1999.

Marandi, Seyed Mohammed. "Reading Azar Nafisi in Tehran." *Comparative American Studies* 6, 2 (June 2008): 179–89.

Marin, Louis. *Utopics: Spatial Play.* Trans. Robert A. Vollroth. Atlantic Highlands, New Jersey: Humanities, 1984. First published as *Utopiques: jeux d'espaces.* Paris: Minuit, 1973.

Maslin, Janet. "A Terrorist in a Fleshpot Before Bidding Farewell to the Flesh," *New York Times,* June 9, 2008. Accessed June 5, 2009. http://www.nytimes.com/2008/06/09/books/09masl.html.

McCarthy, Karen. "Q & A with Bernardine Evaristo." *Valparaiso Poetry Review* 4, 2 (2003). Accessed July 9, 2011. http://www.valpo.edu/vpr/evaristointerview.html.

Melikian, Souren. "Destroying a Treasure: The Sad Story of a Manuscript." *International Herald Tribune,* April 27, 1996. Accessed September 8, 2010. http://.caissoas/CAIS/Art/manuscript.htm.

Merritt, Stephanie. "When slavery isn't such a black-and-white issue," *The Observer,* August 24, 2008, p. 23.

Mitchell, W.J.T. *Picture Theory.* Chicago and London: University of Chicago Press, 1994.

Mohr, Dunja. "Transgressive Utopian Dystopias: The Postmodern Reappearance of Utopia in the Disguise of Dystopia." *Zeitschrift für Anglistik und Amerikanistik* 55 (2007): 5–24.

Moretti, Franco. *Graphs, Maps, Trees: Abstract Models for Literary History*. London and New York: Verso, 2000.

Moylan, Tom. *Scraps of the Untainted Sky: Science Fiction, Utopia, Dystopia*. Boulder, Colorado: Westview Press, 2000.

Moyn, Samuel. *The Last Utopia: Human Rights in History*. Cambridge, Massachusetts: Harvard University Press, 2010.

Mukherjee, Bharati. "The Management of Grief." In *The Middleman and Other Stories*, 177–97. London: Virago, 1990. First published New York : Grove Press, 1988.

Mumford, Lewis. *The Myth of the Machine: Technics and Human Development*. London: Secker and Warburg, 1967.

Murphy, Jessica. "The Moment of Origin." *Profile*, Jan.–Feb. 2008: 40.

Nadler, Steven. *Rembrandt's Jews*. Chicago and London: University of Chicago Press, 2003.

Nafisi, Azar. *Reading Lolita in Tehran. A Memoir in Books*. London: I.B. Tauris, 2003.

Nahai, Gina. *Cry of the Peacock*. New York: Simon and Schuster, 1991.

Nahai, Gina. *Moonlight on the Avenue of Faith*. New York: Harcourt, Brace, 1999.

Nahai, Gina. *Caspian Rain*. San Francisco: McAdam/Cage, 2007.

Nahai, Gina. "So What's With All the Iranian Memoirs." *Publishers Weekly*, November 26, 2007, p. 58.

Nathan, Andrew and Robert S. Ross. *The Great Wall and the Empty Fortress*. New York: Norton, 1997.

Neufeld, Rob. "Interview with Chitra Divakaruni about *One Amazing Thing*." Accessed April 12, 2012. http://the readonwnc.ning.com/special/interview-with-chitra.

Newberger, Julie. "Susan Choi. Interview." *failbetter.com*. September 23, 2008. Accessed February 26, 2009. http://www.failbetter.com/28/ChoiInterviw.php.

Newman, Judie. *John Updike*. London: Methuen, 1988.

Newman, Judie. *Fictions of America: Narratives of Global Empire*. London and New York: Routledge, 2007.

Newman, Judie. "Slave Narratives and Neo-Slave Narratives." In *The Cambridge Companion to the Literature of the American South*, edited by Sharon Monteith. Cambridge: Cambridge University Press, 2013. Forthcoming.

Newman, Judie. "Glocalizing Gilroy." *Journal of Commonwealth and Postcolonial Studies* 17, 1 (Spring 2011): 93–102.

Niven, Alastair. "Alastair Niven in Conversation with Bernardine Evaristo." *Wasafiri* 16, 34 (2001): 15–20.

Nordenson, Bree. "Cowboys and Damsels." *Columbia Journalism Review* 46, 4 (Nov.–Dec. 2007): 59–62.

Oboe, Annalisa and Anna Scacchi, eds. *Recharting the Black Atlantic: Modern Cultures, Local Communities, Global Connections*. London and New York: Routledge, 2008.

Ozick, Cynthia. *Quarrel and Quandary: Essays by Cynthia Ozick*. New York: Alfred A. Knopf, 2000.

Pagels, Elaine. *The Origin of Satan*. London: Random House, 1995.

Parry, Benita. "The Presence of the Past in Peripheral Modernities." In *Beyond the Black Atlantic: Relocating Modernization and Technology*, edited by Walter Goebel and Saskia Schabio, 13–28. London and New York : Routledge, 2006.

Passaro, Vince. "Dangerous Don DeLillo." *New York Times Magazine*, May 19, 1991, p. 36–38.

Poe, Harry Lee. *Edgar Allan Poe: An Illustrated Companion to His Tell-Tale Stories*. New York: Metro Books, 2008.

Popper, Karl R. *The Open Society and its Enemies*. Volume 2. London: Routledge and Kegan Paul, 1945.

Quinn, Susan. *Marie Curie: A Life*. London: Mandarin, 1996.

Rawls, John. *The Law of Peoples*. Cambridge: Harvard University Press, 1999.

Reid, Robert. *Marie Curie*. London: Collins, 1974.

Ribkoff, Fred. "Bharati Mukherjee's 'The Management of Grief' and the Politics of Mourning in the Aftermath of the Air India Bombing." In *Literature For Our Times. Postcolonial Studies in the Twenty-First Century*, edited by Bill Ashcroft, Ranjini Mendis, Julie McGonegal, and Arun Mukherjee, 507–22. Amsterdam: Rodopi.

Rorty, Richard. *Philosophy and Social Hope*. London: Penguin, 1999.

Roushanzamir, Elli Lester. "Chimera Veil of 'Iranian Woman' and Processes of U.S. Textual Commodification: How U.S. Print Media Represent Iran." *Journal of Communication Inquiry* 28, 1 (January 2004): 9–28.

Rowe, John Carlos. "Reading *Reading Lolita in Tehran* in Idaho." *American Quarterly* 59, 2 (June 2007): 253–75.

Rueckert, William. "Some of the Many Kenneth Burkes." In *Representing Kenneth Burke. Selected Papers from the English Institute*, edited by Hayden White and Margaret Brose, 1–30. Baltimore and London: Johns Hopkins University Press, 1982.

Ruthven, Malise. *A Fury for God: The Islamist Attack on America*. London and New York: Granta Books, 2002.

Sargent, Lyman Tower. "The Three Faces of Utopianism Revisited." *Utopian Studies* 5, 1 (1994): 1–37.

Sargent, Lyman Tower. "Ideology and Utopia: Karl Mannheim and Paul Ricoeur." *Journal of Political Ideologies* 13, 3 (2008):263–273.

Sargisson, Lucy. "Religious Fundamentalism and Utopianism in the 21st century," *Journal of Political Ideologies* 12, 3 (October 2007): 269–87.

Sarshar, Houman, ed. *Esther's Children: A Portrait of Iranian Jews*. Los Angeles: Center for Iranian Jewish Oral history/The Jewish Publication Society, 2002.

Scanlan, Margaret. *Plotting Terror: Novelists and Terrorists in Contemporary Fiction*. Charlottesville and London: University Press of Virginia, 2001.

Seaman, Donna. "Review of *House of Sand and Fog*," *Booklist* 95, 11 (February 1999): 961.

Shahvar, Soli. "The Islamic Regime in Iran and its Attitude towards the Jews: The Religious and Political Dimensions." *Immigrants and Minorities* 27, 1 (March 2009): 82–117.

Shelby, Tommie. "Cosmopolitanism, Blackness and Utopia: A Conversation with Paul Gilroy." *Transition* 98 (2008): 116–35.

Shouse, Eric. "Suicide: Or the Future of Medicine. (A 'Satire by Entelechy' of Biotechnology)." *KB Journal* 4, 1 (Fall 2007). Accessed September 14, 2009. http://www.kbjournal.org.

Sick, Gary. *All Fall Down: America's Tragic Encounter with Iran*. New York: Random House, 1985.

Simmons, Ryan. "What is a terrorist? Contemporary Authorship, the Unabomber and *Mao II*." *Modern Fiction Studies* 45, 3 (1999) 675–695.

Smith, Joan. "Blonde Roots," *The Times*, July 25, 2008. Accessed July 10, 2011. *http://entertainment.timesonline.co.uk/tol/arts_and_entertainment/books/book_reviews/article4396396.ece*.

Sofer, Dalia. "Of These, Solitude." In *Yentl's Revenge: The Next Wave of Jewish Feminism*, edited by Danya Ruttenberg, 206–11. New York: Seal Press, 2001.

Sofer, Dalia. *The Septembers of Shiraz*. London: Picador, 2008. First published New York: HarperCollins, 2007.

Solnit, Rebecca. *A Paradise Built in Hell: The Extraordinary Communities that Arise in Disaster*. New York: Viking, 2009.

Solomon, Deborah. "Tales from Tehran," *New York Times*, August 26, 2007. Accessed August 18, 2010. http://www.nytimes.com/2007/08/26magazine.

Spivak, Gayatri Chakravorty. "Can the Subaltern Speak?" In *Marxism and the Interpretation of Culture*, edited by Cary Nelson and Lawrence Grossberg, 271–313. London: Macmillan, 1988.

Stephen, Andrew. "The Truth About the Lie Detector," *New Statesman*, October 16, 2006. Accessed April 1, 2009. http://www.newstatesman.com/200610160033.

Thrift, Nigel. "Intensities of Feeling: Towards a Spatial Politics of Affect." *Geografiska Annaler. Series B. Human Geography* 86, 1 (2004): 57–78.

Thrift, Nigel. "But Malice Aforethought: Cities and the Natural History of Hatred." *Transactions of the Institute of British Geographers*. New Series. 30, 2 (2005): 133–50.

Tipler, Frank J. "The FAP Flop," *New York Review of Books* 33, 19 (4 December, 1986). Accessed March 2, 2010. http:/www.nybooks.com/articles/4946.

Todorov, Tzvetan. *Hope and Memory*. London: Atlantic Books, 2003.

Turkel, Gerald. "Property, Law and Violence: A Thematic Analysis of *House of Sand and Fog*." *Humanity and Society* 30, 4 (November 2006): 378–91.

Uebel, Michael. "Striptopia?" *Social Semiotics* 14, 4 (2004): 3–19.

Updike, John. *The Poorhouse Fair*. London: Gollancz, 1959.

Updike, John. *Toward the End of Time*. New York: Knopf, 1997.

Updike, John. "Elusive Evil." In *More Matters: Essays and Criticism*, 464–80. London: Hamish Hamilton, 1999.

Updike, John. "At the Hairy Edge of the Possible." In *More Matters: Essays and Criticism*, 578–86. London: Hamish Hamilton, 1999.

Updike, John. "A 'Special Message' for the Franklin Library's Signed First Edition Society Printing of *Toward the End of Time*." In *More Matters: Essays and Criticism*, 832–4. London: Hamish Hamilton, 1999.

Updike, John. "Confessions of a Churchgoer." *The Guardian*, January 8, 2000, p. 1, 3.

Waldman, Amy. "Freedom." *Boston Review* (July/August 2009): 39–42.

Waldman, Amy *et al.*, "Guantánamo and Jailers. Mixed Review by Detainees." *New York Times*, March 17, 2004. Accessed 29 June, 2012. http://www.nytimes.com/2004/03/17/world/guantanamo-and-jailers/mixed-review-by-detainees.

Wallerstein, Immanuel. *Utopistics: Or Historical Changes of the Twenty-First Century*. New York: New Press, 1998.

Walter, Jess. *The Zero: A Novel*. New York: Harper, 2007.

Welch, Stuart Cary. *A King's Book of Kings. The Shah-nameh of Shah Tamasp*. New York and London: Thames and Hudson in association with the Metropolitan Museum, 1972.

Welch, Stuart Cary and Martin Bernard Dickson. *The Houghton Shahnameh*. Cambridge, Massachusetts: Harvard University Press, 1981.

Whitaker, Janet, Chela Kaplan and Amy O'Brien, "A Conversation with Kim Edwards." Accessed September 10, 2009. http://www.ket.org/bookclub/books/1999_feb/interview.htm.

Whitlock, Gillian. *Soft Weapons: Autobiography in Transit*. Chicago and London: University of Chicago Press, 2007.

Whyte, Jess. "Critiquing the Violence of Guantánamo: Resisting the Monopolization of the Future." In *Imagining the Future: Utopia and Dystopia*, edited by

Andrew Milner, Matthew Ryan and Robert Savage, 123–35. North Carlton, Australia: Arena Publications, 2006.

Wilde, Oscar. *The Soul of Man Under Socialism and Selected Critical Prose.* Edited by Linda Dowling. Harmondsworth, Penguin, 2001.

Wood, Paul. "Hunting 'Satan' in Falluja Hell." *BBC News*, November 23, 2004. Accessed July 12, 2012. http://news.bbc.co.uk/go/pr/fr/-/1/hi/world/middle_east/4037009.stm.

Worth, Jennifer. "Unveiling *Persepolis* as Embodied Performance." *Theatre Research International* 32, 2 (2007): 143–60.

Wright, Robin. "Chinese Detainees Are Men Without A Country." *Washington Post*, August 24, 2005. Accessed June 29, 2012. http://www.washingtonpost.com/wpdyn/content/article/2005/08/23/AR2005082301362.

Zell, Michael. *Reframing Rembrandt: Jews and the Christian Image in Seventeenth Century Amsterdam.* Berkeley: Ahmanson, 2002.

Index